ALSO BY ADAM ROCKOFF

Going to Pieces: The Rise and Fall of the Slasher Film, 1978–1986

THE HORROR OF IT ALL

One Moviegoer's Love Affair with Masked Maniacs, Frightened Virgins, and the Living Dead . . .

ADAM ROCKOFF

SCRIBNER

New York London Toronto Sydney New Delhi

SCRIBNER
An Imprint of Simon & Schuster, Inc.
1230 Avenue of the Americas
New York, NY 10020

First Scribner hardcover edition May 2015

Interior design by Akasha Archer

Manufactured in the United States of America

1 3 5 7 9 10 8 6 4 2

Library of Congress Control Number: 2014038825

ISBN 978-1-4767-6183-1
ISBN 978-1-4767-6186-2 (ebook)

For Grandma Gladys, who bought me my first *Fangoria.*

And who is stronger than any Final Girl.

"It used to be drink, smoking and drugs.
Then there was a fourth thing, porn,
and now there's a fifth, horror."

—DETECTIVE SUPERINTENDENT PETER KRUGER,
HEAD OF SCOTLAND YARD'S OBSCENE PUBLICATIONS SQUAD

Contents

Prologue

It was the best of times, it was the worst of times . . .

Those immortal words were almost certainly not written to anticipate the horror boom in the early years of the twenty-first century. And yet they most surely apply.

It was the best of times because interest in horror movies, and all the accompanying cultural detritus, is at an all-time high.

I just got back from Barnes & Noble, as good a barometer as any for measuring the zeitgeist. On this day, the magazine rack was stocked with no fewer than eleven titles devoted exclusively to horror and exploitation films. *Eleven!* And lest anyone think I'm exaggerating for effect, here they are: *Fangoria*, *Rue Morgue*, *Scary Monsters Magazine*, *Diabolique*, *HorrorHound*, *Famous Monsters of Filmland*, *Shadowland Magazine*, *Filmfax*, *VideoScope*, *Video Watchdog*, and *The Walking Dead: The Official Magazine*. There were exactly zero magazines dedicated to Westerns. None for comedies either. Zilch for family films, dramas, and musicals. While there were also a handful of general entertainment periodicals, those publications included horror, too, whenever it hit the mainstream.

The 2011 Best Picture Oscar winner, *The Artist*, grossed a total of $44 million. That same year, in just its opening weekend, the *third* installment of the *Paranormal Activity* series grossed $52 million. This is just one example, but it's indicative of what a commercial juggernaut horror has become.

If the genre is as healthy as it's ever been, how can it possibly also be the worst of times? Well, because as incredible as this might seem, the golden age of horror journalism—which I would argue we're in—has a downside: it seems as if everything worth writing has already been written.

I love the *Friday the 13th* series as much as anyone, but after Peter M. Bracke's exhaustive fully illustrated oral history, *Crystal Lake Memories*, as well as both Daniel Farrands's accompanying documentary adaptation and his earlier film *His Name Was Jason: 30 Years of Friday the 13th*, there's absolutely nothing to add to the legacy of everyone's favorite hockey-masked maniac. We now have a handful of books I could legitimately describe as the definitive work on Dario Argento, and with *Mario Bava: All the Colors of the Dark* and *Beyond Terror: The Films of Lucio Fulci*, Tim Lucas and Stephen Thrower respectively have provided the final word on these Italian titans. I can't imagine anyone writing about the grindhouse and trash cinema more lovingly than Bill Landis and Michelle Clifford. And if a Peter Biskind–esque look at horror cinema's most famous feuds and faces is your thing, you probably can't do better than Jason Zinoman's *Shock Value: How a Few Eccentric Outsiders Gave Us Nightmares, Conquered Hollywood, and Invented Modern Horror* or David Konow's *Reel Terror: The Scary, Bloody, Gory, Hundred-Year History of Classic Horror Films*. I could go on and on, and on and on.

So what's the problem with this embarrassment of riches? Twenty years ago, when I was digging around the back of a moth-infested used-book store for a battered copy of John McCarty's *Splatter Movies: Breaking the Last Taboo of the Screen*, I could never have dreamed that some Monday I would be able to order the biography of Peter Cushing, a history of horror fanzines, and a beautiful full-color coffee table book showcasing Metallica guitarist Kirk Hammett's unparalleled horror memorabilia collection, only to have all of them arrive at my front door on Tuesday morning.

The more I thought about it, the more I realized that this was only a problem for *me*. It had been over a decade since my first book, *Going to Pieces: The Rise and Fall of the Slasher Film*, came out, and I had been itching to write a follow-up. But about what?

Then it hit me. I was in the bathroom reading *Fargo Rock City* for the umpteenth time—both on the toilet and in general. I know I sound like some hack comedian, but every single good idea I've ever had has come to me either in the shower or while emptying my bowels. For those of you who don't know, *Fargo Rock City* is Chuck Klosterman's memoir about growing up as a heavy metal fan in rural North Dakota. On the surface, it's both a history and critical analysis of hair metal, but filtered through Klosterman's personal experiences it becomes something much more profound.

What if I could do the same thing with horror movies? To my knowledge, *this* had never been done. Kier-La Janisse's masterful *House of Psychotic Women* comes close. But two things gave me reason to believe there might be room for another voice. One, and most obvious, Janisse is a woman. We may like to pretend that gender has no effect on how we process art and culture, but that's a lie, and everyone knows it. Plus, her hardscrabble life was markedly different from my own uneventful suburban upbringing. Two, and this is equally apparent just from her book's subtitle—*An Autobiographical Topography of Female Neurosis in Horror and Exploitation Films*—Janisse is a far better writer than I'll ever be.

This isn't false modesty. Unfortunately, I have plenty of examples to support this claim. The first testimonial (the *very* first one) on the back cover of *Going to Pieces* states: "Rockoff is no blood-in-his-eye moron." Have you ever heard such effusive praise? I might not be the smartest guy in the room. Or the most eloquent. But hey, at least I'm no moron! I might as well be the thinnest guy at fat camp. Then there's the fact that a signed copy of my book is selling on eBay for less money than a brand-new one. So I have the dubious distinction of being one of the lucky authors whose signature actually *devalues* the work. This reminds me of a hot dog stand near my hometown where a buttered roll actually cost *less* than a plain roll. As adventurous as my friends and I were, we never dared sample that "butter."

So why waste your hard-earned money on this book? As a close friend of mine recently asked, "Who the hell wants to read about *your* experiences? Why is that interesting to anybody except for you?" I realized two things. One, I need some new friends. But two, my experiences, while unique to me, are really nothing more than a window to your own. A mirror to reflect back those memories that may have been forgotten, misplaced, or shelved away in the furthest recesses of your mind. Part of the subtitle of this book is *One Moviegoer's Love Affair*. That's both true and misleading.

I distinctly remember the first time I ever saw the 1978 film *Class Reunion Massacre*. On some level, I understood that hundreds of people were responsible for its conception, production, and release; thousands more had eventually seen it in theaters or on home video. But the film itself was so weird, and my experience of watching it so personal, that at the time I couldn't imagine anyone else even being aware of its existence.

Once I started discussing horror films with like-minded fans, I soon learned that many people were indeed aware of *Class Reunion Massacre*. One or two had even seen it in some shitty theater under its original title, *The Redeemer: Son of Satan!*

Then it became crystal clear. Although I can only write about my own experiences, I can draw on the collective consciousness of horror fandom. And *this* is why you might like this book. Because my memories are yours.

I'm almost forty now, no longer the target demographic for horror movies. And yet I love them more than ever. Lots of my friends do too.

As someone who came of age during the slasher boom in the early eighties, I've seen the genre rise, and fall, and rise again. Since then, horror films have undergone more transformations than even Dr. Moreau could fathom. *Scream* ushered in an era of snarky, self-conscious, postmodern horror. *The Blair Witch Project* obliterated the studio model and proved that any bozo with a camcorder could make a scary movie, while superior documentary-style films such as *The Last Exorcism*, *The Devil Inside*, and the *Paranormal Activity* series proved to be not the exception but the rule. The term "torture porn" was coined to describe the uncompromising films of Eli Roth and Rob Zombie, giving media pundits a perfect sobriquet for the objects of their derision. Films released barely twenty years earlier were remade or "reimagined" in droves, including each of the holy trinity of slasherdom: *Halloween*, *Friday the 13th*, and *A Nightmare on Elm Street*. Vampires were sexy, then gritty, then sexy again. And, eventually, zombies were freakin' everywhere.

The time is once again ripe to ask the question: why do horror films continue to not only endure but prosper? It's a question that will be answered not by the cultural arbiters—forever frustrated by their inability to explain the allure of horror—but by someone on the front lines.

Because to really understand the modern horror film, you have to live it. You have to embrace the outré, dive headfirst into the rabbit hole with eyes wide open (or shut), and not be afraid to slay the sacred cows.

And for those of us who do, it's a helluva ride.

CHAPTER ONE

Crawling to Babylon

In second grade, there's nothing I would have liked more than to have seen my teacher, Mrs. Glassman, meet her demise at the business end of Jason Voorhees's machete. I don't mean this euphemistically. I really would have loved to come to school one day, only to learn that she had been hacked to death by a madman.

After all, she deserved it.

An adorable little girl named Erica Steinberg sat next to me in class. She was sweet with a wonderful sense of humor, which meant she laughed at my painfully unfunny juvenile jokes. She was also pathologically shy and terrified of speaking in class. I'm certain the thought of being called on filled her days with dread. Mrs. Glassman picked up on this vulnerability almost immediately. But instead of gently leading Erica out of her shell, empathically encouraging her to find her voice, Mrs. Glassman badgered her incessantly, demanding she speak up and contribute.

Believe me, this wasn't a calculated strategy to show Erica there was nothing to be afraid of. It wasn't like the time I scooped up my nervous son and slid with him down the waterslide, knowing full well that if he did it once he'd want to do it fifty million more times. This wasn't even an old-school teacher demonstrating tough love. This was cruelty, plain and simple.

Then there was Don Ross. Today, he would no doubt be diagnosed with a variety of syndromes and conditions and monitored round-the-clock by a group of specialists. But back in 1982, he was just considered rambunctious. One day Don was trying desperately to explain something to Mrs. Glassman—just get out a single thought—and she kept cutting him off. Naturally, this made him more and more frustrated. And for a kid who is already high-strung, frustration is like rocket fuel.

Instead of giving Don some time to cool off, Mrs. Glassman threatened him with detention. When he wouldn't stop protesting, she said, "That's one day." This only made him angrier, even more determined to be heard. But she just ignored him, as if he wasn't even there. And with an evil smile, she continued adding days to his sentence. "That's two . . . that's three . . . that's four . . ." A few years later, an almost identical scene would be played out in *The Breakfast Club*. The only difference is that John Bender was a legitimate juvenile delinquent who pulled false fire alarms and hid his dope in Brian Johnson's underwear. Don Ross was a good kid with emotional problems.

Who knows on what number Mrs. Glassman eventually stopped. Or if cooler heads eventually prevailed and the excessive punishment was reduced. It's irrelevant. What matters is that Mrs. Glassman saw a child who was in desperate need of help. Of guidance. Of consolation. And her first instinct was to hurt him.

Now, are the above two stories the absolute worst things

that could ever happen to a child? Of course not. I mean, for crissakes, in nineteen states in the union teachers are still allowed to hit their students.* For real! We spend billions on education reform yet give teachers the right to beat the shit out of the kids in their care. But there are fewer trusts more sacred (at least in the other thirty-one more enlightened states) than that between a teacher and an impressionable student. And Mrs. Glassman obliterated that.

Since I displayed no obvious weakness—although, if my report card is any indication, I was a pretty obnoxious chatterbox—I never personally felt her wrath. That is, until the class was given a writing assignment in which we had to describe what we enjoyed doing when we weren't in school.

My essay wasn't so much a description of my favorite pastimes as it was a laundry list of about two dozen horror films. I had seen maybe one or two of them, such as *Jaws* and *Dracula*; the rest were titles from the cable guide that seemed especially enticing. Logical choices such as *Terror Train*, *Friday the 13th*, *Visiting Hours*, *Happy Birthday to Me*, and *Night School* were interspersed with some puzzling selections like *The Octagon*, *Fighting Back*, and something called *Fire at the Grove*, which I have to assume is a long-lost TV movie since I can't find a single reference to it anywhere.

---

* According to Corpun.com, a site whose stated purpose is the study of corporal punishment around the world, but which is clearly a comprehensive database for spanking fetishists. For those parents with children trying to determine where *not* to live, state-sanctioned abuse is legal in Alabama, Arizona, Arkansas, Colorado, Florida, Georgia, Idaho, Indiana, Kansas, Kentucky, Louisiana, Mississippi, Missouri, North Carolina, Oklahoma, South Carolina, Tennessee, Texas, and Wyoming.

I ended the essay by adding, "I like to go and visit the zoo too."

If I had never seen the majority of these films, what then compelled me to list them? And why did I claim that this was how I liked to spend my free time?

It all began with *The Elephant Man*.

I was six years old when I saw the visage of Joseph Carey Merrick, although since it was in the movie, it was actually the face of John Hurt brilliantly transformed by Christopher Tucker's revolutionary makeup. That was the first time I can actually remember being terrified. Since I was an extraordinarily sensitive child—as demonstrated by my precise recollection of Mrs. Glassman's offenses—I was even more disturbed by the indignities inflicted upon Merrick by the miscreants of Victorian London than I was by the man's actual deformities.

Nature's malice I could accept; that of my fellow man was infinitely more upsetting.

Even before *The Elephant Man*, I knew that the world could be a dark and fearsome place. This revelation came from an unlikely source. Most people are familiar with the elephant Babar as either the main character in a series of classic children's books or as the punch line in one of the funniest scenes from *Fletch*. But to me, he was an unwitting guide into life's ugliness. There's a page in *Babar the King* where a herd of winged elephants representing positive values, such as Courage, Kindness, Intelligence, and Hope, chase away their malevolent doppelgängers Cowardice, Anger, Stupidity, and Despair. The leader of the baddies is Misfortune, a sickly old woman riding some crazy-looking horned giraffe-like thing. Her minions look no less disturbing: Spinelessness is a humanoid gremlin while Sickness is a dachshund blowing smoke from its elongated snout.

Eventually, my mother had to hide the book. When she asked me why I was so frightened of these specific illustrations, from a children's book no less, I couldn't articulate it. But I knew. It was as clear as day. Abstract concepts had been given a face—albeit a crudely drawn one—which was more than enough for my preadolescent brain to process as a tangible threat. I might not have known what "discouragement" meant, but now that I could see it in the form of a porcine monster, I was absolutely convinced that it was coming straight for me.

So what did I do? I did what any kid would do—I slept in my parents' bedroom far more often than I'd like to admit. Ironically, it was there, ensconced in the safety of goose down, that one morning I witnessed something that made the benign terrors of Babar pale by comparison. It was an antismoking public service announcement, and its final image is forever seared into my memory.

The entire PSA was comprised of a single shot of a woman holding up a black-and-white photograph in front of her face. The subject in the photo is attractive, or at least pleasant-looking in a fifties-housewife kind of way. She begins telling a story about how her husband fell asleep while smoking in bed, presumably with her in it. A fire ensued and her husband perished in the blaze. The entire time, the camera moves closer and closer to the photograph until the woman says, "I guess you could say, I was the lucky one." She then lowers the photo. Holy fucking shit. Suddenly the Elephant Man was Cary Grant. I had never seen anything so profoundly disturbing. The woman had been burned beyond recognition. Her face, or what was left of it, was nothing more than a mass of melted flesh, strips of scar tissue crisscrossing each other at unnatural angles. Mercifully, the image was only on TV for a few seconds before cutting away to whatever Saturday morning cartoon followed it. From then on, the moment I saw the first frame of that commercial, I would dive underneath the covers until I heard her final bitterly ironic line of dialogue. *I guess you could say, I was the lucky one*. For years, her voice was the soundtrack to a thousand nightmares. I have absolutely no idea who directed this PSA—probably just some journeyman who went on to make commercials hawking potato chips and antifungal cream—but some enterprising producer should find this dude and sign him up (although he's probably retired or dead by now). Just typing in various search terms, trying to find any information at all on this PSA, literally sends shivers up my spine. I'm not exaggerating when I say it remains the most terrifying thirty seconds of video I have ever seen.

But the Elephant Man, Babar, and "the lady who got burned" had nothing on the scariest *film*. To this day, it's one of only a handful of movies that I still refuse to watch alone in the dark. When my wife and I started dating, I tried to give it another go and it still freaked me the fuck out. This movie is the Walt Disney Company's 1980* release *The Watcher in the Woods*.

The plot of the film is almost inconsequential. A couple and their two daughters temporarily move into a huge English manor. Mrs. Aylwood (Bette Davis), the estate's owner, notices that one of the children, Jan, bears a striking resemblance to

* Technically, *The Watcher in the Woods* was first released in 1980, albeit briefly. However, the version most people are familiar with is the "official" cut, released theatrically in October 1981.

her teenage daughter who mysteriously disappeared nearly thirty years earlier. The melodrama is just background noise. The only thing that matters is that *Watcher* contains some of the most haunting images ever captured on celluloid. Laugh if you want, but the shot of a blindfolded Karen Aylwood, reaching out in desperation while mouthing the words "Help me," is as bone-chilling as anything from *The Haunting* or *The Uninvited*. The fact that this specter only appears when Jan looks at her own reflection makes it all the more unsettling. Between this and the legend of Bloody Mary, I spent most of my childhood avoiding mirrors at all costs.

Of course, at the time, I knew nothing about the troubled history of *Watcher*, whose production and theatrical release were a monumental clusterfuck. *Watcher* was born out of Disney's desire to make more adult-themed films, following their success with *The Black Hole*. What ensued, however, was a struggle between producer Tom Leetch and studio brass about how un-Disney a Disney film should ultimately be. The film's ending was a point of particular contention for all involved. *Watcher* was rushed into theaters to capitalize on star Bette Davis's fiftieth anniversary in the entertainment industry. As a result, the groundbreaking special effects planned for the final scene were jettisoned in favor of an ending that was less complicated to shoot—and completely incoherent. Even in an era where star power actually meant something, can you think of a dumber reason to either see, or not see, a film? Because of some arbitrary date related to the leading lady's history? If I told my wife we couldn't see the next *Sex and the City* installment because I wanted to wait for the thirty-fifth anniversary of *Square Pegs*, she'd rightfully have me committed.

Predictably, when *Watcher* was released in theaters audiences were confused. But when it hit video soon after, it attracted a whole generation of rabid fans like myself, ones less concerned about narrative cohesion than cheap thrills. Kids who came to sit on Uncle Walt's lap but instead got their fright card. Even today, I can still give my thirty-six-year-old sister a heart attack by writing "Nerak" ("Karen" spelled backward)—a plot point in the film—into the condensation on a window.

Recently, I was at a film festival where Gary Sherman, one of the horror film's most underrated directors—*Death Line*, *Dead & Buried*, *Vice Squad*—was talking about how his interest in the genre stemmed from a traumatic event from his childhood. The bodies of three young boys were found naked and bound in a forest preserve near his Chicago home, a case that received national attention as the Schuessler-Peterson murders. Since the victims were around his age, Sherman was terrified. An astute child, he heard that the best way to combat a fear was to learn as much as possible about it. Knowledge wasn't just power, it was a defense mechanism, so Sherman immersed himself in serial killers and aberrant psychology.

I did the same thing with horror movies.

But curiously, after dozens of viewings of *Watcher*, I noticed something else happening. Although I was scared shitless of the film, literally jumping off the couch each time a mirror would shatter and Karen's ghostly countenance would appear, I kind of liked the feeling. I felt energized. Rejuvenated. Alive. I became a fear junkie. Now, this doesn't mean I was a particularly brave addict. I watched *Friday the 13th Part 3* standing in the doorway of my living room, peering around the door frame in case the tension became so unbearable that I had to scurry back to the safety of the kitchen. Just the poster for *Curtains*, with the image of a small doll coming through the elongated mouth of an old-crone mask, shook me up so badly that I couldn't even bring myself to watch the film when it first made the rounds on cable.

So every new horror film became a test, a game to see how much fear I could handle. Like all addicts, I eventually built up a tolerance. And the more films I watched, the more I fell in love with them. With their colorful villains and breathtaking monsters. Mind-bending plots and phantasmagoric imagery. Even their rather reassuring worldview; except for a few daring and downbeat examples, good usually triumphed over evil. Although slasher films were certainly the most prevalent subgenre at the time, I sought out all flavors of horror. Gothic ghost stories. Cold War parables. Seventies devil films. Forgotten independent oddities. Even the dusty old Universal classics and their marginally faster-paced Hammer Films spawn held interest, as I understood that they were part of a lineage that seemed to grow richer and more compelling with every passing generation.

Concurrent with my burgeoning love of horror, seismic changes were taking place in the film industry. The early days of home video were a vast wasteland, mainly of pornography and weird promotional infomercials. Shortsighted as usual, the Hollywood studios were initially wary of this new technology. Just as they had feared nearly every other technological innovation since the birth of the medium, they were convinced it was going to completely upend their business model. Ironically, by the time the DVD market cratered in the late 2000s, home video had come to make up a disproportionate share of the industry's profits. Because discs were priced so low, even casual film buffs could afford to build their own home library. You could buy a new, digitally remastered version of *Casablanca* for hardly more than it once cost to rent it at Blockbuster, especially if you factored in the inevitable late fees.

An unintended result of the studios' trepidation was an immediate boom in low-budget home video distributors, which sprang up to meet the public's insatiable desire for product. Since these distributors couldn't get their hands on studio releases, they were forced to fill their pipelines with the only films they were able to license—more often than not, horror and exploitation titles.

This was a game changer. Before this, these B movies could only be seen in independent theaters, usually in large cities, and at the occasional drive-in, which were already few and far between. Although I lived only forty-five minutes from Forty-Second Street, the mecca of the famed grindhouses, I had as much chance of visiting these fleapits as I did Kathmandu. We went into Manhattan exactly once a year around Christmas to catch a Broadway musical and gawk at Macy's holiday window displays. And although I would have gladly traded in my *Guys and Dolls* or *Oklahoma!* tickets for a showing of *Women in Cages* or *The Corpse Grinders*, I seriously doubt anyone else in my family would have considered this an appropriate holiday excursion.

Once sleaze became available to consume in the privacy of one's home, the grindhouses lost much of their appeal, unless you were an exhibitionist or Pee-wee Herman. The dilapidated seats, atrocious acoustics, and cum-covered floor weren't accoutrements worth preserving.

More recently, we've seen a similar scenario play itself out with pornography, as physical media like magazines and videos/DVDs have gone the way of the dinosaurs. It's all about safety, convenience, and cost. The more I think about it, the more baffling it is that there's still a market for *any* non-Internet-distributed porn. How many copies of *Swank* can the Pakistani owner of my local liquor store possibly be selling? And to whom? Who in their right mind would shell out fifteen bones for a single issue in light of the free and unlimited selection online? And while we're on the topic, what kind of lunatic purchases pornography at an airport newsstand? But a lot of people do, right? I mean, literally *every* airport I've ever been in has a robust selection of dirty magazines. There must be a compelling reason for them to keep stocking this smut. And that reason can only be that there's still a demand for it. Forget religious profiling, which I really don't have a problem with. We would be well served if TSA agents focused most of their attention on travelers buying airport porn. Because any person who *must have it now*, and can't wait until they return to the privacy of their home or hotel room, isn't the kind of person you want roaming the cabin at thirty thousand feet. What do they plan to do with it anyway, join the Mile-High Club with themselves? Plus, anyone who has no compunction about buying porn not only in public, but in an *airport* of all places, in plain view of babies, grandparents, and Franciscan nuns, is obviously a deeply disturbed individual.

That said, I sort of feel bad for kids today. After all, trying to procure pornography before you're old enough is a noble time-honored tradition. Disabling the Net Nanny on the family computer can't possibly hold the same illicit thrill as trying to buy dirty magazines at the corner store, holding your breath in anticipation while the teenage clerk decides which is more important, enforcing the store's age restrictions or possibly pocketing a fiver.

Believe it or not, I still have my family's very first VCR displayed in my office as a retro conversation piece. It's a behemoth of a machine that came with a remote control connected to the system by an actual cord. Ironically, I'd love such an obsolete feature today, as I spend an inordinate amount of time searching between the cushions of the couch for one of our fifty thousand remotes.

In November 2013, the wires were abuzz with the news that Blockbuster had finally given in to the inevitable and closed its remaining three hundred stores. My first reaction was shock. Neither I nor anybody I knew had any idea there were *any* Blockbuster stores still open. We assumed the last one went out of business around the time Andre Agassi started losing his hair. My second reaction, however, was sadness. Unlike my more militant spiritual brethren, I never viewed Blockbuster or any of the larger chains, such as Hollywood and West Coast Video, as the evil empire. They served a necessary function. If I needed to rent *When Harry Met Sally* for whatever reason, I was glad they were well stocked. But since my tastes ran closer to *Shocking Asia*, which, surprise, Blockbuster did not carry, I had little use for them. So although I certainly won't miss anything about the stores themselves, I do lament the end of an era. To me, the video store was what the record shop was to my parents' generation, and what, according to Norman Rockwell, the counter at the corner drugstore was to that of my grandparents.

I remember the huge clamshell boxes, prominently displayed to catch the eye of discriminating cinephiles browsing through rows of tapes. The gorgeous artwork and scenes of carnage on the back covers promised unspeakable horrors, making me dizzy with anticipation. Or that might have been the smell of mildew, day-old popcorn, and industrial disinfectant that hung in the air. But either way, there was no mistaking the ambiance.

Back in the day, my best friend, Mark Cichowski, and I would ride our bikes down "the path," a narrow crumbling concrete bridge that spanned a meandering creek. It connected our hometown of North Brunswick, New Jersey, with the neighboring hamlet of Milltown. Milltown's Main Street looked like a set from a Frank Capra movie, practically unchanged since the 1950s. Nestled among a pizza parlor, Irish bakery, pharmacy, and Catholic church (whose billboards, years later, my cousin would deface because they ran graphic antiabortion ads) was the Book Swap. It was nothing more than an ordinary used-book store that seemed to stock an inordinately large selection of Harlequin romance paperbacks. In the back of the store was a small section of VHS tapes for rental. I can't remember if they were literally *all* horror movies or if those were the only ones that caught my eye. But I *needed* to see them. This was easier said than done.

I am the product of an overprotective mother. Well, overprotective for the seventies; today she would probably be cited by the Department of Child Services for gross negligence. For example, we spent a few weeks each summer at the Jersey Shore, where I attended a "day camp" run by teenagers more interested in huffing glue than looking after a bunch of unruly kids. Despite my being an excellent swimmer, not to mention the oldest in the group, my mother insisted I wear a life jacket into the ocean since "you never know how strong the undertow can be." As a result, I was teased mercilessly by all the other campers, who were probably convinced I was the aquatic version of the boy in the bubble.

On the other hand, my friends and I built a dirt bike course in the middle of the forest, complete with ramps made from rotted wood off of which we'd jump over mini bonfires like pint-sized Evel Knievels. Nowadays, if one of my kids so much as gets on their bike without a helmet, I begin to hyperventilate.

Thankfully, my mother was extremely open-minded when it came to my media consumption. Well, open-minded or clueless. I tend to think, or at least I hope, she might not have known exactly what *Last House on the Left* was when she rented it for me when I was in sixth grade.

By that time, my mother had come to terms with the fact that I loved horror movies. Since the Book Swap was a wholesome family-owned business, they forced her to sign a "consent form" that stated in no uncertain terms that she was giving me permission to rent movies rated R specifically for violence—as opposed to those movies rated R (or even worse, unrated!) because of sexual content. I know, it seems ridiculous. Cultural commentators love to point out the disparity between America's attitudes toward sex and violence, with the latter being *far* more permissible in mainstream entertainment. As opposed to, say, enlightened Europe, where lovers frolic au naturel on public television while violence is severely regulated. I never thought I'd say this, being pro-vagina and antigun, but as a parent with two young kids I actually find it much easier to explain away fictionalized bloodshed. Because of their diet of video games, Cartoon Network shows, and Lego battlefields, my children at least have a frame of reference for death. But two naked people in strange positions and making guttural noises? This is a discussion I'd like to put off for at least a couple more years.

As much as I truly want to shield my kids from the prurient for as long as possible, there is something to be said for good old-fashioned honesty. Oftentimes, the things we say to protect children inevitably create even more confusion. For example, I must have been no more than five or six when I saw my first *Playboy*. Some older kids had stashed it in the woods near my house and my friends and I came across it while we were sledding. When I told my mother, she calmly explained that *Playboy* was just a magazine for grown-ups. Obviously, this was a less than satisfying answer, so naturally I pressed her on what specifically made it so. She finally gave in and told me that *Playboy* featured photos of deer slain by hunters as well as the cancer-riddled lungs of smokers, blackened with tar and other by-products of cigarettes. What's ironic is that I would have found it perfectly understandable that men enjoy looking at pictures of naked women—I certainly did, even at that young age—but I could never for the life of me grasp why anyone would want to see this other shit. To illustrate what a powerful hold childhood lessons have on the psyche, even in the face of conflicting but accurate information, when I was in college and actually *subscribed* to *Playboy*, I would still subconsciously look for the dead deer and diseased lungs between the centerfolds and celebrity pictorials.

But I digress . . . Once Mark and I made our selection from the Book Swap, we would stop at the nearby convenience store to stock up before returning to my house for hours of uninterrupted viewing. Sweet Jane might have been living on reds, vitamin C, and cocaine, but we preferred a cocktail of Hostess CupCakes, Fun Dip, and Jolt to get us through the marathon screening sessions.

Over those lazy weekends we'd plow through quite an eclectic selection of films, determined less by taste than by what the Book Swap currently had in stock. We watched *The Thing* over and over again, marveling at Rob Bottin's makeup effects and fast-forwarding through the "boring" parts, which were, of course, all the talky scenes that didn't include dogs splitting apart and chests bursting open. We found *Mausoleum* unspeakably funny and nearly wore out the VCR's tape head rewinding the scene where tiny heads sprout from the breasts of former Playboy Bunny Bobbie Bresee. And we had our minds blown by *Sleepaway Camp*. Sure, the film's gender politics might have escaped us, but sometimes a girl with a dick trumps all.

Growing up, my family actually owned a video store called the First Row. The reason this doesn't figure more prominently into my childhood is because the store was located about an hour from my house. The more significant family business was actually a dairy farm, founded by my great-grandfather, which, over the years, spawned a chain of convenience stores along the mid-Atlantic coast. How a video store fit into that mix I really don't know, but we owned one nonetheless.

During one of our occasional visits to the First Row, a life-size cardboard advertisement for the exploitation film *I Spit on Your Grave* stood right next to the counter. The image was one of the most well-known and striking in the history of B-movie poster art: the posterior of a woman clad only in a torn undergarment clutching a bloody knife. The tagline is also genius: *This Woman Has Just Cut, Chopped, Broken, and Burned Five Men Beyond Recognition . . . But No Jury in America Would Ever Convict Her!* The display was so overt—and so inappropriate for a family video store—that the film took on a disproportionate sense of importance for me. I assumed it had to be the ne plus ultra of exploitation. Years later, when I finally saw the film, it was one of the few that actually lived up to its billing—it was even more extreme than advertised.

The poster image was so notorious that an urban legend sprang up around it. Supposedly, that tight little behind belonged to none other than Demi Moore. When I finally met Meir Zarchi, the writer/director of *I Spit on Your Grave*, at the premiere of the film's 2010 remake, I asked him about this rumor. He smiled, placed a single finger to his lips, and nodded ever so slightly. Was it an admission? Or was Zarchi, surprisingly playful, just fucking with me? In the spirit of journalistic integrity, I guess I could press him for an answer. But I kind of like the mystery. And since I have the framed poster in my office, I enjoy sharing this tidbit with visitors who pretend to be just as interested.

If the video store quickly became a secular temple, its congregants had an equally compelling reason to stay at home: cable television. Today, in a world where many of us make no distinction between shows on the broadcast nets, basic cable, pay cable, video on demand, and streaming services, it's hard to remember just how revolutionary the concept of cable initially was.

Even more than home video—which required at least a minimal degree of parental involvement, if only for the rental fee or a ride to the video store—cable was the gift horse that deserved a big sloppy kiss on the mouth. For the enterprising kid, nothing was off-limits. And I was nothing if not enterprising. Somewhere in the back of my parents' entertainment center is a battered VHS tape that once contained the soft-core troika of *The Sensuous Nurse*, *The Story of O*, and *Lady Chatterley's Lover*. I recorded these films in the dead of night over a period of months, since I was the only one in my family who knew how to work the timer on our VCR. The movies were captured in the SLP format, which allowed you to cram six hours of footage onto a standard two-hour VHS tape. Sure, the quality suffered, but blank tapes were an expensive accessory, and it was also much easier to hide my growing library of smut on as few tapes as possible.

Some kids are entrepreneurial by nature. Whenever I read profiles of successful business figures their story always contains a fond remembrance about how they got their start peddling magazines, shoveling snow, hawking encyclopedias, or selling hair tonic (this last example is admittedly from the *Brady Bunch*). I was not one of these kids. My days were spent almost exclusively playing sports, watching horror movies, and trying desperately to get girls to notice me.

However, because we had a few extra VCRs lying around the house, I had a short-lived plan to become a professional (and illegal, but at the time I didn't know it) film distributor. I had figured out how to connect two VCRs together with A/V cables. This allowed me to record from one prerecorded tape onto a blank tape. My idea was to dub the highlights from my soft-core library (money shots without the money or the shooting) to create a greatest hits–like video that I could then sell to every red-blooded male in my elementary school for a little more than the price of tape stock.

Unfortunately, my plan hit a snag when I failed to consider the amount of uninterrupted, and more importantly, unsupervised, time that I would need to complete the master tape. It would have to be one day when I was home sick from school. But this posed another problem. Some parents keep their kids home from school for nothing more than a hangnail. My wife actually got "mental health" days where her mother let her play hooky a few times a year just so she could clear her head. This would never have flown in my house. As loving as my parents were, they would have made me roll myself to school in my own iron lung. When I was around nine, I came down with synovitis, a harmless but temporarily debilitating condition in which the membranes lining the joints become inflamed. I couldn't move my legs and was completely incapacitated. Naturally, my parents suspected I was faking and forced me to get ready for school. I swung down the hallway, doorknob to doorknob, like some kind of tree sloth, my useless legs dragging behind me.

Over the next month, I managed to carve out a few hours during which I dubbed about a half a dozen scenes. I sold zero tapes. Vestron Video had no idea how close they came to obsolescence.

In order to compete with the video store, cable systems needed some way to promote and differentiate their offerings. The implementation of a "channel menu" was years away and the venerable *TV Guide* about as compelling as a Bob Ross marathon. So these companies would send out a monthly, full-color supplement to highlight all their new films. Oftentimes, the poster art was featured along with a summary. I would literally spend hours poring over these listings—which is how I got the names of the films listed in my infamous second-grade essay. If I shut my eyes, I'm instantly transported back to 1982. There was *Blood Beach*, accompanied by the image of a screaming woman partially swallowed up by the sand itself. The tagline was sublime: *Just When You Thought It Was Safe to Go Back in the Water—You Can't Get to It*. *The Boogens* also seemed interesting, and not just because the creatures looked and sounded like mucus. Little did I know that I should have recorded this low-budget gem for my defunct distribution company, as it would soon become one of the most sought-after out-of-print titles for collectors. *Are You in the House Alone?* might have been a bloodless TV movie about sexual assault, barely more graphic than an after-school special, but all I knew was that a good-looking teenager was alone in the house. The possibilities were limitless.

Back in the early eighties, if you were a kid with an insatiable urge to know about the newest crop of horror movies, there were few options. There was no Internet. Bookstores were pretty much useless and the public library just as bad. At the most, it would carry a handful of books about the Universal Monsters and maybe a biography of Boris Karloff or Vincent Price. For current films, you were shit out of luck.

Thankfully, there was the Route 1 Flea Market.

Before it was razed in 1996 to make way for a Loews multiplex, this flea market was one of Central Jersey's great landmarks. Ostensibly a place for low-income families to find good deals on tube socks, for a kid whose idea of high culture was professional wrestling, it was like an all-expenses-paid trip to Disney World. Where else could you possibly find Chinese stars, a rattlesnake paperweight, and a "Kill a Commie for Mommy" T-shirt within fifty yards of each other? Since neither of my parents would get within a half a mile of the place, I was fortunate to have a grandmother who would have done anything for her only grandson. Our weekends at the flea market are some of the best memories of my childhood. She would buy me a couple slices of pizza and then some rock candy or gummy worms to wash it down. While digesting, I would play endless games of Jungle Hunt and Dragon's Lair. Before we left, we would always make a stop at the magazine stand. It was here that I was first introduced to *Fangoria* and its grislier sister publication, *GoreZone*.

Fangoria had been around since 1979, when it was spun off as a fantasy film alternative to its science fiction–centric parent, *Starlog*. When the first few issues failed to gain traction with readers, editor Bob Martin shifted the magazine's focus to horror films. Issue 7, with *The Shining*'s Jack Nicholson front and center, solidified *Fango*—as it's affectionately known—as "the First in Fright."

Fango's success was no accident. Its focus was tight, its layout beautiful, and its articles of a much higher quality than any of its competitors. It was also a fortuitous time to launch such an endeavor. Special-effects artists were just coming into their own as the *real* stars of horror films, and there was no better way to showcase the work of Tom Savini, Rick Baker, and Rob Bottin than a full-color spread in *Fango*. The slasher films of the time also ensured a steady stream of product to cover. But arguably, nothing was more important to the long-term health of the magazine than the decision to hire a young NYU grad in the summer of 1985.

Tony Timpone was an unabashed horror fan whose dream job was to work for *Fangoria*. While still in school, he honed his craft writing for some of Forry Ackerman's post–*Famous Monsters of Filmland* ventures. After breaking in through *Starlog*, Timpone rose quickly through the ranks of *Fango*, soon becoming editor-in-chief, a position he would hold with great distinction until 2010. Almost immediately, he put his stamp on the magazine. Forgoing an elitist approach to the genre, *Fangoria* covered *everything*, from studio blockbusters and man-in-a-suit Japanese monster movies to Italian zombie films and underground American trash. Even if some readers didn't appreciate this communal philosophy, it was impossible to dislike Timpone himself. His enthusiasm for horror movies was infectious; although I didn't know him well, I distinctly remember his grabbing me at a *Fango* event in Chicago to rave about this new French film called *Ils*. Plus, he favored finely tailored suits in a genre better known for black T-shirts and denim jackets. I always admired the fact that he took his unofficial role as spokesman for the horror genre seriously enough to look the part.

Perhaps the most remarkable thing about *Fangoria* is that it has remained horror's magazine of record for over thirty years. This is even more impressive when one considers just how many other periodicals have come and gone over this same period. In fact, there is only one other horror magazine that has even approached—some people would argue it has now exceeded—the cultural cachet of *Fango*.

Rue Morgue magazine started as a pipe dream for founder Rodrigo Gudiño. He was working at the now-defunct Canadian music-industry magazine *RPM* when he had his eureka moment.

The first black-and-white issue of *Rue Morgue* hit the street—literally, as Gudiño himself distributed free copies to passers-by—a few days before Halloween 1997. The date was a good omen indeed; for the next few years, Gudiño poured everything he had into his fledging publication. Under his watchful eye, *Rue Morgue* drew upon the talents of the very best, and most opinionated, writers in the business. At one time or another, Chris Alexander, Dave Alexander, John W. Bowen, Jovanka Vuckovic, the Gore-Met, Paul Corupe, and Sean Plummer were (and in many cases, still are) regular contributors. Art directors Gary Pullin and later Justin Erickson abandoned the typical "film still" cover in favor of gorgeous illustrations reminiscent of Basil Gogos's work for *Famous Monsters of Filmland*. Taking a page from the *Fangoria* playbook, *Rue Morgue* eventually moved into other areas, including conventions, film festivals, and most notably, its own film label, Rue Morgue Cinema.

Today, I don't know a single person who reads either *Fangoria* or *Rue Morgue* but not the other. They're the Beatles and the Rolling Stones of horror magazines, despite what other upstarts may claim, or pretend, to the contrary.

But let's get back to Mrs. Glassman, that paragon of elementary education. After the incident with my horror essay, she placed a call to my parents. I understand that in today's post-Columbine, post-Newtown world it doesn't seem unreasonable that a teacher would act with a preponderance of caution. In fact, educators *should* be contacting parents to head off potentially dangerous students. But this was long before the issue of school violence was even a blip on the national radar. And trust me, Mrs. Glassman's intention wasn't to prevent an incident or help diagnose some psychological defect. Like everything else she did, she was simply exerting her unquestioned authority. Thankfully, my parents were smart enough to realize that not only had I not seen most of the films whose titles I transcribed from the cable guide, but the chance that they had a budding psychopath living under their roof was fairly slim. At the meeting, Mrs. Glassman blathered on about how much of my creative writing veered toward the darker side. My parents nodded respectfully. I just sat there, embarrassed, praying for this nightmare to be over.

The only tangible effect this incident had was to strengthen my resolve to see these films. I watched Leatherface, Michael Myers, Jason Voorhees, Frank Zito, Harry Warden, and Andrew Garth saw, hack, slash, and slice their way through hundreds of victims. But they never hurt a child.

That indignity was reserved for Mrs. Glassman.

CHAPTER TWO

Slasherama

In the fall of 1980, America's best-known film critics, Gene Siskel and Roger Ebert, devoted an entire episode of their PBS series, *Sneak Previews*, to "a disturbing new trend at the movie box office."

This trend, of course, was the slasher film.

I moved to Chicago in 1998, only a few months before Siskel's tragic death, so I wasn't particularly familiar with his reviews for the *Chicago Tribune*. I think it's safe to say, however, that I wouldn't have cared for him. Just as I didn't care for Ebert, his cohost and rival at the competing daily, the *Chicago Sun-Times*. I didn't like Ebert's politics, his sense of self-importance, or, quite frankly, his taste in movies. That said, nobody should ever have to endure what he went through in the last few years of his life. The man faced his inevitable death with a combination of grace and strength that I always found inspiring.

I'm not going to lie, it's a lot of fun to dissect this particular episode because it perfectly illustrates just what pompous blowhards these two were. But it's equally instructive to use as a primer to address the most prevalent and enduring criticisms of the slasher film. After all, there has never been a more disreputable genre. Porn, maybe. But even here, you have your radical feminists for whom the choice to fill every conceivable orifice with objects—both animate and inanimate—is the ultimate form of self-expression.

Not so with slasher films. *Everybody* hates them—except those of us who love them.

The show begins with Ebert introducing the episode's topic. Siskel jumps right in, saying, "To put it bluntly, what you see in most of these films is a lot of teenage girls being raped or stabbed to death. Usually both." Now, I don't want to quibble about semantics and nitpick every single word, but for a self-proclaimed journalist, Siskel's reporting certainly leaves a lot to be desired. What films is he talking about? I have to imagine he did at least a little research before the show, if only enough to formulate an opinion about how awful these films are. But I also imagine I've seen *a lot* more slasher films than he has and I can't think of a single one in which the killer rapes a woman, much less rapes and then stabs her to death. But according to Siskel, this "usually" happens. I guess he could be referring to *I Spit on Your Grave*—a film Ebert particularly detested—but not only is the victim not stabbed, she survives the assault and enacts her own even more brutal revenge. Maybe he's talking about *Last House on the Left*, a film in which the victims are indeed raped and then stabbed, and of which, ironically, Ebert was a huge fan. But *Last House* was released in 1972, nearly a decade before the slasher's heyday. More likely, Siskel just doesn't know what the hell he's talking about.

Ebert then chimes in to note that one of the things all these films have in common is "that they portray women as helpless victims." Like his partner, he must have done *some* research. But also like his partner, he's dead wrong. While the term "final girl" might not yet have entered the pop culture lexicon, the conceit was certainly familiar. In almost *all* these films the lone survivor is a woman, and specifically a headstrong resourceful one who either defeats or escapes the killer. Alice in *Friday the 13th*. Marti from *Hell Night*. Anne from *Graduation Day*. Hell, Jamie Lee Curtis alone faced down the masked maniac in no less than three slasher films (more if you count all the *Halloween* sequels she appeared in). I would hardly call any of these women "helpless victims."

For a moment, let's pretend that all the victims in slasher films *are* helpless women, and let's even take it a step further and admit they're usually quite attractive. Is this such a bad thing? Critics would say yes. They would argue that slasher films promulgate the primitive idea that independent women must be punished for asserting their sexuality. And punished in the most severe manner possible. As evidence, they point to the fact that in many slasher films the virginal girl is the sole survivor (never do they acknowledge, as stated before, that this practically negates the argument that these girls are helpless), while her more promiscuous friends meet a gruesome end.

In *Going to Pieces* I argued that this phenomenon is rooted not in an ultraconservative mind-set, as the theory usually goes, but a practical one. It's certainly no secret that filmmakers realized almost immediately the benefits of spicing up their horror with a little T & A. After all, who comprises the audience of most slasher films? Teenagers. And what do young adults want to see? If I have to spell it out, it's been a long time since you've been a teenager. Since you're never more vulnerable than when you're naked, and particularly when you're bumping uglies, it only makes sense that sex and violence are two sides of the same coin. Dario Argento articulates this point perfectly, if not particularly delicately. "I like women, especially beautiful ones. If they have a good face and figure, I would much prefer to watch them being murdered than an ugly girl or man."* Is it wrong to prefer the vicarious thrill the on-screen slaughter of a beautiful woman provides? Who knows? But the damsel in distress is an age-old archetype. And I have to imagine that's for a reason. The dude in distress, not so much.

Another fallacy promulgated by the focus of the show, is that in slasher films, *women* are the predominant victims. This observation has been regurgitated so often by critics of the genre that horror apologists such as myself have instinctively tried to explain the reasons for it, just as I did above. But here's the kicker . . . despite everything we've been told to the contrary, women are *not* disproportionately represented as the victims in slasher films. Not by a long shot. As the eminent statesman Daniel Patrick Moynihan once said, "Everyone is entitled to his own opinion, but not to his own facts." In his book *Blood Money: A History of the First Teen Slasher Film Cycle*, Richard Nowell includes the following appendix: "Victim Gender in Teen Slasher Films, October 1978–April 1982." The grand total: seventy-seven male victims, representing 59.7 percent of the deceased. Female victims number fifty-two, or 40.3 percent. Whatever one may think about Nowell's often impenetrable prose, *Blood Money* is metic-

---

* Argento's English leaves much to be desired, so there's always the question of spotty translation. However, this quote has appeared in so many sources that it must be somewhat accurate.

ulously researched and sourced. But if you're not convinced, if you still find it impossible to believe that the irredeemably misogynistic slasher film is really an equal-opportunity executioner, let's go to another source. In Justin Kerswell's *The Slasher Movie Book*, a much more accessible—not to mention beautifully designed—tome, he includes a similar sidebar. Unlike Nowell, Kerswell is no academic. He is, however, the creator of Hysteria Lives!, one of the oldest and most comprehensive slasher-themed sites on the web, so I'm equally predisposed to accept his findings. He determines that in the 175 slasher films made between 1978 and 1984, generally accepted as the golden age of slasher films, 558 of the 1,046 on-screen deaths were male, while only 488 were female. Now, even if you find the gender discrepancy in both Nowell and Kerswell's findings negligible, which it's really not, it's absolutely impossible to make the case that females bear the brunt of the violence. But why let the truth get in the way of a good argument?

Moving on, to illustrate a "sleazy" movie for his audience, Ebert opts for a clip from *When a Stranger Calls*. He couldn't have picked a worse example. *Stranger* is the absolute antithesis of the slasher film. Aside from a nail-biting opening, and an equally terrifying coda, *Stranger* is a languid character study of a rather pathetic and not entirely unsympathetic sociopath. If it can be criticized for anything it's for being too subtle. Even more perplexing is the specific scene that Ebert chooses to show: it's possibly the most frightening twenty minutes in the history of horror cinema. A bold claim, I know. But I can't think of any phrase more fraught with dread, or more likely to make the blood of my babysitting girlfriends run cold, than "Have you checked the children?" (Not that I would have ever called them and uttered it in those glorious days before caller ID.) Following the clip, Ebert scoffs that this "basic scene has provided the premise for at least a dozen films in the last year." *At least a dozen in the past year?* Seems like Siskel's penchant for exaggeration is contagious. Aside from *Black Christmas*, which five years earlier pioneered the call-coming-from-inside-the-house device, I can think of only a handful of films in the entire slasher cycle that use threatening phone calls in any capacity whatsoever. But according to Ebert, 1979 was apparently a bumper year for prank calls at the movies.

Siskel has an idealized view of "strong women" like Jane Fonda and Jill Clayburgh and laments the fact they can only make one movie or so each year, while slasher films—filled with female representations of which he doesn't approve—are bludgeoning audiences on a weekly basis. Apparently, someone forgot to remind him that Fonda won her Best Actress Oscar for playing a whore and, in his own example of *An Unmarried Woman*, Clayburgh is a woman who defines her self-worth, at least for a large portion of the film, by the men in her life.

Ebert then attempts to make a distinction between movies like *Psycho* and *Halloween*—which both he and Siskel liked—and the current crop of horror films. "These films hate women," he thunders angrily about the latter. "And unfortunately, the audiences that go to them don't seem to like women much either." He complains about being forced to endure the films not in some cushy screening room, but in ordinary theaters with the hoi polloi, an experience he describes as "scary."

Should anyone still be confused about which films specifically comprise this "disturbing new trend," Siskel offers up the names of the worst offenders. *Prom Night*. *Don't Go in the House*.

The Howling. Yes, *The Howling*, which Siskel describes as "a new movie about a woman who goes alone on a vacation and is tortured by the locals." Is he fucking kidding me? Where did he come up with this plot summary? Because he sure as hell didn't see the movie. That's like describing *The Godfather* as the story of an American man living in Italy who must decide whether to take over the family business following the tragic death of his wife. What's ironic is that, had he watched it, Siskel should have loved *The Howling*. It was made by low-budget auteur and Roger Corman disciple Joe Dante and filled with flourishes of black humor. Furthermore, the script was written by indie darling John Sayles and lovingly references many classic horror films and horror film directors from the 1930s and '40s. Siskel continues to drone on, listing additional films: *Terror Train*, *The Boogeyman*, *He Knows You're Alone* (which he calls *He Knows YOU ARE Alone*, adding a touch of class by forgoing the contraction), *Motel Hell*, *Phobia*, *Mother's Day*, *Schizoid*, *Silent Scream*, and *I Spit on Your Grave*, which "is easily the worst of this disgusting bunch." About *I Spit*, Ebert concurs, calling it "the most violent, extreme, grotesque, nauseating R-rated picture I've ever seen."

I'm no *I Spit* apologist. In *Going to Pieces* I described it as "truly a vile film" and "not even a film as much as a series of highly disturbing skits designed to repulse." However, I'm also an enormous hypocrite. In 2010, I wrote the script for the remake of *I Spit on Your Grave* under a pseudonym, Stuart Morse.* My reasons for taking the gig were twofold. One, I

* Anyone who guesses the inspiration for this pseudonym gets reimbursed for their purchase of this book. Just kidding, but it *is* horror related.

needed the money. If it was a choice between my kids being able to attend summer camp and having some egg on my face, well, pass the salt and pepper. Two, there was something enticing about reimagining arguably the most notorious exploitation film ever made. Plus, if truth be told, *I Spit* is not nearly as irredeemable as I proclaimed in 2002. In fact, there's plenty to recommend about it, not least of all its raw energy. This was just the twenty-five-year-old me trying to be cute and self-righteous.

My reasons for adopting a pseudonym were also twofold. At the time, I was working for a company that created educational programs for children. As head of sales, I was oftentimes the only point of contact that prospective clients had with our company. Were they to Google me, I didn't know how good it would look to have this particular credit front and center. In addition, the year before, I had written another controversial film called *Wicked Lake* under my own name. I figured, okay, you write one rape-revenge film and nobody can pigeonhole you. It's just a job. But you write two and suddenly people start looking at you like, "What the fuck is wrong with this guy?"*

Turns out, I picked the wrong film on which to use a pseudonym. *Wicked Lake* was released to nearly unanimously terrible reviews. Ron Jeremy called it the worst movie he had ever seen. The remake of *I Spit*, on the other hand, received surprisingly positive notices. Not from the mainstream press, of course. They're basically a bunch of reactionaries who never understood the film in the first place. But from horror writers.

* Between *Wicked Lake* and *I Spit on Your Grave*, I also wrote a sappy movie for the Hallmark Channel. So make of that what you will.

And I say surprising because if there's one thing that horror critics generally despise it's remakes, especially remakes for which there is no discernible reason. I digress.

Suddenly, Siskel announces that he has a theory. He's absolutely convinced that the prevalence of these films is a backlash against the women's movement. Or as he puts it, "some primordial response by some very sick people." As supporting evidence, he points out that the killer is most often a man who is "sexually frustrated with these new aggressive women, and so he strikes back at them. He throws knives at them. He can't deal with them, he cuts them up, he kills them. Get back in your place. It's against the women's movement." Ebert agrees: "I think you're basically right, Gene."

Siskel's theory makes for good copy. It's quite salacious to imagine that a cabal of demented individuals are playing out their repressed fantasies for mass consumption. But does it hold up to scrutiny? Let's agree that the "sick people" to whom Siskel is referring are the directors, as they're the ones whose creative vision is the driving force behind these films. After all, it's not the actors, as most are just young thespians desperate for a break. Or any of the crew, craftsmen, or honest laborers, far removed from the message of the film. Or even the producers, bean counters who would just as soon make fine-art documentaries if that's what audiences paid to see.

This is hardly a scientific rebuttal, but I've had the good fortune to get to know many of these "sick" directors. They're some of the most delightful and kindhearted people in the industry. John (*Halloween*) Carpenter, while somewhat ornery nowadays, is generally beloved by his female stars. Sean (*Friday the 13th*) Cunningham is a clean-cut family man. Paul

(*Prom Night*) Lynch is a witty Brit. George (*My Bloody Valentine*) Mihalka now makes children's films. Joe (*The Prowler*) Zito is one of the nicest individuals you'll ever meet. Even Meir (*I Spit on Your Grave*) Zarchi, who, judging by his films, must surely be the worst of the worst, was surrounded by his beaming wife and loving family when I first met him. The list goes on and on. For Siskel to claim anything to the contrary, based solely on these artists' (and yes, Gene, they are artists) output, is not only fallacious but completely irresponsible. Remember, he doesn't call their *work* sick—still untrue but at least a legitimate criticism—he calls them sick *individuals* who hate women.

What about the second part of Siskel's theory, where he describes the motivation of the killer as a violent reaction to women's lib? What evidence does he have for this? None, of course. But for the hell of it, let's see if he has a point. Below I've listed ten of the most well-known and successful slasher films, followed by the motivation of the film's killer. If Siskel is right, then at least some—if not *most*—of the films should support his theory.

Halloween: Killer is "purely and simply evil." He has no sexual urges whatsoever.
Friday the 13th: Killer is a woman. Theory not applicable.
Prom Night: Revenge. Killer is avenging the death of his sister.
Terror Train: Revenge. Killer was humiliated by the popular kids.
The Burning: Revenge. Killer was disfigured by mischievous campers.

The Prowler: Revenge. Killer was jilted by his lover.
Night School: Killer is a woman. Theory not applicable.
Happy Birthday to Me: Killer is a woman. Theory not applicable.
My Bloody Valentine: Revenge/insanity. Killer saw his father murdered.
Graduation Day: Revenge/insanity. Killer's girlfriend died tragically.

Not a *single one* of these slashers fits the paradigm that Siskel describes, that of a sexually frustrated man unable to deal with a new breed of sexually liberated woman. Again, not a *single one*. In fact, the only film from this time that might fit the bill is Bill Lustig's *Maniac*, and even that's a stretch, as the maniac's psychosis is rooted in childhood abuse, not sexual frustration.

So what does this prove? Either, A) Siskel has never even seen the films in question (unlikely, but considering his description of *The Howling*, not inconceivable), B) Siskel has seen the films but possesses the cognitive ability of a sea cucumber (equally unlikely; I may disagree with every single thing Siskel says, but obviously he's an intelligent man), or C) for whatever reason, Siskel is so caught up in the mission at large that he's unable or unwilling to deviate from his pet theory, even when incontrovertible evidence to the contrary is staring him right in the face.

There's no prize for the right answer.

Next up is the opening scene of *Friday the 13th* (not counting the film's prologue). A bright-eyed counselor hitchhiking to Camp Crystal Lake accepts a ride with the wrong person. By the time she realizes her mistake, it's too late. She jumps from the car, twists her ankle, and limps off into the forest, where the killer eventually slits her throat. According to Ebert, this scene "demonstrates a very common and probably very significant technique that's used again and again in these films." We see the murder—or at least the chase—from the killer's point of view, whereas "traditional" horror films take the victim's perspective. Or so says Ebert. It seems he forgot all about *Peeping Tom*, the essence of cinematic voyeurism, which he reveres as a masterpiece. Or more recently, the opening scene of *Halloween*, another favorite that he goes on to praise later in the show. Here not only do we see a brutal stabbing from the killer's POV, but the killer also happens to be a six-year-old boy.

Ebert's problem with *Friday the 13th*'s POV technique is that he feels it forces the audience to identify with the killer as opposed to the victim. He's not alone in this belief. Hack film critics will tell you that in taking on the killer's POV, audiences are transformed from passive viewers into active participants, as if we accept some culpability for the on-screen acts. I never bought into this theory because, frankly, it's a load of crap. How does watching a film in which everything is predetermined by the filmmaker have any bearing on personal responsibility? Now, this isn't to say that different shooting techniques can't create a panoply of effects. After all, a POV shot, which by its very nature puts the action front and center, usually heightens emotion. I assume this explains the recent rise in POV porn (well, that and smaller cameras). But does it make us all a bunch of vicarious Jack (or Jane) the Rippers? I think not.

What's especially surprising is that absolutely nowhere in

the program does either Siskel or Ebert touch upon the most obvious, and accurate, explanation for slasher domination: the economic one. Slasher films made a shitload of money. If Sean Cunningham's early film about a Little League baseball team, *Here Come the Tigers*, went on to make $30 million (or even $10 or $15 mil), maybe he would have made *Here Come the Lions*, or *the Bears*, or *the Aardvarks*, but certainly not *Friday the 13th*.

Early on in *Blood Money*, Nowell explains the main thesis of his book, which is in essence a refutation of the prevailing theories about the proliferation of slasher films.

> Thus, where scholars have, to date, commonly applied psychoanalytic models to representation of gender in early teen slasher films in order to claim that they were formulaic, excessively violent exploitation films that were fashioned to satisfy the misogynist fantasies of male visitors to grind-houses and fleapits, by examining the commercial logic, strategies, and objectives of the American and Canadian independents that produced the films and the companies that distributed them in the US, this book demonstrates that filmmakers and marketers actually went to extraordinary lengths to make early teen slashers attractive to female youth, to minimize displays of violence, gore, and suffering, and to invite comparisons to a wide range of post-classical Hollywood's biggest hits, including *Love Story* (1970), *Saturday Night Fever* (1977), *Grease*, and *Animal House* (both 1978).

I'm not sure what's more impressive, that Nowell manages to obliterate the commonly held belief that slasher films were a reaction to *something* other than a desire to make a healthy profit, or that he does so in a single—albeit endless—sentence.

Critics love looking for complex psychological reasons for the creation of art, even when the obvious is staring them right in the face. Besides Wes Craven, usually cited as the slasher film's reigning intellectual, and a few sporadic statements by John Carpenter (which truthfully feel like he's just playing up to the interviewer), none of the slasher film directors have ever said their purpose was anything other than to make an entertaining and, more importantly, profitable movie. This is not to suggest that just because a film makes money it provides any benefit to society at large. But if *this* was the critics' argument, why not explicitly state it? If, on the surface, popular culture is so morally bankrupt as to be self-evident, then why construct, and give credence to, a much flimsier theory?

But I guess I understand the urge to play amateur shrink. After all, let's say you're a freelance writer looking to grab your editor. What's more compelling, that Michael Myers is a projection of sexual repression and stunted adolescence? Or that he was born to suck the teat of good old-fashioned capitalism?

The distributors, who only cared about putting asses in the seats, had a refreshingly sober view on the issue. "You can never go wrong with a movie that makes a girl move closer to her date," said Jere Henshaw, a vice president at American International Pictures, a company that understood the youth market better than anyone. Henshaw couldn't have been more right. I've seen *A Nightmare on Elm Street* close to fifty times. The only viewing I distinctly remember was in seventh grade when two of my girlfriends came over to watch it. For the entire film, I had one of them nuzzled under my left arm, the other under my right. It was the most memorable sexual experience of my life in which no fluids were exchanged.

The irony is that *A Nightmare on Elm Street*, with its themes of familial guilt and subconscious danger, practically begs for a psychoanalytic reading. But I'd just be trying to sound smarter than I am. Now, this doesn't mean that there's *nothing* percolating beneath the surface—no grand themes or deeper meaning. But it *does* mean that most people enjoyed *Nightmare* without giving an ounce of consideration to its subtext. In one of the film's most iconic scenes, the teenage heroine Nancy relaxes in a warm bath. Seconds after she drifts off to sleep, Freddy's finger knives break the surface of the water, right between her legs. It's a chilling, unforgettable image rife with symbolism. I didn't care about any of this. All I was focused on were the girls on either side of me. And if one of them decided to put something between *her* legs, I was going to make damn sure it was my hand.

Despite all claims to the contrary, Siskel and Ebert must have had a soft spot for *Friday the 13th*, as they keep returning to it. In the next clip they show from the film, one of the characters, wearing only panties and a tight T-shirt, hears a noise and goes off to investigate. So as not to offend their more delicate viewers, we cut out before the climax—a graphic ax to her face. Siskel angrily declares, "In the past year I must have seen that scene one hundred or one hundred fifty times. Every movie of this kind has eight or ten scenes just like it. I am sick of them!"

In a weird little aside, Siskel wonders if viewers will watch these films and imitate the behavior of the killers. "Some people may, I don't know," he says dismissively. However, he doesn't seem particularly disturbed by the idea. In fact, he seems a lot more freaked out about the film's theoretical implications than about the possibility that people might actually be inspired to kill one another. For most critics, however, this is their main beef with the slasher: that on-screen butchery leads to real-world violence.

Horror fans, unsurprisingly, take a particularly dim view of this theory, since most of us are well-adjusted, contributing members of society. So instead of addressing it head-on, we choose to deny it. I can't tell you how many times I've read defenses of violent entertainment in which the author states unequivocally that there has never been a reputable study that shows a positive correlation between the consumption of violent media and antisocial behavior. That's bullshit. I could find you dozens if not hundreds of such studies that show a moderate or even significant correlation. Despite what cable news has led us to believe, you can't legitimately win an argument by pretending the opposing view doesn't even exist.

That said, I'm generally skeptical about academic studies. My senior year in college at the University of Wisconsin–Madison, I took a course taught by a lovely older professor well-known for her groundbreaking scholarship on the effects of media. Her class focused on the relationship between fictional violence and aggression in children. For an ongoing class project—which commenced on day one and concluded on the final day of the semester—we had to interview dozens of parents about the viewing habits of their children. Then we would ask them about the children's subsequent behavior. After analyzing all the responses, we would draw our conclusion. Well, it should come as no surprise to anyone who knew me in college that the day before the project was due I had not interviewed a single parent. I think I might have even forgotten about the entire thing were it not for the fact that Feldman, my housemate who was also in the class, inadvertently unearthed his syllabus at the last moment. So we did what any enterprising college student would do—got drunk off our asses, ordered in from the Pizza Pit, stayed up all night, and forged every single one of those questionnaires. I actually felt guilty the next day when, after we made our presentations to the class, the professor complimented us on our work. I was always afraid—though not enough to confess—that one day the professor would publish another one of her well-received books, relying at least in part on our data.

Whenever people question the veracity of scientific studies they're usually concerned about the possible bias of the conductor. What they should be far more worried about is the integrity of those compiling the data. If this usually falls to goofballs like me and Feldman, I can't begin to imagine how many other studies have been corrupted. Maybe everything we know about the universe is suspect. Is regular exercise and a good night's sleep secretly hardening my arteries? Could an all-bacon diet and midmorning cigar really be the key to longevity?

However, let's pretend that all studies are conducted flawlessly by meticulous professionals—not inebriated undergrads—under the most rigorously enforced controls. I could still find ways to dispute the methodology. Or minimize the findings. Or even come up with completely different ways to interpret the results.

There are also correlations that simply can't be easily explained, as they seem to fly in the face of common sense. For example, it's indisputable that violent crimes—even violent crimes among youths—have plummeted over the past twenty years. And yet over this same period I don't think anyone would deny that entertainment has become *far* more violent, even if we take first-person shooter games out of the equation.

Although it might make us uncomfortable, let's accept the fact that people who commit violent crimes watch a disproportionate amount of violent entertainment. Because let's be honest, it's probably true.

What I believe has been lost in the entire debate, and what I'm convinced is the most important component of it, is the reason *why* we watch. After all, we know people have entirely different psychological, emotional, and even physiological reactions to the same stimuli. Whenever NFL Films shows the famous play from *Monday Night Football* where Lawrence Taylor snaps Joe Theismann's tibia like a wishbone on Thanksgiving, I have to look away. Same thing goes for the injury of that Louisville basketball player in the 2013 Final Four, where his bone was sticking clear out of his shin. I assume most people have the same reaction (which makes me wonder, why the hell do they still keep showing it?). On the other hand, my business partner Alex Flaster once directed a documentary about Joe Clark, a seventeen-year-old who abducted a young boy and over the next forty-three hours proceeded to break most of the bones in both his legs. Clearly this psychopath didn't have the same aversion.

Wouldn't it stand to reason then that people watch horror movies for a multitude of purposes? Some, like me, started watching them almost as a dare, then kept watching for the vicarious thrill. Others might get off on the startling special effects. Still others might find comfort in the formulaic archetypes. And some—hopefully very few, but still some—might use horror films to satisfy their actual sadistic tendencies. But if there were no horror movies, and it was all *Mary Poppins* and the Wiggles, I promise you, those lunatics would still be out there. Horror movies don't create real-life monsters and aren't in any way liable for their existence. To use an oft-quoted line from *Scream*, "Movies don't create psychos. Movies make psychos more creative."

Still, horror movies have always been a convenient scapegoat. *Natural Born Killers*, *Child's Play* 3, *Scream*, Rob Zombie's *Halloween*, and countless others have been fingered as the inspiration for gruesome murders. And truthfully, maybe they were. Between the alarmist press, the knee-jerk reactionaries, and the less-than-precise diagnosis of mental illness, determining the actual cause of violence is nearly impossible.

Sometimes, however, the connection is explicit.

On January 18, 2003, the body of twenty-one-year-old Thomas McKendrick was found in a shallow grave. He had been bludgeoned with a hammerlike object and stabbed in the face over forty times. The killer was his best friend, twenty-two-year-old Allan Menzies. Menzies was obsessed with the forgettable (though apparently not for him) film *Queen of the Damned*, based on the bestselling Anne Rice novel. He had watched it at least one hundred times, sometimes multiple times a day. As reality slipped away, Menzies became convinced that the main character Akasha was his queen. He committed the murder at her behest.

Now, clearly Menzies is crazy by any measure. And equally clear, he was definitely motivated by *Queen of the Damned*. But what does this prove? Chapman was inspired by *The Catcher in the Rye*. Hinckley by Jodie Foster in *Taxi Driver*. Berkowitz by his neighbor's dog. All this shows is that mental illness finds a home in a myriad of places. At the risk of sounding like the narrator in those commercials for Time-Life Books, or a second-rate Rod Serling, when you're dealing with the mysteries of the human mind, uncertainty is the only thing that's certain.

As a lifelong (mostly) Chicagoan, Ebert was intimately familiar with Bughouse Square, a nickname for Washington Square Park, which for much of its history was a place for activists, revolutionaries, dreamers, and garden-variety nut jobs to gather and debate the issues of the day. As if channeling the spirits of those long-lost orators, he gets up on his soapbox. "There is a difference between good and scary movies and movies that systematically demean half the human race. There is a difference between movies which are violent but entertaining and movies that are gruesome and despicable. There is a difference between a horror movie and a freak show."

Following this rant, we move on to a scene from *Halloween*, a film that, again, both he and Siskel greatly enjoyed and admired. Jamie Lee Curtis is trapped in a closet while Michael Myers menaces her with a kitchen knife. It would seem that this scene encapsulates everything the duo hates about the slasher film. After all, the dominant image is Curtis cowering in fear, her shirt ripped, as Michael tries to stick a knife in her. There's certainly no discernible difference between this scene and others they've railed against. But as Lee Corso would say, "Not so fast, my friend!" According to Ebert, "*Halloween* is directed and acted with a great deal more artistry and craftsmanship than the sleaze-bucket movies we've been talking about." It's a justification that artists have been using since time immemorial: execution can elevate content.

It's the reason why *Salò, or the 120 Days of Sodom* is considered a masterpiece while Kink.com is obscene. Why *Lolita* is read in college classrooms but online schoolgirl fantasy stories are tawdry. Why Mapplethorpe is a genius and Anthony Weiner a pervert. (For the record, I find *Salò* complete and utter shit [no pun intended], *Lolita* thinly veiled child porn, and Mapplethorpe silly. But whatever, high culture was never my thing.)

The episode is drawing to a close so Siskel needs to wrap things up. With typical hyperbole he says, "These women-in-danger films all really boil down to just one same image. One disturbing image. A woman screaming in abject terror." Ebert ends with what amounts to a public service announcement about how to recognize these films by their posters ("Usually has a knife! Or a hatchet! Or an ax!"),* as if they're some communicable disease to be prevented by hand-washing or slapping on a condom.

In retrospect, the effect of Siskel and Ebert's crusade was negligible. At best, it may have galvanized a few housewives in Des Moines† who were previously unaware of slasher films but now quite worried that their once-innocent teenagers could be exposed to such Hollywood garbage.

It also may have reminded the Motion Picture Association of America (MPAA), under whose purview the film ratings fell, that they really dropped the ball in letting *Friday the 13th*

---

* Ebert unknowingly foreshadows one of the greatest taglines ever conceived: *By Sword, by Pick, by Axe, Bye Bye*, from *The Mutilator*.

† I have no idea why I always use Des Moines as the representative middle-America city. But I mean no disrespect. I've been there once; it's a lovely place.

get by with an R rating, considering how graphic the murders were. Who knows how embarrassed the organization really was—although I've heard reports that MPAA honcho Jack Valenti was furious—but there's no question that the murders in subsequent slashers such as *Friday the 13th Part 2*, *My Bloody Valentine*, *Terror Train*, and *Happy Birthday to Me* were far less explicit—and not by design. Fortunately, most of these films have now been rereleased in uncut versions with all their gore effects restored (in the old days, the naughty bits were only available on bootlegs or foreign imports, which could be prohibitively expensive).

Speaking of naughty, the attack on slasher films in the United States was nothing compared to that of our friends across the pond. Europeans love to paint Americans as puritanical and sexually repressed, but the British are a far more uptight bunch. Until recently, hard-core pornography was basically outlawed. In July 2013, Prime Minister David Cameron announced that Internet service providers (ISPs) would be asked to automatically block access to pornographic sites, unless customers actively decided to "opt in" by contacting their ISP. Can anyone imagine a similar measure being seriously considered in America, other than by some fringe religious group? I was going to write that pornography has become as American as baseball and apple pie, but that's doing a severe disservice to our patriotic smut peddlers. After all, a lot of people hate pie and the 2013 World Series had an average 8.9 rating, meaning about 14.9 million people watched. By comparison, that very day, about 40 million Americans visited an adult website.

Commentators love to bemoan the polarization of American politics. You want an issue that crosses party lines and unites the masses? Try taking away our Internet porn. You'll have New England liberals linking arms in solidarity with Deep South rednecks to protect life, liberty, and the pursuit of cum-shot compilations.

Apparently, the British had their knickers in a twist over home video technology even before questionable content began to dominate the offerings. According to David Kerekes and David Slater in their definitive book on the subject, *See No Evil: Banned Films and Video Controversy*, there was a very real fear that British citizens were becoming addicted to home video. Because these "videoholics" were not constrained by any external safeguard—unlike television, which signed off at midnight—these addicts could theoretically watch forever. One only has to think back to the sparse offerings in the early days of home video to understand how ludicrous this concern was. It seems that VCR theft was also a major problem in Britain. A device called Videoalert, which emitted an ear-splitting siren whenever the unit was moved, was designed to ward off would-be thieves. I don't know which is worse, losing a relatively expensive piece of technology, or enduring the equivalent of a foghorn blast every time I bumped into my entertainment center.

An early opponent of Britain's nascent video industry was the National Viewers' and Listeners' Association (NVALA).* Founded in 1965 by a schoolteacher named Mary Whitehouse,

---

* For whatever reason, this acronym has always reminded me of NAMBLA, the North American Man/Boy Love Association, an organization I still can't believe is allowed to exist, since it advocates for child rape. Through either research or out of curiosity, I've probably Googled every legal sexual perversion known to man, and visiting NAMBLA.org is the only time I've literally felt sick to my stomach.

NVALA's original target was television, but it soon turned its focus to other objectionable mediums, none more famously than videos. Whitehouse was straight out of central casting. With her prim haircut and severe features, she looked the part of a sanctimonious scold. She was both beloved and feared by the establishment, and before her work was done she would be appointed Commander of the Most Excellent Order of the British Empire. Not surprisingly, she was equally detested by the artistic community. The Pink Floyd song "Pigs (Three Different Ones)," from their 1977 album, *Animals*, calls out Whitehouse by name. It's obviously supposed to be a scathing indictment of her hypocrisy, but like most of Pink Floyd's lyrics that I once found brilliant, now it just sounds silly.

While Whitehouse was unquestionably the face of the movement, her ideas found a willing audience in a public already galvanized against horror movies. Newspapers stoked this fear with sensationalist stories about robberies and rapes committed by juveniles who blamed their antisocial behavior on home videos. It did not help that in the early days of the video panic the Yorkshire Ripper was still on the loose. This serial killer murdered thirteen women before he was apprehended in the winter of 1981. When the truth about his grisly crimes came to light, it read like something right out of a slasher script.

Initially, video distributors were not required to obtain certification for their films, unlike theatrical releases, which had to be reviewed by the British Board of Film Censors (BBFC). The result was an explosion in horror and exploitation titles that previously had no chance of seeing the light of day (or light of a projector bulb on a theater screen). The authorities, however, were not completely hamstrung. The Obscene Publications Act (OPA) allowed police to seize videotapes that, in their opinion, had a "tendency to deprave and corrupt." I never understood why obscene materials thought to have a detrimental effect on the general public wouldn't also impact those whose job it was to determine their harmfulness. Apparently, society's moral guardians are made of tougher stuff. Maybe Mary Whitehouse was really a nunsploitation aficionado?

In 1982, *The Driller Killer*, *Death Trap*, and *I Spit on Your Grave* were all successfully prosecuted under the OPA. But this wasn't good enough. Under pressure from the public, the press, and, of course, Mary Whitehouse, the director of public prosecutions drafted a list of thirty-nine film titles that were suitable for prosecution. The films on this list became known as the fabled video nasties.* Over the years, the number of films on the list fluctuated, as some were added and others removed, evidently not depraved enough to still warrant inclusion.

Then, in July 1984, authorities brought out the big guns with the passage of the Video Recordings Act. The thrust of the law, and its most chilling stipulation, was that prior to release all videos had to be certified by the BBFC. The fallout was

* In the absence of any "official" list, the following are the films generally cited as the initial thirty-nine video nasties: *Absurd*, *Andy Warhol's Frankenstein*, *Anthropophagous*, *Axe*, *The Beast in Heat*, *Blood Bath*, *Blood Feast*, *Blood Rites*, *Bloody Moon*, *The Burning*, *Cannibal Apocalypse*, *Cannibal Ferox*, *Cannibal Holocaust*, *Cannibal Man*, *The Devil Hunter*, *Don't Go in the Woods*, *The Driller Killer*, *Evilspeak*, *Exposé*, *Faces of Death*, *Fight for Your Life*, *Forest of Fear*, *Gestapo's Last Orgy*, *The House by the Cemetery*, *The House on the Edge of the Park*, *I Spit on Your Grave*, *Island of Death*, *The Last House on the Left*, *Love Camp 7*, *Madhouse*, *Mardi Gras Massacre*, *Nightmares in a Damaged Brain*, *Night of the Bloody Apes*, *Night of the Demon*, *Snuff*, *SS Experiment Camp*, *Tenebrae*, *The Werewolf and the Yeti*, and *Zombie Flesh Eaters*.

catastrophic. Because the cost of certification was prohibitively high, many small independent distributors who specialized in videos of questionable content were forced out of business. The remaining few that tried to play the government's game saw their films shredded so badly as to be almost unrecognizable. After all, if you try to eliminate all the offensive content from, say, *I Spit on Your Grave*, you're basically left with a fifteen-minute promotional video for some lakeshore real estate.

One unintended but completely predictable consequence was a robust video black market that sprang up virtually overnight. Nasties that once couldn't be given away now commanded several hundred dollars. It's a principle familiar to any student who ever took an introductory econ class: value is inversely proportional to supply. Then there's the principle familiar to any parent, or to any person with a lick of common sense: the more forbidden something is, the more attractive it becomes. I can't imagine someone actually wanting to watch *Night of the Bloody Apes*. That is, until being told they're not allowed to.

Part of the fun of revisiting moral panics surrounding slasher films, the video nasties, and other forms of controversial entertainment is watching nostalgia slowly replace indignation. Even the most alarmist campaigns eventually lose steam. Manufactured outrage has a relatively brief shelf life. I mean, is there anybody out there who still believes that comic books portend the end of the Western civilization? Today, that mindset is more quaint than threatening.

Except when it isn't.

In October 2009, Montreal makeup artist Rémy Couture met with a prospective client. A man and his girlfriend wanted

Couture to help them stage a series of provocative photos. But they weren't really a freaky couple; they were undercover officers. Couture was handcuffed, thrown in the back of a squad car, and charged with "corrupting morals," which sounds like something out of Orwell, not an actual crime in North America's most liberal country.

This whole sorry saga began back in 2006 when Interpol received complaints out of Germany and Austria about Couture's website, www.InnerDepravity.com (don't put the book down and run over to your computer; the site has since been disabled). The site was created from the perspective of a fictional psychopath and sexual sadist. It contained dozens of photos and two short films of women being raped, tortured, and mutilated (not necessarily in that order). The material is some of the most disgusting I have ever seen. And Mr. Couture is one of the most talented makeup artists around.

Although the videos on Couture's website have production credits at the end (hardly what you would add to a super-secretive snuff film), an Austrian pathologist determined that the photos showed "possible manslaughter." This was enough "evidence" for Interpol to pass the information on to the Royal Canadian Mounted Police.

As word of the arrest began trickling out, Couture's plight became something of a minor cause célèbre for the horror community. Editorials and articles detailed the perceived injustice while blogs posted relevant updates. Tom Savini lent his support and the 2011 documentary *Art/Crime* focused on the case. A website was created to collect donations in order to help defray the cost of Couture's legal defense, which ran into the tens of thousands of dollars. T-shirts were printed with the slogan

"Art Is Not a Crime," as were G-strings emblazoned with the phrase "Corrupt Me."

In December 2012, the case finally went to trial. A seven-woman, five-man jury acquitted Couture on all three charges of corrupting morals by distributing, producing, and possessing obscene material.

He narrowly avoided up to two years in prison—for being too good at his work.

Although they were certainly no proponents of outright censorship, somewhere, Siskel and Ebert were smiling.

CHAPTER THREE

Horror High

I love lists. They're the reason I still cite *Sgt. Pepper's Lonely Hearts Club Band* as the greatest album ever made,* even though I actually think it's only the sixth-best *Beatles* album.†

Sometimes when I'm having trouble sleeping, which is often, I will seek out random lists of things in which I'm interested. In the last year alone, I've Googled "Greatest Heavy Metal Album Covers," "Most Beautiful Swimming Holes," "Greatest Professional Wrestlers," "Top 10 NCAA Football National Championship Teams," "Longest Underground Rivers," "Most Underrated Led Zeppelin Songs," "Coldest Temperatures on Earth," "Top 10 NBA Centers," "Greatest Horror Movie One-Sheets," "World's Deepest Caves," and "Most Painful Diseases."

So it would stand to reason that there needs to be a chapter

---

* According to *Rolling Stone*'s 2003 special issue "The 500 Greatest Albums of All Time."

† For those who care, I prefer, in descending order, *Abbey Road*; *Magical Mystery Tour*; either *Rubber Soul* or *Revolver*, then the other; and finally the White Album.

in which I combine my love of lists with my love of slasher films. But then I figured, there has to be a more compelling way to celebrate these films. I mean, would you be surprised that *Black Christmas*, *Halloween*, and *Friday the 13th* would be vying for the top spot? Or that Canadian imports like *Prom Night*, *My Bloody Valentine*, and *Happy Birthday to Me* would be rounding out the top ten? And how would I account for precursors to the slasher film, like *Psycho* and *Peeping Tom*? Plus, my opinions on these films change all the time, influenced by a variety of factors. Today, I might prefer *The Burning* to *Terror Train*, while tomorrow I might be high on *He Knows You're Alone* or *Night School*.

I started thinking about the most common characteristics of these slasher films, from their formal elements (final girl, revenge-minded psychopath, ineffective authority figures) to their stylistic flourishes (POV shots, jump scares). It occurred to me that with only a handful of exceptions (I'm looking at you, *My Bloody Valentine* and *Curtains*), the main characters in slasher films are in either high school or college. And what encapsulates this particular time better than a yearbook? Because the typical categories—Most Popular, Most Athletic, Class Clown, Most Likely to Succeed—aren't really applicable, I had to get a little creative. So sit back, crack open your brand-new copy of the Slasher Yearbook, and Keep in Touch . . . that is, if you manage to stay alive!

GREATEST KILLS

Slasherdom is chock-full of films that contain a single unforgettable murder. The decapitation in *The Mutilator* seems to be the *only* reason for the film's existence. But if we're going to choose one film that best represents the crème de la crème of slasher slayings, it would be a sacrilege to pick one not blessed by the work of Tom Savini.

Horror fans are as familiar with Savini's biography as they are their own. As a child, he would save the money he made from shining shoes in order to buy makeup. His experience as a combat photographer in Vietnam, where he found a measure of safety behind the camera, informed the realism of his later work. His makeup effects in *Friday the 13th* are iconic. In *Maniac*, infamous. In *The Burning*, the murders were too realistic for the censors and were subsequently watered down. *Friday the 13th: The Final Chapter* continues his Crystal Lake carnage, and the demise of Jason might be his most impressive set piece.

It's somewhat ironic, then, that it's one of Savini's lesser-known films that contains his best work. *The Prowler* is a tour de force of the master's magic. A bayonet is driven through the top of one unlucky victim's head, slicing through his cranial, sinus, and oral cavities until his eyeballs roll back into white and the blade emerges from beneath his chin. This scene concludes with a bloody pitchforking in the shower. There's also a cringe-inducing neck slashing in a swimming pool and a final exploding head that exceeds a similar effect in *Maniac*. Genius, all of it.

Distribution issues kept *The Prowler* from achieving the same notoriety as similar slashers, until Blue Underground gave it a proper DVD release twenty years later. For the collectors out there, the film's Mexican lobby card—on which it's called *Rosemary's Killer*—features some gorgeous artwork of the murders.

MOST LIKELY TO SUCCEED (BUT DIDN'T)

If only there were a surefire formula for box office success. But until someone comes up with a viable sabermetrics-like system, the closest thing we have to a Rosetta stone is William Goldman's famous adage "Nobody knows anything." The truth is, there's oftentimes no discernible reason why some films succeed while others fail. It's like trying to understand the logic behind Molly Ringwald's becoming a sex symbol in the eighties while the girl from *Can't Buy Me Love* couldn't get arrested. After all, any red-blooded teenager who had his first orgasm during the Reagan administration who says he didn't beat off at least once to Cindy Mancini is either lying or secretly in love with Patrick Dempsey.

Even the slasher film, the most formulaic of genres, can't beat the odds every time. Some films strike a chord while others don't. Some get picked up by a distributor that knows exactly what it's doing, while others are allowed to wither on the vine. But sometimes you see a film that for all intents and purposes *should* have done better. And *The House on Sorority Row* is one of those films.

We start with the perfect slasher setup. After a brief prologue of a traumatic pregnancy twenty years earlier, we jump to the present (in this case, 1983), where a bunch of sorority sisters are holding a final party before their house is closed for the summer. A practical joke (though I would use the term loosely) goes awry and their hated housemother, Mrs. Slater, is killed. Rather than turn themselves in, the girls realize the show (er, party) must go on! During the festivities, the girls are killed off one by one. Could Mrs. Slater have cheated death? Or is it her homicidal son, Eric, the baby from the prologue, who is very much alive and has been living in the attic all these years?

Director Mark Rosman was Brian De Palma's first assistant director on *Home Movies*, a forgettable film De Palma made between *The Fury* and *Dressed to Kill*. Right from the beginning of *The House on Sorority Row*, it's obvious the young acolyte learned well at the master's knee; an early tracking shot through the sorority house is vintage De Palma. I wouldn't go so far as to call it horror's *Touch of Evil*, but it's a classy bit of filmmaking for a genre in which class is a rare commodity. There's also a languid pan across the guilty faces of the partygoers that recalls *Carrie*'s ill-fated prom. If subtle camerawork isn't your bag, there's also a nice head-in-the-toilet gag that I'm surprised hasn't been ripped off more frequently.

Looking back, I'm blown away by how well *The House on Sorority Row* actually did at the box office. Released by exploitation specialist Film Ventures, as opposed to one of the majors, it took in over $10 million, beating out that year's better-known horror titles like *Amityville 3-D*, *The Hunger*, and *Something Wicked This Way Comes*. So why then do I say it didn't "succeed," when clearly it made back its budget multiple times over? Probably because it never *felt* like a success.

Released in January 1983, at the tail end of the slasher cycle, *The House on Sorority Row* was never spoken of with the same reverence as a *My Bloody Valentine* or a *Prom Night*. Or even lesser but earlier entries like *The Burning*, *Graduation Day*, or *Night School*. The poster art never beckoned to me from the shelf of the video store; it looks more like soft-core porn than horror. In fact, before I wrote *Going to Pieces*, I had seen the film exactly one time. That said, I have no doubt that if *Sorority Row* had hit theaters in the months following *Friday the 13th*, the name "Eric" would be as infamous as "Jason" or "Freddy" (or at least "Cropsy" or "Harry Warden"), and sequels in which a new crop of giggling coeds move into the vacant sorority house would have been churned out. The film was a victim of circumstance, as opposed to incompetence, which I suppose is the fairest thing you can say about it today.

MOST FUTURE STARS

Admittedly, slasher films are usually far from acting showcases, hardly training grounds for budding Oliviers. They are, however, perfect vehicles for young thespians looking to break into the business. The list of slasher alumni who have gone on to bigger and—at least in most people's eyes—better things is fairly impressive: George Clooney (*Return to Horror High*), Brad Pitt (*Cutting Class*), Kevin Bacon (*Friday the 13th*), Johnny Depp (*A Nightmare on Elm Street*), Renée Zellweger (*Texas Chainsaw Massacre: The Next Generation*).

So which slasher film had the best farm team? After a hard-fought battle, the victory goes to *The Burning*. Other films might have had bigger future stars—*He Knows You're Alone* featured Tom Hanks in his film debut—but none had so many solid prospects. This summer-camp slasher, which was cowritten by Miramax cofounder Bob Weinstein, stars Best Actress Oscar winner Holly Hunter, future *Seinfeld* funnyman Jason Alexander, the always solid Fisher Stevens, and, although he never did much else, *Fast Times at Ridgemont High*'s lovable nerd, Brian Backer.

Runner Up: *The Final Terror* (a.k.a. *Campsite Massacre*), with Rachel Ward, Adrian Zmed, Joe Pantoliano, and Daryl Hannah.

BIGGEST WTF MOMENT

It's not the ending of *Sleepaway Camp*. That would be too easy. After all, the film traumatized a generation of kids and became well-known—even to those who never saw it—as the one with "the chick with a dick." Oh, and in case you were worried about the young actress's well-being, they didn't strip her down and add a six-inch (I'm being *very* generous) pecker to her thirteen-year-old anatomy; it was an actor (so the penis was real) wearing a mask.

Luckily, there are plenty of other candidates, as the genre is filled with more than its share of head-scratchers, scenes that make you sit back, throw your hands up in submission, and just say, "What the fuck?" Scenes such as the finale of the Xmas slasher *Christmas Evil*, where the killer Santa makes his getaway by driving a van off a bridge—but instead of plummeting to his fiery death, he defies the laws of gravity (and coherent filmmaking) and continues flying toward the winter moon. Or what about the rocket scientist in *Slaughter High* who, after watching her friend's intestines explode from his stomach, somehow finds a working bathtub in a deserted high school and decides to strip naked for a soak! Solid choices for sure, but it's probably the ending of the survivalist slasher *Just Before Dawn* that takes the cake. The film's final girl, Constance, faces off against a backwoods behemoth by the light of her campfire.

It shouldn't be much of a fight—a petite blonde against a hulking maniac—until Constance literally shoves her tiny hand into the killer's mouth. She keeps pushing until her arm is halfway down his throat, eventually suffocating him. Constance is all fucked up after she realizes what she's done and the film ends on this rather downbeat note. You almost can't believe what you just saw. I guess it's a little less shocking today, where you have plenty of websites seemingly created for the sole purpose of proving that the human forearm can in fact fit into orifices you never thought imaginable.

Director Jeff Lieberman cites *Just Before Dawn* as his favorite among his films. It actually owes far more to movies like *Deliverance* than it does the slasher film. But the timing of its release (1981) and its stylistic trappings place it firmly in the slasher canon. Lieberman also directed the nature-run-amok (more accurately, the worm-run-amok) film *Squirm* (*my* favorite of his films) and the LSD-themed *Blue Sunshine*, which I guess makes the hallucinatory ending of *Just Before Dawn* all the more understandable.

BEST HOLIDAY SLASHER

Even as a Jew, I love everything about Christmas. I love the songs. "Dance of the Sugar Plum Fairy" is wonderfully creepy, "Carol of the Bells" sounds like metal,* and I have a soft spot for

* The main reason I make this connection is because the Savatage song "Christmas Eve/Sarajevo 12/24" is really just a hard-rock version of this carol.

"The Little Drummer Boy." I love the idea of mistletoe, that you can con a girl into kissing you by holding a parasitic plant above her head. I love the fact that the holiday's color scheme looks like Freddy's sweater. I love the pageantry, and as an unapologetic capitalist, I even love the crass commercialization of the holiday. If that offends the devout few, and you'd prefer to spend December 25 (even though Jesus was almost certainly not born on that day) dicking around a manger instead of tearing through presents and getting fucked up on eggnog, have at it.

As such, I feel a little bit like the Grinch for not choosing one of the many Christmas slashers for my favorite holiday horror. After all, most of them have something to recommend. *Black Christmas* is an indisputable classic. *Christmas Evil* is nutty. Both *Don't Open Till Christmas* and *Silent Night, Deadly Night* are sleazy fun. *Silent Night, Bloody Night* is a historical curiosity, while David Hess's *To All a Goodnight* proves, at the very least, that the man who immortalized Krug Stillo wasn't actually a criminal.

That said, they don't hold a (votive) candle to *My Bloody Valentine*. As the most popular of the so-called Canadian tax shelter films, *Valentine* was produced by John Dunning and André Link. In 1962, this legendary Canadian duo cofounded Cinépix (which would eventually become Lionsgate Films) and were responsible for some of the very best Canuxploitation, including Cronenberg's early films and the *Last House on the Left*–ish *Death Weekend*. Excuse the shameless name-dropping (although it's not like I'm tossing around Spielberg and Lucas), I knew Dunning very well before his unfortunate passing and am also friendly with *My Bloody Valentine*'s director, George Mihalka, so the film will always have a special place in my (bloody) heart.

But even without the personal connection, *Valentine* must be at the top of every self-respecting slasher fan's list. It has everything you could ask for in this type of film. The cast isn't comprised of clueless teenagers, but young adults struggling with life in a blue-collar town; think *All the Right Moves* with mines instead of mills and a pickax-wielding madman instead of Craig T. Nelson. The script is lean and economical, Mihalka's direction flawless, and the fact that it was shot in an actual mine (though closed down at the time) lends an air of authenticity that couldn't be duplicated on a soundstage, at least not on the film's budget. You also have a cheesy theme song that I have to imagine was done in jest but actually sounds like (or at least not worse than) fellow Canadian Gordon Lightfoot's "The Wreck of the Edmund Fitzgerald." When an Irish alt-rock trio christened themselves My Bloody Valentine, it also became the best horror film to lend its moniker to a rock band, although with the other contenders being *White Zombie* and *Two Thousand Maniacs!* (inspiring 10,000 Maniacs), there wasn't too much competition.

THE WORST . . . THE ABSOLUTE WORST SLASHER

It's embarrassing how much time I've spent considering the options.

From past experience, I narrowed down the finalists to *New Year's Evil*, *Home Sweet Home*, and *Don't Go in the Woods*. I have no idea which of these three celluloid atrocities is the genre's absolute nadir. To say all are stupefyingly bad is an insult to other awful films. This trio elevates ineptitude to an entirely new level. I guess the most remarkable thing is not that they were made at all—after all, a chimpanzee can make a film—but that anybody picked them up for distribution.

New Year's Evil is the most professionally made, and by this I mean the least incompetent. Roz Kelly, who played Pinky Tuscadero, Fonzie's main squeeze on *Happy Days*, is cast as Blaze, the on-camera host of a televised New Year's Eve rock special. During the show, she's terrorized by a caller who promises to murder one victim each time the clock strikes midnight in different time zones across the country. He identifies himself as "Eeevil" and uses an electronic device to make his voice sound like Stephen Hawking's. If this actually seems like a cool premise, don't worry, it's not. The killer is revealed as Blaze's ex-husband, who wears a sweat suit like a Russian mobster and hides his identity behind a Dick Nixon (I think) mask. The highlight of the entire film, aside from the end credits, is when the ex-husband tries to get into another character's pants by telling her, "There's a big party up at Erik Estrada's place."

For being so irredeemably terrible, *Home Sweet Home* has a strangely compelling pedigree. It's produced by and features Don Edmonds of *Ilsa: She Wolf of the SS* fame. Alex Rebar, star of *The Incredible Melting Man*, is the executive producer. A five- or six-year-old Vinessa Shaw, who went on to play the HIV-positive prostitute in Kubrick's *Eyes Wide Shut*, is the young daughter. But the star of the whole shebang is Jake Steinfeld, creator of Hollywood's Body by Jake fitness empire, as a drooling, homicidal, PCP-injecting, recently escaped mental patient. I've heard that Steinfeld has no sense of humor about his involvement with the film, which makes watching this travesty almost worthwhile.

Just before, I said I didn't know which of these three films was the worst. I was wrong. It has to be *Don't Go in the Woods*, since I just rewatched it and can't remember a single thing about the film other than some mountain man murders a bunch of hikers. I hate the fact that the sheriff in the movie is so morbidly obese it's distracting. I hate the fact that the film is sometimes referred to as *Don't Go in the Woods . . . Alone!* on poster art and home video for no reason whatsoever. I hate the actors, the script, the effects, and everything about it except for some nice travel shots of the Utah wilderness. But most of all, I hate it for simply existing. It's the worst slasher film ever made. And not in a so-bad-it's-good way. It just sucks. And at barely eighty minutes, it's seventy-eight minutes too long.

Postscript: A few weeks before I turned in this manuscript, I was perusing one of my favorite books, *Nightmare USA: The Untold Story of the Exploitation Independents*, by Stephen Thrower. To my complete and utter surprise, as soon as I began reading the section on *Don't Go in the Woods*, I remembered that Thrower had quite a bit of praise for the film he calls the "*quintessential* video nasty" (emphasis his). I had no choice. If an author who wrote two* of the most important works of horror criticism saw something so special about *Don't Go in the Woods*, there had to be something I was missing. So I went back and watched the movie *three fucking times*: on YouTube,

* As I mentioned in the prologue, Thrower also wrote the definitive tome on Lucio Fulci, *Beyond Terror: The Films of Lucio Fulci*.

off my old VHS tape, and finally the twenty-fifth-anniversary edition DVD. Was there some longer, uncut version that I had never seen that would finally allow me to see the light? Turns out, there wasn't—the film (all three versions) was as awful as I remembered. In fact, all this painfully long episode did was reinforce something I already knew—even the most brilliant writers are sometimes dead wrong.

MOST ANNOYING CHARACTER—MALE

Insert your own joke here. I mean, there's a reason the audience cheers following a good 95 percent of the killings in slasher films. The *Friday the 13th* series alone has a murderers' row of folks who can't die soon enough. There's Ted from *Part 2*, who "welcomes" his friends to Camp Crystal Lake by having their truck towed, and *Part 3*'s Shelly—also a contender for Character Least Likely to Get Laid—who unintentionally gives Jason his trademark hockey mask. And finally, good old Teddy Bear, Crispin Glover's foil from *The Final Chapter*, who gets stoned, watches an eight-millimeter stag film, and then gets put out of his sexless misery with a knife to the back of his skull. But all are more lovable losers than anything else. For someone who really engenders loathing, who makes you want to crawl into the screen and throttle him, we have to return to *Home Sweet Home*.

With this sentence—and certainly with the previous section on the worst slasher—I've undoubtedly written more about *Home Sweet Home* than it deserves. But we can't hold that against "the Mistake." You see, that's what all the grown-ups call the teenage rocker son of one of the characters: the Mistake. As in, he was a "mistake." They also spend the better part of the film musing about popping Valium and killing the kid. So it's not really a surprise that the Mistake retaliates by spying on them while they have sex and taunting them with priceless lines like "Rock and roll forever!" and "Let's get it on, baby!"

I once described the black-and-white-face-painted Mistake as a "KISS wannabe," but he's obviously much closer to a squirrelly Marcel Marceau with diarrhea of the mouth. And although we can blame his behavior on his worthless parents, unfortunately, that doesn't make him any more tolerable. When he finally ran into Jake Steinfeld, I was so grateful that this was the end of him, I went to the Body by Jake website and almost bought a Body Balance Air Pod for $29.99, a contraption that looks like it's guaranteed to break your ankle.

MOST ANNOYING CHARACTER—FEMALE

Sleepaway Camp may have been passed over for Biggest WTF Moment, but it returns stronger than ever to claim this category for everybody's favorite deranged aunt. Don't worry, though, this is no consolation prize born of pity. We don't have an Al Pacino Oscar situation on our hands. As most people will remember, Pacino was denied the statuette for *The Godfather*, *Serpico*, *The Godfather: Part II*, *Dog Day Afternoon*, *. . . And Justice for All*, and *Scarface*, until 1992, when he finally won Best Actor for *Scent of a Woman*, condemning him to a subsequent career of screaming guttural noises at the audience.

No, Aunt Martha is more than deserving of this honor. When we first meet her, she's about to send her son and niece, Angela, off to sleepaway camp. She's dressed like a gay sailor and ponders rhetorical questions out loud, but we can almost excuse this bizarre behavior since, as the previous scene revealed, the saintly woman adopted Angela after her father and brother were killed in a tragic boating accident. But quickly Aunt Martha becomes more grating than Freddy's nails on a chalkboard. Every word, every mannerism, reeks of purposeful overacting. But since there's no context for any of it, we're left scratching our heads. Watching her, I'm reminded of the audition scene from *True Romance*. In it, we have Michael Rapaport (a good actor), pretending to be Dick Ritchie (a bad actor), reading for the role of a good actor. I have no idea which one Aunt Martha really is—a good actor pretending to be bad, or a bad one trying to be good. I do know, however, that she has less than four minutes of screen time in the entire film and yet every second feels like an eternity.

At the end of *Sleepaway Camp*, we learn that Aunt Martha is not only annoying but batshit crazy. In reality, she adopted her *nephew* after the accident; her niece was the one actually killed. However, because she always wanted a daughter, she raised "Angela" as a girl, turning the poor kid into some kind of gender-confused homicidal freak.

I don't know why I feel compelled to add this, but from the interviews I've read it seems like the actress who played Aunt Martha, Desiree Gould, is a lovely normal woman. She became a successful real estate agent and appeared in only a handful of additional films. I still have no idea if she's a good actress, or why she made the creative choices she did, but it's pretty clear she's not the kind of person who, in real life, goes around psychologically castrating orphans.

MOST MISUNDERSTOOD

I loved *April Fool's Day* the first time I saw it. It's one of my favorite movies, period, and one of only four horror movie posters I have framed in my office (the others being *Creepshow*, *I Spit on Your Grave*, and *The Watcher in the Woods*). Unfortunately, few others seem to share this sentiment. Before writing any more, I feel obligated to give the mandatory spoiler alert. So if you've never seen the film twenty-nine years after its original release—but still plan to—please stop reading.

The film starts off like a typical slasher film by way of Agatha Christie's *And Then There Were None*.* Muffy St. John, a wealthy college student, invites a group of her friends to spend the weekend on her family's private island. After the requisite practical jokes, the cast is picked off one by one. The big twist, which comes with only a few minutes left in the film, reveals it all to be the ultimate April Fool's prank. It turns out that Muffy is set to receive the estate as part of her inheritance, but only if she can prove that it can pay for itself. To do so, she plans to stage murder mystery weekends. This was a trial run and her friends were the unwitting guinea pigs.

Ironically, it was the critics who seemed to appreciate the

* One of my favorite pieces of trivia, which absolutely nobody believes, is Christie's novel's original title. It's too offensive for me to even write but 100 percent true. Just go and Google it. Trust me.

joke the most. While the reviews were hardly glowing, most acknowledged that *April Fool's Day* was a cut above (my bad pun) its contemporaries, mainly slasher sequels, which were starting to be released with some regularity (the notable exception was Joel Rubinoff of the *Toronto Star*, who called the ending "so inept it could have been plucked from an old *Laverne & Shirley* episode"). Horror fans, on the other hand, hated the film (although it did make nearly $13 million). From what I can ascertain, they felt tricked (maybe the title should have given them a clue?), like when a particularly surreal episode of a TV series turns out to have been a dream. How this ruins the previous seventy-five minutes I don't know, but audiences clearly felt it was all a big joke that they weren't in on. That's too bad, because if you just sit back and enjoy the ride, then *April Fool's Day* is a lot of fun.

You have director Fred (*When a Stranger Calls*) Walton, who obviously knows a thing or two about suspense, expertly pulling the strings; one of the all-time best final girls in Amy Steel; Thomas F. Wilson, fresh off of *Back to the Future*; the always interesting Clayton Rohner; and Deborah Goodrich, the hot chick from *Just One of the Guys*. The real scam was that she bamboozled the twelve-year-old me into believing that all college girls were into casual sex and S & M. April Fool's indeed.

MOST RIDICULOUS TRIGGER

Look, I'm not trying to justify murder. But sometimes, I feel that the killers in slasher films get a raw deal. I mean, what if you were a harmless geek and the popular kids stuck your head in the toilet, yanked off your underwear, and burned off half your face with acid (*Slaughter High*)? Upon recovering, you probably wouldn't run right to the principal. Or what if you saw your sister die (*Prom Night*), your father murdered (*My Bloody Valentine*), or your poor young son sink to his watery grave because his camp counselors were making love (*Friday the 13th*)? You'd probably be pretty pissed off. Pissed off enough to pick up a convenient weapon and mete out some good old-fashioned vigilante justice.

In *Christmas Evil*, little Harry experiences nothing as traumatic. He sneaks downstairs to find his father, dressed as Santa Claus, sniffing his mother's crotch. Seriously. These two are either the most chaste couple I have ever seen or far too kinky for me to comprehend. The kids are asleep and they're finally alone—and *this* is the way they choose to work off their holiday stress. Mommy stands in front of the tree while Santa-suit-clad Daddy kneels in front of her, massaging her thigh and . . . smelling. Eventually, little Harry grows up, but instead of this oedipal episode leaving him with a distinct distaste for Christmas, it only exacerbates an obsessive love of the holiday. So of course, he takes it upon himself to spy on the neighborhood boys and girls and mark down which have been naughty and which have been nice. Oh, and he also murders those people who don't share in his seasonal glee.

The adult Harry is played by actor Brandon Maggart, father of singer Fiona Apple. Back in the nineties, Apple had a huge hit with the single "Criminal." The opening line is "I've been a bad bad girl." Every time I heard that fucking song—and I heard it *a lot*, since they played it everywhere—I would imagine Papa Maggart adding his daughter's name to his list. Since

Fiona had been *very* naughty, for her sake, I hope life didn't imitate art.

MOST INFLUENTIAL (PRE-*BLACK CHRISTMAS*)

It's often referred to as the first true "body count" film. It's also referred to as *A Bay of Blood*, *Blood Bath*, *Carnage*, *Chain Reaction*, and *Ecology of a Crime*—and this is to say nothing of its many non-English titles. I call it *Twitch of the Death Nerve*, both because that's the title under which I first saw the film and because it's my favorite of all the nonsensical appellations.

With *Twitch*, Mario Bava unknowingly created the template for the dozens of eighties slasher films that can trace their lineage back up to this bloody bay. The plot is a whodunit about a group of contemptuous individuals who are trying to lay claim to a prime slice of bayside real estate. Most people find this one of Bava's most linear films, but I have to confess that most of the time I have no idea what the hell is going on. Maybe it's because some of the characters look remarkably alike and I have trouble telling them apart. But no matter, it's not the plot but *Twitch*'s unique combination of ultraviolence and jet-black humor, not to mention the surreal ending, that makes it so delicious. I am, however, convinced that Bava was getting paid per use of his zoom lens. For some reason, the Italians as a whole have always unabashedly embraced this stylistic gimmick, but *Twitch* takes unnecessary zooming to absurd extremes.

Over the years, as *Twitch* became more accessible on home video, a minor controversy erupted over the similarity between certain scenes and those in *Friday the 13th Part 2*. And when I say "minor controversy" I'm being generous. It's the kind of thing only horror obsessives give a shit about. Like the unending and heated debate over the proper way to refer to the group formerly known as the Quarrymen—is it "The Beatles" or "the Beatles"? Never has the proper case of a "T" been more relevant. But as inconsequential as this seems to normal people, fans were convinced that *Friday the 13th Part 2* stole from *Twitch*.

Sean Cunningham denied having ever seen *Twitch*. So did Steve Miner, the director of *Friday the 13th Part 2*, as did *Part 2*'s writer, Ron Kurz. Fans were not satisfied. The similarities were too pronounced. You can almost explain away a machete to the face, as you can the death of a character in a wheelchair. But the famous "shish kebob" scene—in which a pair of lovers are impaled on a spear while in the throes of ecstasy—is literally identical. Leave it to author Peter Bracke to get to the bottom of things. In *Crystal Lake Memories*, Kurz reminisces about collaborating closely on *Part 2*'s script with Phil Scuderi, whom he describes as "a cross between Roger Corman and Michael Corleone." He gives Scuderi credit for coming up with the aforementioned scenes, including the human shish kebob. Why does this matter? Because as the shadowy investor behind not only *Friday the 13th* but *Last House on the Left*, Scuderi also ran Hallmark Releasing. And what was an early film that Hallmark distributed? You guessed it, *Twitch of the Death Nerve*, which Scuderi actually retitled *Last House on the Left 2*! Self-righteous fans consider this outright theft. But I don't know, I think it's kind of cool that an American sleaze merchant could plumb the depths of Italian exploitation and appropriate the tropes in a Hollywood blockbuster.

MOST SEQUEL-WORTHY KILLER

In many ways, *The Burning* is the quintessential slasher film. Aside from the fact that the "final girl" is a boy, it stays as close to the slasher paradigm—by this time, fairly well defined—as any film in the subgenre: a tragic accident disfigures an innocent character who in turn becomes a homicidal maniac and seeks his revenge, on both the responsible parties and anyone else who gets in his way.

However, in many other ways, *The Burning* is just plain weird. It's best known today as the first original production from the Weinstein brothers; Harvey Weinstein takes the unusual (in fact, it's the first time I've ever seen it) credit of "Created and Produced By," laying the groundwork for an entire career of fearlessly promoting himself as the driving creative force behind a project. Then there's the score from Rick Wakeman, the keyboardist from Yes, which gives the film a distinct giallo-like feel, especially in the early scenes before we arrive at camp. Tom Savini turned down *Friday the 13th Part 2* in order to work on *The Burning* and his effects are without a doubt the highlight of the film. But *unlike* any of the *Friday the 13th*s, which sliced and diced many counselors but drew the line at prepubescent campers, *The Burning* has no such compunction. The kids are brutally murdered in broad daylight; poor Fisher Stevens even has his fingers snipped off.

Therefore, it's really a crying shame that good old Cropsy lasted only a single film. As anybody who ever attended overnight camp knows, every place has its own local legend; even my childhood day camp had Zacharia, who, from what I remember, had one mangled eye, which, of course, made him evil. Upstate New York, where the Weinsteins were from and where *The Burning* was shot, was home to Cropsy. The legend was so pervasive that it was also the basis for *Madman*, another slasher in production at the exact same time. However, once the *Madman* team got wind of the rival production, they called an audible, tweaked the script, and renamed their villain Madman Marz.

Obviously, I'm cheating a little bit in nominating Cropsy as a perfect candidate for jump-starting the never-happened *Burning* franchise. After all, Michael, Jason, and Freddy are all vaguely supernatural beings, which allowed audiences to suspend their disbelief and welcome them back for each subsequent sequel. But Cropsy was just a crotchety old caretaker who was burned to a crisp. And at the end of *The Burning*, there's no question that a well-placed ax to the face prior to a second immolation polishes him off for good. Still, if the film had done a little better at the box office, and the Weinsteins didn't have such an art house hankering, I like to think there might have been a way to bring the melted madman and his trusty garden shears back for an encore.

BEST FOREIGN INTERLOPER

As a rule, the slasher film has essentially been an American phenomenon. The cast, the setting, the insipid teen jargon—everything about them seems straight out of small-town USA. The irony, of course, is that many of the most popular slashers are Canadian made, but these all did their best to scrub away any trace of specificity to their home country.

Given the worldwide success of slasher films, what's most surprising is how few international productions actually tried to jump on the gravy train. There was *The Day After Halloween* and *Nightmares* from Australia, and *Bloody Moon* from Spain, courtesy of Jess Franco, but none of these films gained much traction. This might have been because slasher films themselves drew heavily from foreign influences. Or maybe it was because these films were so distinctly American that they were hard to duplicate.

An obvious choice for this category would be *Pieces*, a film so wonderfully awful that it needed *two* legendary taglines: *You Don't Have to Go to Texas for a Chainsaw Massacre!* and *It's Exactly What You Think It Is!* This fan favorite was directed by Spaniard Juan Piquer Simón and shot predominately in his homeland. Even though it's atrociously dubbed, relies on the "talent" of many well-known European faces, and rounds up extras who look straight out of old World War II newsreel footage, it still *feels* like a badly made American production—not unlike *Slaughter High*, another film from *Pieces*'s two American producers, Dick Randall and Steve Minasian.

On the other hand, Michele Soavi's *StageFright*, while nonspecific about its geographical setting, could only have come from the country that birthed the giallo. Today, Soavi is best known for the 1994 Rupert Everett favorite *Cemetery Man*. But in 1987, he was ready to make his feature directorial debut following a successful career as an actor and assistant director with collaborators Dario Argento and Lamberto Bava. With shades of *Happy Birthday to Me* and *Curtains*, *StageFright* finds a group of rehearsing actors locked somewhat unbelievably in a theater—while being stalked by a murderer dressed up as the killer from the play. It's actually less convoluted than it sounds. But you don't come to *StageFright* for the streamlined story. As with the gialli that influenced it, you come for the visuals. The fact that Soavi hides his killer behind an oversize owl mask without it once approaching the absurd is a testament to his skill as a director. And the scene in which the big bird sits among his victims, posed in a gory tableau, as a fan blows random feathers through the air, is as beautifully surreal as anything composed by his esteemed former employers. The film's final shot, of the impossibly alive madman winking at the audience—far more slasher than giallo inspired—is a nice shout-out to its American counterparts, which understood better than anyone that sometimes you just can't keep a good maniac down.

CHAPTER FOUR

Terror on Tape, or How I Turned Down a Hand Job for Ninety Minutes of Bloodthirsty Mutants, Killer Kids, Homicidal Hillbillies, Demonic Priests, and Eurotrash

"Nothing can be said to be certain, except death and taxes," Benjamin Franklin wrote to his friend the French physicist Jean-Baptiste Le Roy.

Evidently, Franklin knew a lot more about electricity (although if you think about it, one would have to be either daft or certifiably insane to fly a kite in an electrical storm) than he did about teenage boys. Because if there's one absolute certainty, it's that no self-respecting fourteen-year-old would turn down a hand job.

Yet that's exactly what I did in the fall of 1988.

About eight of us were hanging out at Marcy Fillipelli's house—her parents were either dead or out for dinner; I can't remember which, but I don't recall ever meeting them. It was my job to choose the movie for the night, and although we all understood that this was only a pretext to a night of dry-humping and hickeys, it was a responsibility I took *very* seriously. Only two types of films would be acceptable: a comedy in which some preppy dude dressed in tennis whites would inevitably be doused with mud . . . or oil . . . or garbage. (Today's comedies are much raunchier, so there would undoubtedly be some sort of bodily fluid involved. But curiously, they showed a lot more bush back then. And it being the eighties, it was *a lot* of bush.)

Or a horror movie.

This, of course, was my domain. The girls might have preferred the high jinks of William Zabka and his Cobra Kai chums, but I wanted something that would hit 'em right in the amygdala. My motivation was self-indulgence, not sadism. The way I figured it, the more terrified they were, the better chance I had of getting my girlfriend at the time, Krista Vicenzi, to cozy up to me. The fear response, at least physiologically, is far closer to sex than is unbridled laughter. Sweating, heart palpitations, shortness of breath, versus the braying of a hyena.

There were no doubt some good reasons (although I can't recall any of them) why I bypassed the usual staples of such teenage gatherings—*Carrie*, *The Exorcist*, any number of slasher films—in favor of *Terror on Tape*, an obscure compilation of clips from the great exploitation distributor Continental Video.

Terror on Tape casts Cameron Mitchell as the owner of the redundantly named Shoppe of Horror Video Store. Although Mitchell was one of the founders of the Actors Studio, the famed Manhattan collective that rose to prominence under Lee Strasberg and became a mecca for disciples of Stanislavski, he will forever be identified (somewhat unfairly) with

Italian sleaze. And *Terror on Tape* is nothing if not wonderful, full-blown, glorious sleaze.

The film opens with a bow-tie-wearing rube wandering into the store and, after confusing a decorative skeleton for the proprietor, being greeted by Mitchell doing his best Grandpa Munster imitation. The customer asks for a recommendation, something scary but not *too* scary, as he suffers from what in layman's terms can only be described as being a gigantic pussy. So Mitchell shows him an example of what he considers a "mild" horror film, thus plunging us into the film proper.

The first clip on tap is from 1983's *The Deadly Spawn*, here retitled *Return of the Aliens: The Deadly Spawn*, allegedly in an effort to cash in on the success of Ridley Scott's 1979 masterpiece. How anyone could conceivably think that a bargain-basement independent feature about marauding alien "fish" that look like sperm with razor-sharp teeth could have anything to do with a 20th Century Fox release from four years earlier is beyond me. Questionable marketing decisions aside, and despite its inclusion on the *Terror* compilation—leading it off, no less—*The Deadly Spawn* is actually a superior creature feature, a heartfelt albeit bloody homage to the invasion films of the 1950s. What the makeup team managed to pull off on a virtually nonexistent budget is nothing short of extraordinary. Although I tend to think that practical-effects purists are a smug lot—the kind of folks who claim that Rick Baker's astonishing transformation in *An American Werewolf in London* can't hold a candle to Jack Pierce's slow dissolves to more and more yak hair for 1941's *The Wolf Man*—it's tough to envision how CGI could have added anything to the expertly applied latex and Karo syrup of *Spawn*.

There was something else that struck me about *Spawn*, leaving me with a vague and inexplicable sense of unease. It didn't *look* like any of the films I was used to. Even the cheap, ultra-violent ones. This was back before any idiot with a C-note could buy an off-the-shelf video camera and create their own *Blair Witch Project*. Making a movie, even a movie as inept as, say, *Bloodthirsty Butchers* (an actual film from Staten Island auteur Andy Milligan, arguably the worst director to ever get behind the lens), required some serious dough. Film stock, and by "film stock" I mean the strip of celluloid onto which photographic images are captured, was prohibitively expensive. Whatever one's artistic shortcomings, if you could shell out enough to purchase a reel of thirty-five-millimeter (or sixteen-millimeter, or even eight-millimeter) your film was going to look like a film.

I had also seen enough behind-the-scenes photos in *Fangoria* to have at least a rudimentary understanding of the film-making process. Movies involved sets, klieg lights, and camera rigs. Yet *The Deadly Spawn* looked as if it was made in my basement, cast with my grandmother and some of her mahjong buddies. Years later, I met the director, Doug McKeown, at a horror convention. I was surprised to learn he was a fellow New Jerseyan, and was even more surprised to find out that this specific scene from *Terror on Tape* really was shot in a basement in New Brunswick, the town adjacent to my own. *Rosemary's Baby* is often lauded as the film that removed horror from its Gothic trappings and placed it in a modern context. But unless you were John Lennon, the fictional Bramford (actually the Dakota) wasn't familiar at all. Even though it was right across the Hudson River and up Central Park West, it felt foreign. *The Deadly Spawn*, on the other hand, felt like home.

The next bunch of clips was pretty forgettable. They came

from *Vampire Hookers*, whose name is the most memorable thing about it; *Blood Tide*, which I've never seen in its entirety but stars James Earl Jones and seems to rip off scenes from *Jaws* wholesale; *Cathy's Curse* and *Madhouse Mansion*, which looked equally dull, although the latter did star Marianne Faithfull; and *Frozen Scream*, whose clip ends with a man being held down in a hospital bed while a syringe is forced into his eyeball. The scene is shot from the perspective of the victim, so as soon as the needle touches his cornea (read: camera lens), fake blood is squeezed into the frame. I used this very same effect in a student film I made my sophomore year in college, although I honestly can't remember if I was consciously referencing *Frozen Scream* (seems unlikely, because I had no particular affinity for the film), incorporating motifs I had filed away deep within my subconscious (even less likely, since my biggest concern was probably finding female classmates willing to go topless), or doing neither (almost definitely). What I do remember, however, and the proof is somewhere deep within the bowels of the University of Wisconsin's Vilas Hall, is that I managed to carry out the effect just as (in)competently as the professionals behind *Frozen Scream*. And I was one of the least talented students in the class.

Just in case this memory has you yearning for ocular trauma done right, I would refer you to Gary Sherman's *Dead & Buried* (a classic eighties creepfest even absent the relevant scene) and, of course, the granddaddy of all orbital obliteration, Lucio Fulci's *Zombi*.*

---

* So as not to incur the wrath of angry film students, I feel compelled to give a shout-out to Luis Buñuel's 1929 surrealist masterpiece *Un Chien Andalou*, which begins with an eyeball sliced open by a razor.

After this, *Terror on Tape* began to pick up a little. In *To the Devil a Daughter*, Christopher Lee takes a pregnant woman in the throes of late-stage labor and ties her legs together, resulting in a spontaneously bloody birth. I thought it was pretty cool that the new addition to the family looks like the thing on the cover of Black Sabbath's *Born Again* LP, but a whole lot cooler when the woman takes the demon baby and forces it back into her vagina!* Although *To the Devil a Daughter* was not actually the last offering from Britain's Hammer Films, it is the one that put the proverbial nail in the once-esteemed company's coffin. Aside from its general distastefulness, the film features a *well*-underage Nastassja Kinski going full frontal. I never understood how producers are allowed to get away with what would be considered illegal under any other circumstances, but apparently they can. Just look at most of Brooke Shields's early career. I guess it's like the old joke about how paid sex between two consenting adults is illegal, while paid sex between two consenting adults in front of a camera is a legitimate enterprise.

Nastassja Kinski is, of course, the daughter of deranged German actor/madman Klaus Kinski. Revered by cinephiles for his collaborations with Werner Herzog, such as *Aguirre: The Wrath of God* and *Fitzcarraldo*, and by horror and exploitation fans for his refusal to turn down almost any paying role, Kinski (who died in 1991) was recently accused by his oldest daughter, Pola, of sexually abusing her from the age of five to nine-

* This isn't exactly what happens in the film itself. But the way it's cut together in *Terror on Tape*, it sure seems like it. Either way, this is how I perceived it.

teen. When the allegations came out, Nastassja admitted her father tried to molest her as well.

Knowing what I knew about Kinski, I didn't find any of this the least bit surprising. I bet he was guilty of even worse things—though there are few I find more repellent. In light of Werner Herzog's close but complicated relationship with Kinski—they were, at different points in their lives, best friends and worst enemies—I figured there would be no one more qualified to weigh in on the accusations. In 1999, Herzog even produced a documentary, *My Best Fiend*, about his life and work with Kinski.

Strangely enough, I could not find a single statement from Herzog about the revelations that, at least for one news cycle, were lighting up wire services all over the world. His silence was particularly conspicuous since he is usually willing to weigh in on any number of social issues. But now, he had absolutely nothing to say. Not even a prepared statement about the horror of the allegations. Now, is there any reason to believe Herzog was aware of Kinski's crimes and opted for willful ignorance? No. This is a man who positions himself as something of a conscience of the documentary community. He just made a critically acclaimed documentary about the inhumanity of capital punishment. Surely his sympathy for cold-blooded murderers must extend to innocent little girls?

Figuring the notoriously prolific Herzog might just have been busy, I reached out to him through his production company to request an interview. Were this not possible, I asked if I could send him a few brief questions to answer via e-mail. I didn't have to wait long for a reply. The following was Herzog's response through his spokespeople: "Due to his extremely busy schedule it is unfortunately impossible for Mr Herzog to answer questions. We hope for your understanding."

I guess there's just never a convenient time to talk about your once-best friend raping his daughter.

Meanwhile, on the *Terror on Tape* front, things were just getting good, helped by a gory crucifixion from *The Eerie Midnight Horror Show* that was a helluva lot more fun than the one in *The Passion of the Christ*. So it was unfortunate that the aforementioned bow-tie-wearing customer, now completely gray and crazier than Renfield as a result of viewing the tape, decides to leave the store.

A tough-talking construction worker complete with hard hat comes in to take his place. The dude claims to have seen it all and requests a good zombie film. So naturally, Mitchell shows him a clip from *The Kidnapping of the President*, which has absolutely nothing to do with zombies. For what it's worth, I'm not entirely convinced that the clip is actually from *President*, although that's how it's labeled. I've seen *President*, and I don't remember the scene at all. But since none of this matters anyway, I won't perseverate.

Then came *Nightmare*, which was released theatrically (if barely) in October 1981, right in the sweet spot of the slasher cycle. Well directed, brimming with soft-core sex, and filled with some spectacular gore effects, the film seemed to have all the necessary elements. Even the plot was derivative of earlier slashers, which usually translated to success: a psychotic inmate in a mental institution, haunted by a gruesome nightmare, escapes to Florida to hunt down his ex-wife and young son, leaving a trail of bloody corpses in his wake. Unfortunately, the film also had a lot going against it. For one thing, it was financed by David Jones, a New York City gold broker supposedly using the film as a tax write-off. Nor was *Nightmare* ever acquired by a major studio that could use its marketing muscle and national distribution pipeline to maximize exposure. Maybe most importantly, it was directed by an Italian, Romano Scavolini. And as everybody knows, Italians—at least in the film business and especially in the horror genre—are completely nuts.

Nightmare's notoriety is based mainly on things that have absolutely nothing to do with the film itself, unfortunately, since it would make a perfect triple feature of Manhattan malaise alongside Bill Lustig's *Maniac* and Abel Ferrara's *The Driller Killer*. For the film's British home video release, the distributor held a contest in which participants had to guess the weight of a human brain preserved in a glass jar; some swear the specimen was genuine, others claim it was a poorly made mockup. Either way, subsequent to this promotional stunt, David Hamilton Grant, company secretary at the film's British distributor, bought himself a six-month stay in the pokey for releasing a film deemed obscene under the Obscene Publications Act. The film is also a bone of contention for Tom Savini, who, despite receiving on-screen credit as special effects director, categorically denies having anything to do with the film. Savini was riding a wave of success with *Friday the 13th*, *Maniac*, and *The Burning*, and claims that Scavolini just wanted to glom onto his fame. He maintains that makeup artist Les Larrain, who tragically took his own life shortly after the film was released, was the real wizard behind the effects (which even today hold up surprisingly well). Since I have a photo of Savini from the set of *Nightmare*, instructing the actors on how to properly swing an ax, he's either lying or in the throes of full-blown dementia.

Shortly after I finished writing *Going to Pieces*, I began the research for what was to be my next book. The working title was *Dissecting Depravity: Behind the Scenes of the Ten Most Controversial Movies Ever Made*. In addition to *Nightmare*, the book was to include *Cannibal Holocaust*, *I Spit on Your Grave*, *Nekromantik*, *Guinea Pig* (the entire series), *In a Glass Cage*, *Snuff*, *Bloodsucking Freaks*, *Henry: Portrait of a Serial Killer*, and *Silent Night, Deadly Night*. Just as DVD killed off VHS, these shiny discs also derailed my project. Because director commentaries were now de rigueur for every new release, I saw no reason why people would want to *read* my version of events when they could *hear* them firsthand from the filmmakers. And probably at a fraction of the cost.

Still, before I put the kibosh on the project, I managed to wrangle up an interview with Scavolini. Because his English isn't particularly strong and my Italian is nonexistent, we decided to conduct the interview via e-mail. I sent him a list of mundane questions that could have been conceived by any reasonably intelligent third grader. The kind of questions that "artists" detest answering because they limit their ability to pontificate on their delicate genius. Of course, these are exactly the types of questions that are instrumental if we are to draw a complete picture of the film in question. *What was the genesis of the film? How was it financed? Where was it shot? Describe your working relationship with the cast. With the crew. Any on-set anecdotes? When was the film released? How much did it gross?* Scavolini gamely answered every one of these questions. And then, in signing off, he wrote: *Adam, Keep digging. You may be onto something bigger and more important than you could ever imagine.* Admittedly, at first, I was kind of creeped out. What the fuck was he talking about? For a fleeting second, it even crossed my mind that I had uncovered some sort of deeper conspiracy, not unlike the plot of the film, where looking too closely into the particulars of *Nightmare* would sow the seeds of my own destruction. Then I remembered something . . . the Italians are completely nuts.

Because the next two clips from *The Slayer* and *City of the Walking Dead* were so boring, I thought it might be a good time to get back to the matter at hand (job). By now, Krista was nestled into me, and at some point, most likely during the *Cathy's Curse* segment, I began feeling her up. The only reason I remember this at all is because she wore one of those underwire bras. Getting underneath was no less difficult than wedging your hand into a closed door. Most of the other couples had lost interest in the movie following the opening credits and had wandered off to find a secluded spot of their own, so I placed Krista's hand on my crotch. It was fortuitous timing: the construction worker, lasciviously sucking on a toothpick or matchstick, had just requested some T & A. Mitchell obliged, so we were treated to an orgy from *Vampire Hookers*, some more erotic weirdness from *The Eerie Midnight Horror Show*, and a striptease from *Nightmare* that pushes its protagonist over the edge.

Because I assume Krista didn't want to jerk me off in the middle of the living room, even if there was no one left but the two of us, she suggested we retire to one of the unoccupied bedrooms. I took her hand and was about to lead her out when *City of the Walking Dead* caught my attention. A zombie stabs a woman in the breast and slices off her nipple. I sat right back down. I don't know what this reveals about me, that I would rather have seen a nipple removed on-screen than exposed in person (and frankly, I don't even want to speculate), but Krista left in a huff. And I'm glad she did, because the next clip was from *Color Me Blood Red*.

In a scene that reeks of a 1960s aesthetic (at least as I imagined the sixties to be), a Bettie Page–looking woman berates her underachieving painter boyfriend. But instead of meekly enduring her insults, he stabs her in the fucking face. Then he smears her bloody maw across his canvas. When a pompous art buyer shows up—and we know he's pompous because he wears a beret—he proclaims about the painting, "There may never be anything like it!" A sentiment that could easily apply to the film's director, Mr. Herschell Gordon Lewis.

Throughout his illustrious career, H. G. Lewis has been bestowed with a number of monikers: the Sultan of Sleaze, the Baron of Blood, the Mad Hatter of Splatter, and the most enduring, the Godfather of Gore. And these all fit him to a T. But Lewis was, more than anything, a contradiction.

He was a soft-spoken and erudite English professor who, oh, just happened to make the most depraved films up to that time. An exploitation pioneer who had little passion for cinema, especially for the genres in which he plied his trade. A spectacularly sadistic showman who, under the surface, was a rather prudish family man. If those who discover Lewis for the first time are disappointed in the discrepancy between the man's films and the man himself, they can find solace in his longtime business partner, David Friedman. Friedman was everything Lewis wasn't and everything an exploitation film producer was supposed to be. Born in Birmingham, Alabama, he was a former carnival barker who, with his omnipresent cigar, traveled across the South making pictures for the drive-in circuit. Once they teamed up, this dynamic duo made a few classic "nudie cuties" before quickly realizing that mainstream cinema was breaking out of its puritanical cocoon, making the bare breasts on which their films depended less of a novelty. Always eager to exploit or, quite often in Lewis's case, initiate a new trend, the two set out to create a new breed of fear film.

Lewis's first gore film, the revolutionary *Blood Feast*, came along barely three years after *Psycho*. Yes, *Psycho* traumatized audiences. They screamed, they fainted, they refused to ever take showers again. You have no idea how many horror directors have told me that as a result of seeing *Psycho* at a young age they still only take baths. I've never had the guts to question why lying naked in the water offers any additional protection from a knife-wielding maniac than standing upright under a spray. I can certainly appreciate *Psycho*'s cultural significance and can easily understand how it might have shocked unsuspecting audiences in 1960 (I find it less easy to believe that theatergoers in the 1930s actually passed out cold from watching *Frankenstein*). But come on, it's still an exercise in restraint and subterfuge—classic Hitch—over explicitness.

Lewis, on the other hand, doesn't fuck around. *Blood Feast* opens with a young woman relaxing in a bathtub (she must have seen *Psycho*!). A minute later, some lunatic breaks into her home, hacks off her leg, and gouges out her eye. Following this, we are treated to a scalping, some back-room open heart surgery, and in the film's most notorious scene, an impromptu tongue removal. Lewis's later films *Two Thousand Maniacs!* (the next clip in *Terror on Tape*), *The Wizard of Gore*, and *The Gore Gore Girls*, in which a woman's nipples are snipped off only to squirt out regular and chocolate milk, are even more deliriously gory.

Conventional wisdom holds that even isolated from its sociological impact—*Psycho* quickly became a part of mainstream culture while *Blood Feast* was relegated to a drive-in oddity—*Psycho* is a much more terrifying film because of its *realism*. Oh, really? Let's put aside the plot of both films for a moment and agree that they're both absurd. And before anyone has a conniption, I'm well aware that *Psycho* was adapted from the Robert Bloch novel, itself based on the real-life case of Wisconsin murderer Ed Gein.* But if I tried hard enough, I guarantee you that I could find a host of ritualistic murderers who killed for reasons no less laughable than in order to create an Egyptian feast to resurrect a long-dead goddess, which is the story line of *Blood Feast*. So when critics discuss realism, what they really mean is the way that the two directors, Hitchcock and Lewis, utilize the tools of their craft to reflect the authenticity of the events within the film. Now, would anyone dispute that Hitchcock was a brilliant visionary while Lewis was a two-bit hack? Probably not. But I'll tell you something equally indisputable. *Blood Feast* is a much more realistic film than *Psycho*.

The shower scene in *Psycho* is the most overanalyzed and deconstructed three minutes in the history of cinema. This one scene is the subject of entire books, documentaries, and even

---

* Gein has served as the inspiration for so many fictional madmen that it's hard to believe he was only responsible for two murders. Nor was there any hard evidence that he was a cannibal or a necrophiliac. That said, I still wouldn't want him as a neighbor.

a memoir. It was painstakingly planned and meticulously executed, requiring more than a week of shooting to accommodate the more than seventy-five camera setups. As I mentioned before, its effect on theatergoers was unprecedented.

It's also totally overrated.

I realize that Hitchcock was somewhat at the mercy of the censors, but never once does Norman's knife really look like it's making anything close to contact with Marion's body. The frenetic editing tries to create the effect of steel piercing flesh, but if we examine it objectively (trying to ignore the fact that we're talking about a revered director at the height of his powers), it fails miserably. After Norman hacks away a good six or seven times, there's still no sign of an entry wound. In fact, the only thing we see is Marion's unblemished torso. Is she that adept at fending him off with her flailing arms? Is Norman such an inept mama's boy that he completely misses her with every slash? Even the blood doesn't look like blood, especially in black and white. It looks like Hershey's syrup, because it is. The entire scene, especially divorced from Bernard Herrmann's shrieking violins, is one big letdown.

Now let's take one of the aforementioned scenes from *Blood Feast*. (I just called my eight-year-old daughter into my office and asked her to pick one of four words: "bathtub," "brains," "heart," or "tongue." She said "tongue," and with the egocentricity of someone her age, didn't even ask what this nonsense was all about.) The killer, Fuad Ramses, tackles a young woman onto a bed and rips out her tongue with his bare hands. Rumor has it that the actress was cast solely because her mouth was large enough to accommodate the sheep tongue used for the effect. Ramses holds up the organ, now dripping with bright red blood.

It looks like a tongue because, well, it is. The victim, still alive, but ostensibly in shock, rolls around moaning as blood pours from her mouth. Granted, I've never been privy to a tongue extraction. But my elementary knowledge of anatomy tells me that the crimes in *Blood Feast* are far closer to reality than the shower murder, and not just because they're shown in glorious Eastmancolor while *Psycho* was famously shot in black and white.

Again, I'm not oblivious to the fact that social mores change, and what is acceptable content at one time would have been completely inappropriate at another. This is the reason that Mae West can exude as much sexual tension as Brando sticking his butter-covered fingers up Maria Schneider's ass. But again, *Psycho* and *Blood Feast* were made *three* years apart. Although I guess the Beatles were laying the groundwork for the flower power juggernaut, things hadn't yet changed *that* much. The fact is that Hitchcock, by this time universally acknowledged as a genius par excellence, didn't push the envelope nearly as far as he receives credit for. And Lewis, a footnote in film history, had a set of balls that even AC/DC would covet.

At the risk of shattering the illusion of Lewis as the avuncular and cultured elder statesman of exploitation, I feel compelled to offer up a personal anecdote about the Godfather of Gore. In 2011, Lewis was in Chicago as the guest of honor at a horror film festival put on by local impresario Rusty Nails.*

---

* Rusty takes his nom de guerre extremely seriously, refusing to comment on, or even talk about, his birth name. In addition to being a director in his own right—he's years into the making of what will be the definitive documentary about George Romero—Rusty holds regular horror and sci-fi marathons at Chicago's wonderful old movie palaces.

Rusty has always been extremely generous to me, often inviting me to conduct Q & As with the directors he flies in for events. I'll never forget the experience of hosting a *Friday the 13th* panel with actors Adrienne King, Betsy Palmer, and Ari Lehman, and score composer Harry Manfredini, in front of a packed house before a screening of a new thirty-five-millimeter print of the film. So I figured it was the least I could do to take Lewis, Rusty, and a few of Rusty's friends out to dinner before a screening of Lewis's *The Wizard of Gore*.

Dinner was delightful. At eighty-two, Lewis had a memory that was far better than mine and he regaled us with tales from his days in the trenches. At the table behind us was a family with a small child. Granted, the kid was rambunctious, yelling out at random intervals as kids are prone to do. It wasn't too distracting. Not only has my tolerance for such things increased exponentially after having children of my own, but we were in a crowded pub on Saturday night.

Apparently, Lewis didn't feel the same.

After one particularly loud shriek, Lewis stopped—midsentence—and screamed, "Would somebody shut that kid up!" At first I thought he was joking. After all, the guy is like the grandfather whom everyone loves. But after waiting for his mouth to turn up in that trademark grin, which it never did, it became clear he was dead serious. I giggled nervously and looked at Rusty. He just shrugged. Luckily, it was so loud I'm not certain the parents of the child heard. Or at least, they probably couldn't believe it came from the nice old man sitting behind them. Lewis, for his part, composed himself and continued on with whatever story he was telling.

I've yet to meet a single person who knows Lewis describe

him as anything but a gentleman and a scholar. For the remainder of the festival, he was characteristically humble and patient with the throngs of fans who wanted to meet their hero. So the dinner episode really doesn't change my opinion of the man. What it does do, however, is make me kind of curious about his 1967 children's film *The Magic Land of Mother Goose*. I always assumed it was typical kid's stuff. But maybe it really harkens back to the source material, where the old lady in the shoe can't deal with all her children so she puts them on a low-calorie diet, beats the hell out of them, and then sends them to bed.

But back to *Terror on Tape*. The next customer to arrive at the ol' shoppe is Michelle Bauer, an eighties scream queen probably best known for her roles in *Hollywood Chainsaw Hookers* and *Sorority Babes in the Slimeball Bowl-O-Rama* (and yes, these are real films; I'm not clever enough to make up such ridiculous titles). She's dressed like a vamped-up dominatrix and, in the horror equivalent of *Deep Throat*, is on a quest to find a film so terrifying it will induce orgasm. Barely able to contain himself, Mitchell queues up some additional clips, mainly from films he's already shown the two other goofballs: death by pitchfork from *The Slayer*, a film that many think Craven ripped off for *A Nightmare on Elm Street*; highlights from Lewis's first three horror films, affectionately dubbed *The Blood Trilogy*; a scalping from *Scalps*; the climax of *Nightmare*, in which a woman is decapitated in flagrante delicto and spews a geyser of blood onto the lover between her legs. Apparently, these scenes do the trick because Bauer promises to "do anything" if Mitchell will rent her a copy. *Terror on Tape* concludes with Bauer clutching a VHS cassette of the eponymous film against her ample bosom, moaning in ecstasy as Mitchell cackles wildly.

I'm well aware that normal people might have a difficult time understanding the transformative nature of *Terror on Tape*. Looking back, the entire episode probably sounds like nothing more than a night of shitty horror movies and blue balls. But the video was my perfect gateway drug. It was a window into a weird and wild world I never knew existed. A world of circular logic and dreamscapes. Ambiguity and nonsense. Every -philia in existence and many that weren't. *Alice in Wonderland* as distilled through the prism of knives, tits, synthesizers, pills, and black magic.

Now, sitting alone in the living room, my friends long gone in search of their own carnal pleasures, I was ready. Ready to be indoctrinated into a world of films that wouldn't have made sense for the majors to release but that were the bread and butter of fly-by-night distributors with delicious names like Gorgon, Wizard, Thriller, and Midnight.

And if turning down a hand job was the price of admission into this exclusive club, that was a small sacrifice to make for a lifetime of celluloid perversion.

CHAPTER FIVE

Sounds of the Devil

Horror movies and heavy metal have been inextricably linked since that fateful day when an English blues band, inspired by a Mario Bava film, changed its name from Earth to Black Sabbath.*

If Altamont represented the spiritual demise of the 1960s, then the release of *Black Sabbath* was the decade's sonic deathblow. The eponymous single from this eponymous album was more than a shot across the bow of contemporary rock, it was a fucking guided missile. The song doesn't even start with a melody, just the sound of softly falling rain. Next, the somber toll of church bells. Then a sinister clap of thunder, warning us this ain't no sun shower. Then feedback. Distortion. Until lead singer John "Ozzy" Osbourne plaintively wails, "What is this

* In his autobiography, Sabbath's mutilated-fingered guitarist Tony Iommi refutes the direct appropriation of the film's title. Although he admits that he and bassist Geezer Butler used to watch horror films at the cinema across from Earth's rehearsal space, he states that neither he nor Butler had ever seen *Black Sabbath* at the time.

that stands before me? Figure in black which points at me." To steal the tagline from Bob Clark's *Black Christmas*, if your skin doesn't crawl, it's on too tight.

Since the beginning, the debate has raged over which was the first true heavy metal band, Sabbath or Zeppelin, with some trying to get cute by throwing Deep Purple or esoterica like Blue Cheer and Uriah Heep into the mix. It's a ridiculous argument. Zeppelin can be as heavy as anyone ("Achilles Last Stand," "Immigrant Song") and downright creepy ("No Quarter"), but there's nothing *scary* about them. The "red snapper incident" aside, they weren't a dangerous band. For all his name-checking of Mordor and Valhalla, Plant was still a zonked-out hippie singing about going to California to meet a girl with love in her eyes and flowers in her hair. Ozzy, on the other hand, was certifiably insane. At a 1981 meeting with CBS Records executives he bit the head off a live dove. At a concert in Des Moines the following year, he bit the head off a bat. Had PETA been more visible at the time, there's good reason to believe he would have bit the head off Ingrid Newkirk.

In *The Dirt: Confessions of the World's Most Notorious Rock Band*, the collective memoir of Mötley Crüe, Nikki Sixx cites a particularly extreme display of the Ozzman's lunacy. The Crüe were opening for Ozzy on his *Bark at the Moon* tour. During a stop in Lakeland, Florida, following an afternoon of heavy drinking, Ozzy proceeded to snort up a column of ants marching across pavement, as if the scurrying insects were nothing more than a line of finely cut Colombian blow. Following the aperitif, Ozzy took a piss on the ground and lapped it up.

Throughout the 1970s, metal and horror movies flirted shamelessly. Alice Cooper sang about Frankenstein and engaged in Grand Guignol–style theatrics. KISS dressed like creatures from another planet and spit blood and fire. The Misfits, more punk than metal but still pretty damn heavy, built a career on lyrics inspired by films such as *Blood Feast*, *Night of the Living Dead*, *Halloween*, and many others. Even their now-iconic logo was lifted from the obscure 1946 serial *The Crimson Ghost*.

It wasn't until the 1980s, however, that this marriage was officially consummated. For a kid with a budding love of the macabre, heavy metal LPs were a sonic conduit to horror. Since "real" metal was never played on FM radio, save for the occasional spinning of "Paranoid" and Judas Priest's "Living After Midnight," the only place I could actually *hear* it was at the house of a friend who had an older deadbeat brother. But I could *see* it at the local Caldor* whenever my mother would drag me shopping with her. Just as the great exploitation film posters promised a smorgasbord of bloodshed usually found nowhere in the actual film, record labels knew how to sell the sizzle. The very first heavy metal album I ever bought was Iron Maiden's *The Number of the Beast*.† The legendary artwork will be familiar to anyone with even a passing interest in metal. In the foreground, the devil lords over fields of destruction. Behind him hovers Eddie, Maiden's monstrous mascot, three times as large and twice as mean as Old Scratch. I knew the

---

* It's somewhat ironic that Caldor was the place where I discovered metal. In 1993, it refused to carry Howard Stern's autobiography, *Private Parts*, because of the book's objectionable content.

† In another metal/movie parallel, Maiden founder Steve Harris wrote the album's title track following a nightmare caused by watching *Damien: Omen II*.

devil was a badass, and if this creature held dominion over him, then I just *had* to hear the music he represented.

Iron Maiden eventually became my all-time favorite metal band. In fact, they're the only band, in any musical genre, from whom I still buy every single new release, partly out of blind loyalty and partly in the misguided belief that maybe, even by accident, they'll once again capture the transcendence of "Phantom of the Opera" and "Hallowed Be Thy Name." Sometimes I wonder if I would have fallen just as hard for, say, Saxon, had they sounded the same but used Maiden's iconography. Probably not. After all, except for a few decent songs, Saxon basically sucked, while Maiden is metal royalty. But there's also a good chance that had music been consumed in bytes and files as it is today, instead of ensconced in tantalizing artwork, I might not have even heard of Maiden until 1986, when their single "Wasted Years" kinda went mainstream.

Looking back at this union, there's no question that metal made out better. Horror practically informs the music. On the other hand, the few times that horror films tried to incorporate heavy metal into their soundtracks, they were unequivocal disasters. Exhibit A: when Dario Argento slapped Maiden's rather obscure "Flash of the Blade" into a chase scene in *Phenomena*. I've already established my love of Maiden, and Dario Argento was at one time my favorite director before he seemingly decided to make movies that sucked. I also love ice cream and good Scotch, but that doesn't mean I want to make a Macallan float. Maiden's galloping riffs and power chords not only seem grossly out of place among Argento's dreamscapes, but they absolutely destroy any tension the director hoped to build. Since I'm basically tone-deaf, I'm completely unqualified to deconstruct the acoustics, but there's a reason that the most effective horror scores draw from classical sources. Winds and strings just *sound* spooky. They evoke mystery and dread, the cornerstone of most horror films. Metal, on the other hand, evokes power. After all, the gods were given a hammer, not a harpsichord.

I'm assuming Dokken's "Dream Warriors," the title song from the third *Nightmare on Elm Street* film, and Alice Cooper's "He's Back (The Man Behind the Mask)," from *Friday the 13th Part VI: Jason Lives*, were meant to be taken seriously at the time. Although listening to them again, and watching the accompanying videos, it's almost impossible to understand how. Then there were the outright parodies, the most egregious being the Fat Boys' "Are You Ready for Freddy?" I detested this video, in which Freddy Krueger raps, "Elm Street's the place / You got the time / Listen to this / You'll bust a rhyme," as it officially completed Freddy's inevitable decline from terrifying screen presence to pop culture buffoon.

So let's recap: Metal drew from horror films with great success; horror films incorporated metal to their detriment. Then there were the times when each was lonely; maybe they had a bit too much to drink and decided to see what would happen. Their offspring—horror films *about* heavy metal—were a wacky bunch indeed.

The first out of the gate was 1986's *Trick or Treat*, most memorable for cameos by Gene Simmons, who's wasted (as in misused, not fucked up) as a radio DJ, and by Ozzy Osbourne, who's surprisingly believable as a television evangelist railing against heavy metal. The film stars Marc Price, whom most folks from my generation fondly remember as lovable loser

Skippy Handelman on *Family Ties*. Here he plays lovable loser Eddie Weinbauer, a heavy metal–obsessed high schooler who inadvertently resurrects his dead idol, rocker Sammi Curr. Initially, Sammi helps Eddie take revenge on the classmates who have bullied him. But soon, as Tygers of Pan Tang once warned, "If you mess around with fire, you're gonna get yourself burnt," and Eddie is forced to destroy his own creation. Making nearly $7 million at the box office, *Trick or Treat* was hardly a failure. But coming out when it did, at the tail end of the slasher cycle, it quickly disappeared into obscurity. Forgettable metal outfit Fastway was responsible for the title song and accompanying soundtrack. This is their legacy, which should probably tell you everything you need to know about the band.*

Even if *Trick or Treat* didn't exactly kick open the floodgates, like an earnest opening act, it prepped the crowd for the headliner. Enter John Fasano, the John Hughes of low-budget, heavy metal–themed horror movies. It's rare when a director perfectly captures the zeitgeist, and even rarer when he has the balls to try it twice—failing spectacularly each time. Fasano wasn't even a fan of metal. The Long Island–born director preferred Bruce Springsteen and hometown hero Billy Joel to anything by Armored Saint. It was only after he teamed up with the Canadian jack-of-all-trades "Rock Warrior" Jon Mikl Thor that he made two of the most surreal rock films of all time.

The first of the two, *Rock 'n' Roll Nightmare*, opens with a prologue in which a young kid witnesses the charbroiled body

---

* Fastway was named for its founders, "Fast" Eddie Clarke of Motörhead and Pete Way of UFO. The duo's previous bands are two of the most respected early metal outfits.

of his mother come shrieking out of the kitchen oven. Actually, it *might* be his mother, or it might be a demon. I've seen the film a handful of times and I'm still not exactly sure. Ten years later, the heavy metal band Triton, led by lead singer Thor, arrives at the same location with their girlfriends. For some reason, the basement of this desolate Ontario farmhouse has been converted into a recording studio. According to Thor, if they can't come up with some new material they will be forced to return their advance. And in light of their "talent," these guys will desperately miss the money. For rock stars, the band spends an inordinate amount of time washing dishes, discussing washing dishes, and fighting about washing dishes. Then a one-eyed penis monster appears and turns one of the girlfriends into some sort of demon.

The majority of the film entails the band members rehearsing, wandering around the property, fooling around with their respective ladies, and then disappearing. During this time, we're treated to the longest and least sexy shower scene in the history of cinema, during which Thor does something vaguely resembling French kissing with his tongue. At about the one-hour mark, the kid from the prologue returns, unaged but now possessed. Shortly after, Thor's girlfriend turns into the devil and summons all the other penis monsters. Thor doesn't seem overly concerned or even surprised at the sequence of events, and proceeds to give the devil an oral history of Satanism. Thor then reveals that he may or may not be alone at the farmhouse—the entire film thus far could be a figment of his imagination—and tears off his shirt to battle the devil in a spiked Speedo. Eventually, Thor defeats the devil through the power of rock 'n' roll or some shit like that.

Obviously, the film doesn't make much sense, which is why played straight it's such a beloved piece of mid-eighties cheese. According to a 2013 *Fangoria* interview with Fasano, *Nightmare* was made for around $52,000 and ended up grossing $400,000. As a result, the film's distributor wanted to see what Fasano could accomplish on a $400,000 budget. The result was the similarly themed *Black Roses*.

In the small town of Mill Basin, the popular heavy metal band the Black Roses arrives to play a series of shows. The local townspeople are all up in arms. Surprisingly, it's the mayor—who might have the worst hair in all of human history—who convinces them that it's nothing more than good clean fun. But of course it's not. During the next night's show, the Black Roses' lead singer, Damian, turns some of the concertgoers into the Martians from *Mars Attacks!* The rest of the kids in the audience are transformed into sexpots and murderers. The reason for all this has something to do with black magic, but just like *Rock 'n' Roll Nightmare*, none of it is very clear. Eventually, the well-liked high school English teacher figures something is amiss. Why? Probably because during class his once-model students begin chanting, "Damian! Damian! Damian!" By the end of the film, Damian has all the kids under his spell, so he yanks off his wig and turns into an evil salamander. Luckily, the English teacher sets the amphibian on fire, freeing the children from the power of Satan and restoring law and order to Mill Basin.

In every respect, *Black Roses* is an improvement over *Rock 'n' Roll Nightmare*. That's hardly a ringing endorsement, but it's the most diplomatic thing I can say. After all, neither is a very good film. But if you read some of the glowing online reviews of *Black Roses* you might assume it's a lost David Lean masterpiece. I guess this just goes to prove that fans eat this shit up and are exceptionally forgiving when it comes to the fondly remembered films of their youth.

One thing for which Fasano, who died unexpectedly in July 2014, should be commended is his stunt casting. Julie Adams has a small role, since the first movie Fasano ever saw was *Creature from the Black Lagoon*. One member of the fictitious Black Roses is played by Carmine Appice, the legendary Vanilla Fudge drummer who inspired a host of other hard-rock skin beaters. Vincent Pastore, still years away from *The Sopranos*, has one of the best and most politically incorrect lines of the film when he tells his recently ear-pierced son, "Only two kinds of men wear earrings. Pirates and faggots. And I don't see no ship in our driveway."

Bada bing!

It might seem as if it was only their aesthetic similarities (to grossly simplify, both were hard, brash, and uncompromising) and analogous fan bases (comprised of misfits who wore their outsider status not as a scarlet letter but as a badge of honor) that made heavy metal and horror movies perfect partners. But where they really made a formidable tag team was in the battle for the hearts and minds of America's youth.

There was, however, one big difference between the responses they provoked. Whereas Siskel and Ebert's antislasher campaign disappeared faster than a coed going to get her boyfriend a beer, heavy metal faced a more formidable opponent.

Contemporary music came under the scrutiny of Tipper Gore when she realized that not everything on Prince's *Purple Rain* album might be appropriate for her eleven-year-old daughter. "She bought it because she liked 'Let's Go Crazy,'" explained Tipper about her daughter's purchase. "But then I heard the words to 'Darling Nikki' with its lyrics about a girl masturbating with a magazine, and I started paying attention."

And she started talking. And voicing her concerns to her fellow members of the privileged class. She soon discovered that more than a few of them shared her views on the issue, including Susan Baker, wife of Treasury Secretary James Baker.

In the spring of 1985, Tipper and Baker formed the Parents Music Resource Center (PMRC), along with their compatriots Sally Nevius, wife of former Washington city council chairman John Nevius; Pam Howar, wife of real estate developer and Republican fund-raiser Raymond Howar; and Ethelynn Stuckey, wife of former Georgia congressman William Stuckey.

The PMRC's mission was to inform parents about the potentially offensive lyrics their children might be listening to and persuade the recording industry to adopt a voluntary rating system—similar to that used by the MPAA—that would be clearly visible on the album packaging.

To their supporters, they were culture warriors, protecting innocent children from the dangers of rock. To their opponents, they were blue-blooded yentas, busybodies who simply had too much time, too much money, and too much self-righteousness to be ignored. But whatever one may think of the PMRC's mandate and its methods, it's impossible to deny the subtle—and sometimes blatant—sexism they faced. Even their nickname, the "Washington wives," defined them not by their own convictions but by the success of their husbands.

As one of their first orders of business they released the "Filthy Fifteen," a list of fifteen particularly objectionable songs. Some of the choices were understandable; W.A.S.P.'s "Animal (Fuck Like a Beast)" is self-explanatory. Some were curious; why the center would choose the forgettable Ian Gillan–era Black Sabbath ditty "Trashed," somewhat of a cautionary tale against drunk driving, is beyond me. Especially since Sabbath has far more well-known songs—"Snowblind" and "Sweet Leaf"—that practically sing the praises of cocaine and weed. I guess any group that lumps songs by Sheena Easton, Madonna, and Cyndi Lauper together with those of Venom and Mercyful Fate, for any reason whatsoever, is begging not to be taken seriously.

However, when you have the ear of the country and the balls of the men who run it, you're taken seriously by default. The center scored an early victory in August 1985, when nineteen of the largest record companies agreed to place parental guidance labels on albums with explicit lyrics. But before the labeling was put into effect, the Senate convened a hearing on the issue. Officially, this was held under the auspices of the Committee on Commerce, Science, and Transportation, whose grouping of disparate disciplines makes about as much sense as the Bureau of Alcohol, Tobacco, Firearms, and Explosives. But hey, that's Congress for ya!

On the morning of September 19, 1985, the hearing commenced in the Russell Senate Office Building. The committee chairman, Senator John Danforth (R-Missouri), an ordained Episcopal priest, opened the festivities with an assurance that "the reason for this hearing is not to promote any legislation . . . [b]ut to simply provide a forum for airing the issue itself, for ventilating the issue, for bringing it out into the public domain." Of course, nobody believed him. At least no metal fans, opponents of censorship, civil libertarians, or concerned taxpayers, who wondered what the fuck this committee was doing in the first place. Still, one has to give Danforth some credit for trying to assuage these fears.

The hearing started off fairly predictably.

Senator Fritz Hollings (D–South Carolina) commends the PMRC for bringing this issue to the "nation's attention," then calls the current state of rock "outrageous filth" and openly wishes there was "some way constitutionally to do away with it."

His cohorts are equally disdainful. Senator Paul Trible (R-Virginia) quotes Plato, poet John Donne, and some nineteenth-century Irish activist before remarking that this might be "the most important hearing conducted by the Commerce Committee this year"—which should have sent chills down the spine of anyone listening who actually cared about commerce. Susan Baker spells out the word "fuck" since she apparently can't bring herself to say it, decries "the proliferation of songs glorifying rape, sadomasochism, incest, the occult, and suicide," and then tries to give some context to teen suicide statistics by invoking three songs—"Suicide Solution," "(Don't Fear) The Reaper," "Shoot to Thrill"—that have absolutely nothing at all to do with suicide.* Jeff Ling, a PMRC consultant, quotes objectionable lyrics from dozens of bands, from Metallica to the Mentors. The net effect is less shocking

* "Suicide Solution" is about the dangers of alcohol; in this context, "solution" is used as a synonym for "liquid." "(Don't Fear) The Reaper" is about eternal love. "Shoot to Thrill," like 99.9 percent of AC/DC's other songs, is about fucking.

than it is an unintentional indictment of the quality of modern songwriting.*

Now, in defense of the PMRC, or at least in defense of Tipper, when asked point-blank by Senator Jim Exon (D-Nebraska) about the center's purpose she is unequivocal.

Senator Exon: I guess a key question that I would like to ask you is, if there is one thing that has come through loud and clear to me at least, it is that you do not want federal legislation and you do not want federal regulation, at least at this time. Is that correct?

Tipper Gore: Yes, that is correct. We do not want legislation to remedy this problem. The problem is one that developed in the marketplace. The music industry has allowed the excesses that you saw and we believe the music industry is the entity to address those excesses. We would like them to do this voluntarily. We propose no legislative solution whatsoever.

Senator Exon: When you say "legislation," do you also include the term that I use, "regulation"?

Tipper Gore: Yes.

Naturally, there were those who questioned Tipper's sincerity on this point. After all, most of the PMRC harpies would have been positively ecstatic to see legislation introduced. But

---

* I don't really know why I feel compelled to include this here, but one of the most unintentionally funny things about the hearing—at least to me—is that in one of the supporting documents the band Dokken is referred to as Kokken. I guess this just says more about my sophisticated sense of humor than anything else.

one thing was certain: they weren't going to go unchallenged. The "friendly witnesses," those either from the PMRC or called in to validate their concerns, were only the appetizer. What anybody who had a rooting interest in the issue really wanted to see were the "opposing witnesses," the artists themselves, for whom even the slightest hint of censorship was unacceptable.

Things get off to a weird start. Chairman Danforth explains that although John Denver was slated to speak, he was forced to leave the hearing for another engagement, as if it was just a neighborhood barbecue and he had somewhere else to be. But, Danforth assures the room, "he plans to be back."

So instead, Frank Zappa is called upon. And now the fireworks really begin.

Admittedly, I've never been a huge fan of Zappa's, mainly because I was never entirely sure what was shtick and what wasn't. I do know that he's incredibly well respected by his fellow musicians and considered one of the smartest minds on the rock scene, which gives further credence to my theory that I'm the one who's missing something.

Zappa is dressed in a suit and tie—and not for a gag; he looks damn good—and is accompanied by his LA-based lawyer, Larry Stein. In order to amend his opening remarks, in response to the previous witnesses' testimony, Zappa asks Danforth to clarify if legislation is in fact being proposed. Danforth dismissively tells him just to stick to his statement and not worry about asking questions. However, Senator Exon jumps in to assure Zappa that the suggestion is "for voluntarily policing this in the music industry." At the very least, credit Exon for being a straight shooter. He candidly admits he might support "some kind of legislation and/or regulation unless the free enterprise system, both the producers and you as the performers, see fit to clean up your act." In remarks not captured in the official transcript, Zappa then mutters, "Okay, thank you, so that's hardly voluntary."

After quoting the First Amendment to the Constitution, Zappa really goes on the offensive. He calls the PMRC proposal an "ill-conceived piece of nonsense" that does nothing to protect children and infringes on the civil liberties of adults, comparing it to "treating dandruff by decapitation" and a "sinister kind of toilet training program."

Then shit gets real. Zappa basically accuses various senators of collusion with the recording industry. He questions the legality—or at least the appropriateness—of having the husband of a PMRC member sit on a committee ruling on the "blank tape tax," which is an industry-specific levy on recordable media. Finally, he declares the entire PMRC hearing a smokescreen to take the public's mind off the latest incomprehensible tax bill.

Before Zappa becomes too enraged, Al Gore steps in. He compliments Zappa as a "true original" and the two, in a particularly boring discussion, debate the merits of printing song lyrics on album sleeves. Meanwhile, to Gore's left, Senator Exon lights up a pipe!

Next comes an exchange that gets to the heart of the issue. Senator Gore believes that Zappa trivializes the concerns of parents regarding the content of their children's entertainment. Zappa vehemently refutes this and clarifies that in fact, it's *only* the parents' concern, not the government's. Gore tells him that the PMRC agrees, to which Zappa replies that up until now the center's demands have "smelled like legislation."

After some more back-and-forth, Senator Slade Gorton (R-Washington) is called upon. Gorton looks like a mentally challenged Henry Fonda. He calls Zappa "boorish" and "insulting to the people that were here previously" (meaning the other witnesses), and then accuses him of not having the slightest understanding of the Constitution. He then snickers to himself and looks around, ostensibly waiting for a show of support. The room basically ignores him.

Clearly, Gorton only wanted to make a splash, having nothing substantial to add to the discussion. He is a founding member of the Discovery Institute, an organization whose stated mission is to "advance a culture of purpose, creativity and innovation." That sounds pretty good, until you realize that the institute's actual purpose is to promulgate an anti-evolution, pro–intelligent design agenda. So while he might have a deep understanding (unlike Zappa) of the United States Constitution, he does not possess even a rudimentary grasp of the basic tenets of science.

Next, Senator Exon confesses he's not familiar with Zappa's music. Gore interrupts him. "You probably never heard of the Mothers of Invention," he chortles in a pathetically transparent attempt to look hip. Exon, who clearly doesn't know what the fuck Gore is babbling about, asks Zappa if he ever performed with Glenn Miller and Mitch Miller. The crazy thing is that I don't think he was trying to be funny. And the even crazier thing is that Zappa, also not trying to be funny, responds that he actually took music lessons in grade school from Mitch Miller's brother! Finally, *now* attempting to be funny (and admittedly, he is), Exon replies, "That is the first sign of hope we've had in this hearing."

There's some more debating and a bizarre exchange in which Zappa invites Senator Paula Hawkins (R-Florida) over to his house to inspect the toys his wife has purchased for their children. To conclude her questioning, she asks Zappa if he makes a profit from the sale of his rock records. He answers in the affirmative. She looks around, sort of confused, and instead of making a point says, "Thank you. I think that statement tells the story to this committee." It does not.

John Denver is now back from his previous engagement. He makes a rather eloquent statement about the dangers of censorship and offers up an anecdote about how his hit song "Rocky Mountain High" was misconstrued as a pro-drug song. He then goes into some hippy-dippy shit about ridding the world of nukes, ending hunger, and living together in peace and harmony. In 1985, I had absolutely no idea who John Denver was and now, looking back, I'm most struck by how much he looked like Cousin Oliver from *The Brady Bunch*.

Chairman Danforth thanks Denver for his "excellent statement" and reassures him that the PMRC only desires additional information, not censorship. Denver responds by reminding the committee that some of the senators at this very hearing have already admitted they would support censorship if it was done constitutionally.

After Gore finishes drooling over Denver, they discuss the appropriate role of the record companies. Just as it threatens to become a somewhat illuminating debate, Danforth interrupts and reminds Denver that, once again, he has somewhere else to be. Denver then announces that he has a noon appointment with NASA and Gore wishes him luck in getting on the space shuttle!*

---

* Apparently, this exchange wasn't nearly as funny as I first thought. Denver was a huge supporter of NASA and desperately wanted to secure a spot as a civilian on a shuttle mission.

After Denver shuffles out, it's time for Dee Snider, the lead singer of Twisted Sister. If Denver was the witnesses' ego, and Zappa was the superego, Snider was definitely the id. At the time, I worshipped Snider. He was an East Coast guy responsible for the best goddamn videos in the history of MTV, as well as one of the most underrated heavy metal albums ever, *Love Is for Suckers*.*

Unlike Zappa, who came dressed to the nines, Snider arrives in a sleeveless jean jacket and sunglasses. He begins his statement by wishing everyone both good morning and good afternoon since, he admits, he has no idea which it is. Watching the full hearing it's abundantly clear that Snider is making a small joke, referencing the fact that the hearing is entering its third hour and many, himself included, have lost track of time. But for those predisposed to cast judgment on a grown man who looks like Shirley Temple on acid, this statement is further proof that Snider is completely detached from reality.

However, those people are in for a rude awakening. From the moment he opens his mouth, Snider is surprisingly articulate and comports himself better than friend and foe on both sides of the issue. He lacks the smugness of the friendly witnesses and comes across as guileless and genuine. Nor does he seethe with Zappa's self-righteous anger or, like the milquetoast

---

* As someone who grew up with MTV, all I can tell you is what we talked about on the playground. And we talked about the videos of Twisted Sister. I'll concede that "Thriller" was groundbreaking, but it was also bloated and pompous. Plus, call it unfair, but I can't even look at Michael Jackson anymore without thinking about his nose falling off. As far as *Love Is for Suckers* goes, even the band doesn't hold it in very high regard. On their greatest-hits album, they have a cover of a Stones song but nothing off *Love Is for Suckers*. I don't care; I still love the album.

Denver, seem willing to accept the committee's assurances at face value. He's forceful but endearingly nervous, passionate but not closed-minded. But above all, Snider is *likeable*.

In a rather impressive bit of oration, Snider intends to "show just how unfair the whole concept of lyrical interpretation and judgment can be and how many times this can amount to little more than character assassination." He lays right into Tipper, calling her a liar and slanderous, and challenges her claim that the lyrics to his song "Under the Blade" encourage sadomasochism, bondage, and rape. On the contrary, he says, it's a song about the fear of surgery.

Snider also deserves credit for being one of the few to inject the concept of parental responsibility into the debate. Danforth wonders how, if Snider is against parental guidance labels, parents can possibly be aware of the type of music their children are listening to. Snider's answer is nothing if not practical. "Well, quite simply, as a parent myself and as a rock fan, I know that when I see an album cover with a severed goat's head in the middle of a pentagram between a woman's legs, that is not the kind of album I want my son to be listening to."

Before Gore can chime in, Snider asks him if he will also profess to being a fan of his music, a reference to Gore's sycophantic fawning over Zappa and Denver. Gore, humorless and stiff as always, declares he is not, in fact, a fan of Twisted Sister. He then tries to nail Snider right away by asking him what the letters "SMF" in the Twisted Sister Fan Club refer to. Snider replies that they stand for the "Sick Motherfucking Friends of Twisted Sister." Gore sarcastically asks if this fan club is also a "Christian group," mocking Snider's self-proclaimed characterization of his religious beliefs. Without missing a beat, Snider counters, "I don't believe that profanity has anything to do with Christianity, thank you." And of course, Snider is correct. Now, I realize most people wouldn't want their preacher dropping F-bombs from the pulpit, but I have at least a layman's understanding of the Bible and nowhere does it say, "Thou shalt not say 'shit,' 'piss,' 'fuck,' 'cunt,' 'cocksucker,' 'motherfucker,' and 'tits.'" That wasn't God, it was George Carlin. Come to think of it, the Bible doesn't say much about profanity besides warning against taking the Lord's name in vain. *That's* one of his commandments, whereas rape, child molestation, and spousal abuse don't make the list. To be honest, I might have picked a different set of ten, but then again, I'm no theologian.

Now we come to my favorite part of Snider vs. Gore. In a bogus attempt to find some common ground, Gore asks Snider to concede that it's at least conceivable that the lyrics to "Under the Blade" could be interpreted in a variety of ways. Snider replies, "Ms. Gore was looking for sadomasochism and bondage and she found it." Gore responds with a hoarse, "Yeah," and clears his throat, possibly trying to process the newfound revelation that his wife might be up for a little B & D.

In one of the most illuminating exchanges, Senator John D. Rockefeller IV (D–West Virginia) asks Snider why he feels compelled to attack "Senator Gore's wife" so vehemently. Snider clarifies that he's not attacking the senator's wife, but rather the head of the PMRC. It's a seemingly minor but actually extremely important distinction, one that Rockefeller fails to recognize but of which Snider is all too aware. As I previously mentioned, this entire charade reeked of chauvinism if not misogyny—and not on the part of the artists. Although this was certainly not his intent, Rockefeller demonstrates his myopic view on women. To him, and presumably to his fellow senators, judging by their silence, being the wife of Al Gore *is* Tipper's raison d'être. But to Snider, she's a worthy adversary, the leader (or at least figurehead) of an organization devoted to fucking with his livelihood. Snider might not pull his punches—he's explicit about his disdain for Tipper and her ilk—but in his condemnation he pays her far more respect than Rockefeller and his cronies do with their support.

In hindsight, one of the most striking things from Snider's testimony is just how closely it fits the popular image of a staunch conservative circa 2014. In fact, if you ignore the fact that Snider *looks* insane, his rant could be ripped right from the playbook of the Christian Right. Married? Check. A loving father? Check. Proudly religious? Check. Abstains from tobacco, drink, and drugs? Check, check, and check. Forget any of this "it takes a village" bullshit; Snider is strident in his belief that the sole responsibility for raising his child falls to him and his wife. When Gore declares it's not reasonable for parents to listen to all the albums they buy their children, it's Snider who reminds him that being a parent isn't always easy.

Honestly, I'm not sure exactly what this observation proves. That Snider was always a stealth pilgrim, hiding in plain sight under a cloak of denim, spandex, and lipstick? Or that cultural mores change so rapidly from generation to generation that what was once considered aberrant is now the status quo? Still, there's something telling about the fact that it was Snider, one of the few heavy metal icons to embrace his Christianity, who chose to suffer the slings and arrows of his persecutors and plead his case before Congress.

Years later, Twisted Sister released what I consider to be

the greatest version of "O Come All Ye Faithful" ever recorded, proving you can take the boy out of the church, but you can't take the church out of the boy. Of course, in the video, which hearkens back to their classic "We're Not Gonna Take It," Snider makes a prim housewife so hot with his religiosity that she tears open her blouse and head-bangs with a life-size candy cane.

Eventually, the PMRC got its way. Parental Advisory labels were slapped on any album with questionable content. The labels were a godsend to two groups: 1) brain-dead parents who were either too lazy or too apathetic to decide for themselves what was appropriate for their children, and 2) those very same children, who now had a guide to the good stuff.

Although they couldn't be bothered to attend the hearings, artists of every stripe lashed out at the PMRC, specifically Tipper. On his 1989 album, *The Iceberg/Freedom of Speech . . . Just Watch What You Say*, Ice-T speculates in the crudest of terms that she might be sexually frustrated, while in "Sucks," KMFDM wants to "strip" her. Usual suspects like the Dead Kennedys, Rage Against the Machine (who really rage against anything), Danzig, and Sonic Youth also added their own denunciations.

This might be heretical to admit, since she was public enemy number one for a generation of heavy metal fans, but I always felt somewhat bad for Tipper. She always seemed more overwhelmed and, quite frankly, clueless than hell-bent on the censorship effort that was ascribed to her. Watching the hearings again, I'm struck by another thought: only thirty-seven years old, Tipper was already saddled with four young children. In another life, she should have been rocking out to the artists she was pit-ted against, not serving the agenda of a bunch of old men who hijacked her well-intentioned but misguided campaign.

Some of Tipper's fellow culture warriors carried on the good fight. Evangelical minister and PMRC friend Bob Larson, author of numerous books with catchy titles like *Rock: Practical Help for Those Who Listen to the Words and Don't Like What They Hear*, continued publishing dire warnings about metal, Satanism, and anything else fun. Admittedly, I've never read *Rock*, but if the fact that there are dozens of copies on Amazon listed for $0.01 is indicative of anything, I probably won't. More recently, Larson has devoted much of his time to performing exorcisms with his drop-dead-gorgeous nineteen-year-old daughter, Brynne, a self-described virgin who looks like a younger Jessica Chastain. In 2013, Vice Media produced a short documentary following Brynne Larson and her two friends Tess and Savannah Scherkenback, who bill themselves as "the Teenage Exorcists." The film, in which the group travels to Ukraine to ply their trade, is both heartbreaking and laugh-out-loud funny—neither of which was the intention of the miniature Merrins.

Years later, Tipper would basically admit that the PMRC hearings were a disaster. "If I could rewrite the script, I certainly would," she told *Daily Variety*. Her husband, however, was far less conciliatory, blaming the entire mess on the Republicans on the committee. "I was not in favor of the hearing," Gore told a group of high-powered Hollywood executives. Anybody who watched the hearing for half a second can see what a huge, steaming pile of bullshit this is. Gore clearly relished his prominent role, especially the opportunity to spar with Snider, one of Tipper's fiercest critics.

The truth is, there are few politicians as contemptible as Al Gore (full disclosure: I voted for him in the 2000 presidential election). In 2006, he traveled to Saudi Arabia, birthplace of eighteen of the 9/11 hijackers, and apologized for America's treatment of Saudi nationals. While taking a break from kissing Saudi ass and flogging his Oscar-winning PowerPoint on global warming, he managed to sell his fledgling network, Current TV, to the Qatar-owned Al Jazeera Media Network. Now, even if you don't subscribe to the belief that Al Jazeera is a font of anti-Americanism and anti-Semitism, and find nothing cynical about a staunch defender of the 99 percent rushing to close the deal in order to avoid an impending tax increase on his estimated $100 million profit, you'd have to have the sense of humor of, well, Gore not to find it deliciously ironic that the crown prince of everything green sold out to one of the world's largest oil producers. When asked about the incongruity between his espoused beliefs and the chief revenue source of his Qatari buyer, the best defense Gore could muster was some dubious claim that Al Jazeera has "outstanding" and "extensive" coverage on climate change. In light of the purchase, Gore can certainly afford the best PR flacks that money can buy. And *this* is what they came up with? It's kind of like defending a serial rapist because he makes a donation to a women's shelter around the holidays.

In the tradition of Dylan, I want to wrap this chapter up by bringing it all back home. I think there's a seminal moment in everyone's life when they realize they're getting old, and for me, this was tied to Ozzy.

One of the unapologetically geeky things that I love to do is attend haunted houses around Halloween. In the old days, these were held in high school gymnasiums or park district headquarters where the extent of the decorations were papier-mâché bats and Styrofoam tombstones. If you were lucky, a volunteer from the local church or Girl Scout troop might pop out of a darkened corner and shriek in your face. But in recent years, a burgeoning industry of high-end, temporary haunted house attractions has sprung up. These feature real actors (or more accurately, real wannabe actors), lifelike props, animatronics, and old-school carnival staples like the "Vortex Tunnel" and the "Hall of Mirrors" updated with a Halloween twist. The more elaborate ones even have a gift shop for those who can't pass up a T-shirt emblazoned with the phrase "I survived ______." These itinerant attractions are virtual cash registers because really, when I was a kid, I would have paid anything for twenty minutes of sanctioned darkness alone with my girlfriend. To have her terrified and clinging to me the entire time would have been just the cherry on top. In fact, to all you comptrollers out there, bitching about bankruptcy and your dying cities, you want a surefire way to increase seasonal revenue? Pour all your discretionary funds into the biggest, baddest haunted house you can afford. It will pay you back in spades. I promise you, people will happily shell out twenty bucks a pop for the pleasure of being groped by some part-time barista in a rubber vampire mask.

But I digress . . . So I was with my business partner Alex and Lance Hori, a friend of mine from college and fellow television producer. We were waiting to buy tickets for one of these haunted houses in a strip-mall parking lot in some nameless suburb. A middle-aged father chaperoning his teenage daughter and her friend stood behind us in line. The girls were yapping about the *The Osbournes*, which that March had become the hottest reality show of the season. It introduced America to Ozzy's dysfunctional but lovable brood and recast the Prince of Darkness himself as a tatted-up, unintelligible Ward Cleaver. "You know," said the father, playfully admonishing them, "Ozzy didn't always used to be a joke. He was once in a band called Black Sabbath that scared a lot of people." The girls considered this for a moment, pondering how the perpetually confused TV dad with whom they were familiar could have ever scared anyone. Then the daughter's friend looked up, as if something clicked. "Oh, yeah," she said hesitantly. "I think my mom has some Black Sabbath albums." Her fucking *mom*! My rapidly receding hairline spontaneously pulled back a few centimeters more. Moms were supposed to listen to Sinatra or Engelbert Humperdinck. I pictured my own mother rocking out to "War Pigs" and shuddered.

Now, twelve years later, this story doesn't sound so funny. Or scary. I'm now the father of an eight- and ten-year-old. And when I listen to the shit they have on their iPods—and "shit" is an apt description, not a synonym for "stuff"—I realize that moms, and dads, do listen to Sabbath.

Thirtysomething years ago I bought my first Iron Maiden album because, as one of our greatest pop songsmiths once sang, "I'd rather laugh with the sinners than cry with the saints. The sinners are much more fun."

I guess that's what getting old means. You end a chapter on heavy metal with a quote from Billy fucking Joel.

CHAPTER SIX

Making Steak from Sacred Cows

I'm ashamed to admit it, but growing up in a predominately Catholic town, there were plenty of times when I wished I wasn't Jewish. It had nothing to do with the religion itself, mind you. Quite frankly, I found the secular strain of Judaism that we practiced far more sensible than what I heard was going on at the church down the street; before I had any understanding of the symbolic nature of the Eucharist, you can only imagine what the horror-obsessed nine-year-old me thought when a bunch of my friends swore that each Sunday they would eat the body of their Lord and Savior.

No, my reason was far more egocentric. While all my friends would worship together at a handful of churches nearby, I was shipped off to an adjacent town three times a week for Hebrew school, where I was thrown together with a bunch of misfits whose idea of fun was making up silly lyrics to Jewish folk songs.

But there was one thing I never envied about my gentile friends: confession. They were forced to take a weekly pilgrimage and spill their guts to a mere acquaintance. I, on the other hand, had only to unburden myself once a year, on the High Holy Day of Yom Kippur. Plus, since masturbation isn't a sin in Reform Judaism, I didn't really have much for which to apologize.

Still, I can appreciate the cathartic nature of confession. So I'm going to admit some things that will undoubtedly brand me a heretic in the exceptionally protective horror community. Things that would be inconceivable for any devotee to utter without getting their horror card summarily revoked. After all, so ingrained are these truths for the horror community that it's almost like challenging the tenets of a religion. So in keeping with the religious theme, I'm going to play Martin Luther (not King Jr.). And here are my grievances.

Horror Commandment: *The Exorcist* is the scariest movie ever made.
Grievance: Not only is it definitely *not* the scariest movie ever made, but in some places it's rather funny (and not by design).

Let me clarify. Obviously not *everybody* feels *The Exorcist* is the scariest movie ever made. Lots of people of my generation, including my wife, will point to *The Shining*. Then you'll have the old-timers, for whom nostalgia is more powerful than any semblance of common sense, who might cite a Universal classic or Hammer film. These are the same kind of people who maintain that the 1945 Army team, with Mr. Inside, Doc Blanchard, and Mr. Outside, Glenn Davis, is the greatest college football team in NCAA history. At the time, maybe they were; I'm not qualified to argue. But anybody who thinks for even a split second that any Division 1 team circa 2014 wouldn't completely annihilate the '45 Black Knights doesn't know the first thing about football. The players today are just so much bigger, faster, stronger, and more athletic that it would be a massacre—and not a proverbial one; somebody might actually die. At the very least, today's teams would score on every single play and Army would have negative net yards both passing and rushing.

You also have those people who project their own fears onto a film, so that one particular scene or aspect of it takes on a disproportionate degree of importance. These are the people so terrified of clowns that they cannot bring themselves to watch *Poltergeist* or *It*. Entomophobes who feel the same about *Them!*, *The Swarm*, or *Empire of the Ants*. A claustrophobic might even name the 2010 Ryan Reynolds film *Buried*.

However, it's safe to say that 95 percent of those asked will choose *The Exorcist*. The remaining 5 percent will place it in their top five. When it was originally released in 1973, just in time for the Christmas holiday, many in the audience vomited. Some fainted. Others had to seek therapy or religious counsel.

I'll fully concede that *The Exorcist* is a terrific film and certainly deserves all the accolades bestowed upon it. I'll even concede that it might be the *greatest* horror film ever made, an absolutely devastating treatise on the loss of faith, the limitations of science, and the ultimate triumph of good over evil. But scariest? Not by a long shot.

It is possible that as a non-Catholic the metaphysical underpinnings of the film failed to resonate with me. Or to put it another way, if you don't believe in the devil, how can he frighten you? But this explanation doesn't hold up to scrutiny.

At least not when applied to me. I don't believe in ghosts, possession, or any form (neither spiritual nor corporeal) of an afterlife, and I still find *The Changeling*, *Audrey Rose*, and the *Paranormal Activity* films scary as hell.

Even for true believers, the kind of Bible thumpers for whom life is nothing more than an eternal struggle for the soul, the demon in *The Exorcist* leaves quite a bit to be desired. This is an entity whose power is second only to that of God himself. So one might assume his dastardly deeds would fall mainly in the realm of genocides, natural disasters, and human suffering on a grand scale. But instead, the best he can do is make an adolescent girl say "cock" and "cunt." I understand his disdain for, as he tells Father Karras, vulgar displays of power, but this torrent of profanity still seems like something concocted by a mischievous twelve-year-old, not the Antichrist.

I also understand that most commentators on the film agree that Regan is not the demon's ultimate prize. She's just a conduit to get to Karras, a vessel through which the demon can decimate the priest's already shaky spiritual foundation. Even if this is true, again, I have to ask, why settle for a single man when humanity is ripe for the taking?

My opinion of *The Exorcist*'s dwindling power was somewhat validated when the film was rereleased in 2000. This was big news, mainly because the originally excised but long-rumored "spider walk" sequence had been reinserted into the film at the behest of William Peter Blatty, who wrote the novel the film was based on as well as the screenplay. My wife and I attended a sold-out midnight showing, as this was still early enough in our marriage where she would indulge me with things like this.

The first disconcerting thing I noticed was the inordinate

number of families with young children. I don't mean teenagers. I mean kids two, three, four, five years old. Admittedly, my wife and I are pretty anal about sleep schedules; when they were that young, our kids both went to bed extremely early and, whenever possible, in their own crib or bassinet. Still, I can understand those people who drag their infants everywhere with them; since babies basically sleep all the time anyway, who am I to judge? But who the fuck brings a child to a midnight showing of *The Exorcist*? The obvious answer is that these were shitty parents, ill equipped to understand the possible consequences or too selfish to care. The more I watched them, however, the more I realized this wasn't the case. Most of them were loving, attentive, and fairly hands-on parents. As long as I live I'll never forget the spectacle of a mother feeding her toddler a handful of Pepperidge Farm Goldfish while the kid asked, "Mama, what's an ex-nist?"

Then I considered the possibility that maybe the majority of these folks didn't actually know what the hell the film was about. But really? These people weren't ignorant. Plus, since the majority of them were Hispanic, and most likely Catholic, they were probably at least vaguely familiar with the exorcism ritual.

So what explains the discrepancy between being a responsible parent and taking your underage kids to see *The Exorcist* in the dead of night? I found out once the film began. The audience laughed when Regan's head spun around 360 degrees. They howled with glee when she projectile-vomited pea soup. Call me a prude, but I was more than mildly disturbed watching a preteen girl jab a crucifix into her vagina; however, this didn't seem to faze them in the least. The bottom line is that they just didn't find any of it that *scary*. In fact, the only part of the film during which they were visibly uncomfortable was when Regan undergoes a battery of medical tests to rule out a physical cause of her condition (Blatty also found this scene the most upsetting).

For what it's worth, I happen to find 1990's *The Exorcist III* absolutely terrifying. I'm not saying it's necessarily superior (although it is a great film), but it does make the hair on the back of my neck stand up in a way that Regan and co. simply don't. Although I may be crazy, I'm not alone. Legendary *New York Times* film critic Vincent Canby actually called *The Exorcist III* a better film than its predecessor. Of course, he also hated *The Godfather: Part II*, so maybe he just doesn't know what the fuck he's talking about.

Horror Commandment: *Suspiria* is Argento's masterpiece.

Grievance: *Suspiria* is overrated and far from Argento's best work.

I discovered the great Dario Argento when I stumbled upon his 1985 film *Phenomena*, which was retitled *Creepers* for its US release on VHS. *Creepers* is an interesting film; fans usually place it in the middle of Argento's body of work, although the more dreadful his current films are, the more it's pushed toward the top. It's something of a hybrid, a combination of supernatural fairy tale and straightforward giallo.

Like many pivotal moments in my horror education, my mother was inadvertently responsible. I had been watching so many horror films that I think she suffered a crisis of confidence, second-guessing her decision to allow me to rent R-rated ones. In order to mitigate the potential danger of a diet of on-screen murder, rape, and other antisocial behavior, she implemented a new rule: going forward, I could only see horror movies in which animals or monsters killed people. Man-on-man violence was no longer allowed. I wasn't too concerned. After all, I could still watch *The Thing*, *Nightwing*, *Orca*, *Grizzly*, or any number of nature-run-amok films from the seventies. And truth be told, like most of my mother's other rules, I figured this one would last like half a day, at most.*

However, during this particular trip to the video store, the rule was still in effect. Therefore, I chose *Creepers*, since the VHS box had a picture of a girl whose face was half-eaten by bugs. The tagline promised, *It Will Make Your Skin Crawl* . . . I got home expecting *Squirm*. Boy, was I wrong. *Creepers* certainly has plenty of bugs, but it also has a decapitation, torture, and a razor-wielding chimpanzee. *Them!* it ain't. I didn't love *Creepers*—although I appreciate it far more today—but even then I knew there was something different about it. The garish colors, the stylized violence, the plot that was completely wacked. I knew I was in the hands of a maestro. After that, I sought out everything I could from Argento. It wasn't until a few years later that I got my hands on the film that is generally considered his masterpiece: *Suspiria*.

---

* Another of her arbitrary rules was that I couldn't watch horror movies in which the victims were killed on camera. The aftermath of the killing was fine to show, but not the act itself. That rule lasted about fifteen minutes.

The film stars Jessica Harper* as an American ballerina boarding at a prestigious ballet academy, which, as she soon discovers, is a front for a coven of witches. One would think they'd choose far less obvious digs than the world's preeminent dance school, but whatever. The plots of Argento's films generally fall into two categories: complicated to the point of being impenetrable, or so flimsy as to be inconsequential. *Suspiria* falls into the latter camp. Not that it matters much. Argento has always been accused of favoring style over substance. It's one of the reasons I fell in love with his work and a criticism also leveled against my favorite American director, Brian De Palma. Still, you would think that Argento's crowning achievement would manage to meld the two much more cohesively than it does. But if you've come only for the style you won't be disappointed. *Suspiria*'s opening airport scene is something out of a dreamscape—or a nightmare. The hiss of the automatic doors foreshadows the whispers of witches. When Jessica exits through them into a rainstorm of biblical proportions, reds, yellows, and blues explode across the screen. It does nothing to advance the story, but that's what makes it so intriguing. American horror would never be so unnecessarily indulgent.

Once Jessica arrives at the academy, another of Argento's limitations is on full display—the awfulness of his scripts. In an interview in *Spaghetti Nightmares* by Luca M. Palmerini

* Daria Nicolodi, Argento's cowriter and sometime muse, originally wrote the starring role for herself, but the US financiers wanted an American lead instead. However, according to Asia Argento, Dario's daughter, it was Dario who didn't want Daria for the role.

and Gaetano Mistretta, Lucio Fulci had this to say about his chief rival: "Everyone thinks he's a very good writer and a very bad realizer, whereas, in fact, it's the other way around." Quite possibly there has never been a more apt characterization of Argento. In a completely telling but otherwise superfluous scene, one of the students taunts Harper and her friend, who are named Suzy and Sara, by saying that names that begin with "S" are the names of snakes. Then she hisses in their faces. My eight-year-old daughter might find this juvenile. Some of this nonsense Argento explains away as a result of his battle with the Italian distributor; Argento scripted the girls in *Suspiria* as eleven-to-fourteen-year-olds, but the distributor wanted them cast much older. Such an excuse might be easier to accept if his other films weren't filled with similar abysmal scripting. I don't know why no one has ever taken him aside and said, "Listen, Dario. You're a brilliant visionary. You paint the screen like an artist paints his canvas. But you should never ever write another script."

I guess the main problem I have with *Suspiria*—aside from the fact that the ballet instructor, Miss Tanner, played by the great Italian actress Alida Valli, looks *exactly* like Jim Carrey in *The Mask*—is that its highlights have been surpassed in other Argento films. His sweeping camera is more evocative in *Opera*. The maggot storm and barbed wire pit-o'-death are combined to greater effect in *Phenomena*. I know that *Suspiria* was first, but that doesn't make it better.

Most consider *Suspiria* the pinnacle of Argento's career; I find it a worthy appetizer.

In case anyone is wondering, the Argento films I'd rank higher are, in descending order, *Tenebrae*, *Opera*, *Deep Red*, and *The Bird with the Crystal Plumage*. And I wouldn't argue with *Inferno* or *Phenomena* either.

Horror Commandment: *Red Dragon* is a poor imitation of the classic *Manhunter*.

Grievance: *Red Dragon* is the superior film.

The amount of animus directed at Brett Ratner is so disproportionate to what the filmmaker deserves that I'm fully convinced the dude must have done something in a previous life to warrant this karmic punishment. *Money Talks* and the *Rush Hour* films aren't your cup of tea? Okay, I get it. Not mine either. But there are many worse filmmakers who have made much worse films. Still, when it was announced that Ratner would be directing the fourth entry of the series based on Thomas Harris's cultured cannibal, there was a collective gasp. The directorial lineage of the series thus far was Michael Mann, Jonathan Demme, Ridley Scott, and now . . . Brett Ratner.

In 1992, when *The Silence of the Lambs* swept the four major categories at the sixty-fourth Academy Awards—the first time this occurred since 1975's *One Flew over the Cuckoo's Nest*—there was a rush to revisit *Silence*'s predecessor, 1986's *Manhunter*, based on Harris's novel *Red Dragon*. Soon came the whispers that *Manhunter* was actually superior to *Silence*. It was called an unforgivably ignored masterpiece that was finally receiving its just due. But although *Manhunter* could never usurp *Silence* in the public's imagination—Anthony Hopkins's portrayal of incarcerated killer Hannibal Lecter all but exsanguinates Brian Cox's—it could at least claim the mantle as the *rightful* adaptation of *Red Dragon*. So Ratner was fucked from the start.

What's interesting to recall, however, is just how irrelevant *Manhunter* was upon its original release. For one thing, it bombed, making back only $8 million of its $15 million budget. The critics also hated it, although it's clear they were really using *Manhunter* as a way to critique *Miami Vice*, director Michael Mann's television series that pretty much *was* the zeitgeist at the time. Looking back, I was surprised to see that *Manhunter* was released at the peak of *Miami Vice* mania. I could have sworn the series had by then long overstayed its welcome, and was even more shocked to learn that it actually ran all the way through 1990. Most of the criticism leveled against Mann alluded to his reputation as a self-indulgent filmmaker, a specious claim that meant he had the balls not to be boring. Not surprisingly, it's the once-derided aspects of the film—lighting, sound design, acting—that were now championed by the revisionists.

If there's one thing Ratner is not, it's stupid, and he was more than aware that both critics and fans would be out for blood. Anticipating such, he made a series of shrewd preemptive strikes with *Red Dragon*. Writer Ted Tally, who had won the Oscar for *Silence*, was brought in to script. *Manhunter* cinematographer Dante Spinotti returned with an entirely new aesthetic, replacing the cold blues of the original with a muted color scheme, especially in the scenes set in the Dolarhyde Nursing Home. It was the casting, however, that was the real stroke of genius. The roles were all filled with critical darlings—Edward Norton, Harvey Keitel, Ralph Fiennes, Emily Watson, and Philip Seymour Hoffman replaced William Petersen,

Dennis Farina, Tom Noonan, Joan Allen, and Stephen Lang. Anthony Hopkins reprised his role as Lecter. It is in this pivotal role that *Red Dragon* far surpasses *Manhunter*. Brian Cox has his backers—mainly annoying contrarians—but he can't hold a candle to Sir Tony. Half the time I can't tell if Cox is British or recovering from a mild stroke. In fact, I actually prefer Hopkins's interpretation of Lecter in *Red Dragon* to that in *Silence*. It's less hammy. More manipulative. Irredeemably evil without the shtick. Providing the Tooth Fairy with Will Graham's home address is a helluva lot worse than telling Clarice Starling she's not more than one generation from poor white trash.

One aspect of *Manhunter* that critics did laud, however, was Mann's decision to portray Dolarhyde not as a caricature—some drooling lunatic—but as a deeply troubled human being. Noonan is always great, and at six feet seven inches he can't help but come across as creepy as hell, but Fiennes brings a sense of pathos to the character absent in the original. Ratner takes extraordinary care in reminding us that Dolarhyde, as Graham says, "wasn't born a monster" but "was made one through years and years of abuse." This notion is reinforced by chilling audio flashbacks, played over contemporary scenes of Dolarhyde's crumbling childhood prison, which detail snippets of the abuse he suffered at the hand of his sadistic grandmother.

The biggest difference between the films lies in their endings, with *Manhunter* heralded as a tour de force of filmmaking while *Red Dragon* is dismissed as typical Hollywood pabulum. In *Manhunter*, Graham barges through a glass window and makes a beeline for Dolarhyde. It's a moment of catharsis as much as strategy, as his obsession with the case has reached a boil. Shot in slow motion with the strains of Iron Butterfly's "In-A-Gadda-Da-Vida" played over the scene, it's great cinema. It's also a tad absurd.

In *Red Dragon*, Dolarhyde fakes his own death, burns down his entire estate, and then sneaks off to Graham's home to seek revenge. The fact that his final targets are those closest to Graham (his wife and son), whom the detective himself put in jeopardy by his actions, raises the stakes exponentially.

I'll concede that Dolarhyde's *Red Dragon* death ventures a bit too close to Michael Myers/Jason Voorhees territory. That said, the way Graham disarms Dolarhyde as the killer holds his son at gunpoint is pretty inventive. The terrified boy has wet himself, and Graham mocks him cruelly. This triggers Dolarhyde's memory of his own similar abuse and prompts him to refocus his rage on Graham, not his son.

The bottom line is this: sometimes Hollywood doesn't fuck it up. And if we're willing to suspend our prejudice against Ratner, studio largesse, and unnecessary remakes, it becomes evident that *Red Dragon* is one of these times.

Horror Commandment: *Alien* is brilliant.
Grievance: *Alien* is boring.

In the proposal for this book, which I put together in order to convince the publisher that my idea had merit, I included a summary of each chapter. For this one, I promised to point out how "*Alien* is an extraordinarily boring film. And worse, a rip-off of Mario Bava's equally boring sci-fi epic, *Planet of the Vampires*." The truth is, I had never seen *Planet of the Vampires*.

But I had heard so many times about how it provided the template for *Alien* that I took it as a matter of faith. Eventually, I got around to watching it. Oh, my god. What an interminable piece of crap. So my apologies to Ridley Scott—he absolutely did not rip off Bava's film.

Having said that, *Alien* is still a snoozefest.

Alien opens with one of the most boring sequences since *2001: A Space Odyssey*, although mercifully much shorter.* While I have nothing against films with a slow build, the first "face hugger" doesn't make its appearance until thirty-five minutes in. That's a pretty long time to go with little to do but admire the scenery and get to know a rather unlikeable bunch of people. My biggest gripe, however, is that despite all things to the contrary, *Alien* isn't really that scary. In fact, I happen to find *Event Horizon* much more frightening (no joke, it's a criminally underrated film). Scott even undercuts the few appearances of the creature by telegraphing its presence with a stray tentacle or string of intergalactic drool. I'm now reminded of Hitchcock's famous interview where he pontificates about the difference between suspense and shock (unsurprisingly, he prefers suspense), but in a movie as deliberate as *Alien*, you need a few good cheap scares. That's why my favorite scene is the creature's appearance in the airshaft with Tom Skerritt. Jesus Christ, check my underwear.

I don't mean to insinuate that there's *nothing* to recommend about the film, which most consider the greatest sci-fi/horror

---

* Apropos of nothing, in college when I couldn't sleep, I would sometimes pop in a classic movie that I was supposed to love but that I really found ridiculously boring. *2001* was always a favorite for this purpose. Others were *Nashville* and *8½*.

hybrid ever made. The sound design is brilliant and the sets, awe inspiring. At a time when *Star Wars* claimed space as a world of childlike wonder, *Alien* proved that the universe was still filled with very bad things. The aliens themselves, designed by Swiss surrealist H. R. Giger, have become iconic monsters, the inspiration for an incalculable number of interstellar baddies. Even the archetype of Ripley, imitated so many times since that it's become, well, an archetype, was relatively fresh in 1979. Her transition from by-the-book company woman to all-around badass gave a generation of women's studies majors fodder for term papers and a generation of fanboys a funny feeling down below.

The scene that everybody remembers, and admittedly, the film's crowning achievement, is when an alien baby bursts out of John Hurt's chest and scurries away from the stunned crew. Allegedly, the cast had no idea this was going to happen, and their surprise captured on celluloid is as genuine as the audience's. I never bought this. With the incredible amount of preparation such a scene would entail, are you going to tell me that no one knew, or thought to ask, how the scene was going to play out? After listening to the DVD commentary, however, I stand corrected. If we're going to believe Ridley Scott—and I have no reason not to—the actors really were kept in the dark and certainly weren't ready for the creature's violent emergence. The entire "birth" was filmed in a single take with multiple cameras. So as good an actress as Veronica Cartwright may be, her blood-spattered look of utter shock is as real as it gets.

The *Alien* franchise trudged on with 1986's *Aliens—The Godfather: Part II* of horror, meaning many people feel that James Cameron's sequel actually surpasses the original. Well, it certainly moves a lot faster. *Alien 3* is today best known as the film that nearly ended David Fincher's career before it started. I think there are a few more sequels—at least one in which the aliens battle the creatures from the *Predator* movies—but since I can't remember a single thing about any of them, how much can there really be to say?

Horror Commandment: *Halloween* is the greatest slasher film. Period. End of conversation.

Grievance: *Friday the 13th* is better . . . or at least as good.

When the drafters of the Declaration of Independence declared "we hold these truths to be self-evident," clearly they did not mean that *Halloween* was the greatest slasher film ever made. That said, judging from the reaction of fans and critics alike, this is *exactly* what they meant. Don't get me wrong. *Halloween is* a slasher film. And a remarkable film, period. I have referred to it at different times and in different places as "the first true slasher film," "the granddaddy of slasher films," and "the quintessential slasher film." What I will say now is that it seems that as the stature of *Halloween* grows, that of *Friday the 13th* declines. And that's a shame, because they're both excellent films.

Their plots are equally preposterous, or, at the very least, highly unlikely. *Halloween* asks us to believe that a virtual catatonic has waited fifteen years to bust out of prison and go on a rampage, while *Friday* expects us to accept something similar about the mother of a dead child. But from the way that critics cream over *Halloween*'s script, you would think it's Beckett. It's a good tight story, but certainly not markedly better than *Friday*'s.

The characters in *Halloween* are no more complex or well defined than their Camp Crystal Lake counterparts. Yet again, if you listen to the pundits, Nancy Loomis and P. J. Soles are the second coming of Hepburn and Bergman, while *Friday*'s collection of unknowns are unworthy of a high school play. In fact, I'd actually make the argument that as fine as Jamie Lee Curtis is, Adrienne King is a much better actress. Although actually younger than Curtis, she brings a depth and maturity to her role as Alice that Curtis never approaches with Laurie Strode. As for the old-timers, sure, Betsy Palmer is hilariously over-the-top, but Donald Pleasence chews so much scenery that I'm convinced he's really looking for Michael's knife in order to extricate the wooden splinters from between his teeth.

Why is *Halloween* beloved while *Friday* is despised (except by its hard-core fans)? One word: blood. *Halloween* is sterile; *Friday the 13th* is an abattoir. And if there's one thing the critics hate, it's gore. In Carpenter's film, a victim is bloodlessly impaled on a door. Michael hides under a sheet, doing his best Casper the (Un)Friendly Ghost impression. A body is splayed out on a bed underneath a headstone. These are striking images to be sure, but hardly graphic. Cunningham on the other hand forgoes any semblance of subtlety. Jack gets an arrow through the neck, Marcie an ax to the face. And poor Mama Voorhees loses her head.

By the time that Tom Savini joined *Friday the 13th*, fresh off of *Dawn of the Dead*, he was already something of a living legend. By comparison, I can't even name the person who handled the makeup effects on *Halloween*. Simply put, you don't hire Savini and then handcuff him, any more than you would buy a Ferrari and keep it in the garage.

What's unfortunate is that most people assume that a lack of subtlety implies a lack of suspense, which doesn't have to be true at all. The first interview I ever gave was way back in the late nineties for the website Buried.com. I discussed watching *Friday the 13th* with Alex; the two of us were working for the same company but were not yet business partners. Alex is a casual film buff but certainly no horror nut. He did however first see *Alien* from an eight-millimeter print projected on someone's basement wall, which I always thought was super cool. Leaving the movie, I asked Alex which was his favorite scene. His response shocked me. It wasn't one of the unforgettable kills or the even more unforgettable ending, which made it a requirement for the maniac in all subsequent slashers to return for one last scare. Instead, it was a rather nothing two-minute sequence of Alice walking around the cabin, making coffee, waiting for Bill to return (which of course he never does). Before Alex brought it to my attention, I barely remembered the scene, but looking back, I was struck by how incredibly suspenseful it actually is. In the interview, I even invoked Hitchcock when describing it. A bit of hyperbole? Perhaps. But it does support my larger point that Cunningham never received his just due for these types of expertly constructed moments.

Had Carpenter shot the exact same scene we'd still be talking about his uncanny restraint. Had it been Bob Clark, it would be his genius for suggestion. Romero, fuhgeddaboudit. Making coffee would be interpreted as a metaphor for the encroachment of modernity into the untouched wilderness. But Sean Cunningham? He's just a hack who needs to fill some time between mindless murders.

I have no idea if Cunningham is particularly bothered by this perception of him. I suspect not, since in interviews he usually mocks those who point to *Friday the 13th* as high art (or even those who refer to it as a "film"). Then again, this could be an elaborate defense mechanism born from years of being told your industry-changing movie is a piece of shit. Either way, Cunningham has always seemed to have a sense of humor about his involvement with the series. Which I suppose is a lot easier when you're laughing all the way to the bank.

Horror Commandment: *An American Werewolf in London* is the best werewolf film of 1981.

Alternate Horror Commandment: *The Howling* is the best werewolf film of 1981.

Grievance: *Wolfen* is as good, if not better, than both.

To steal a quote from Clive Barker, "I like my horror *dark*." You'd think this would be par for the course among my contemporaries, but you'd be wrong. Indeed, I've found that horror fans generally love nothing more than to inject a little comedy into the proceedings, from *The Evil Dead* to *Return of the Living Dead*, as long as it's done respectfully, whatever that means. Not me. After a horror movie I want to feel like I've been punched in the gut, not tickled in the tummy.

So you can understand why I wasn't particularly giddy with anticipation when I started reading in *Fangoria* about two new werewolf films, *The Howling* and *An American Werewolf in London*, that promised to reinvent the moribund werewolf genre with as many laughs as scares. With coverage focusing almost exclusively on the makeup special effects, created by rising stars Rick Baker and his protégé Rob Bottin, it was clear these weren't going to be your father's *Wolf Man*.

Both *Howling* director Joe Dante and *American Werewolf* director John Landis were first-generation Monster Kids, horror-savvy fanboys—long before the term was coined—weaned on *Famous Monsters of Filmland* and TV broadcasts of the Universal classics. Dante got his start in the business working for Roger Corman and had just finished *Piranha* when he decided to adapt Gary Brandner's novel *The Howling* for the screen. He originally had Baker slated to handle the effects, who at the time was best known for creating the creatures in *Star Wars*'s Mos Eisley Cantina. Although Dante and Landis were friendly contemporaries, when Landis heard this he allegedly freaked out, as almost ten years before, Baker had promised to work on *his* werewolf film.

Way back in 1969, while working as a production assistant on location in Yugoslavia, Landis had witnessed a Gypsy funeral. It inspired him to write *An American Werewolf in London*. He had been trying to get the film made for almost a decade to no avail. Studios were flummoxed by the script's unique brand of horror and comedy. They found it either "too scary to be funny, or too funny to be scary." (This is my exact problem with the film, although history would prove both me and the studio executives wrong.) It wasn't until Landis had built up enough goodwill with *Animal House* and *The Blues Brothers* that PolyGram decided to take a shot (according to David Konow's *Reel*

Terror, a $250,000 producer fee to company heads Jon Peters and Peter Guber didn't hurt either). So even though Dante was further along than Landis, Baker kept his promise to his friend and signed on to *An American Werewolf in London*. As a consolation prize, Dante got Rob Bottin, which, in retrospect, was a helluva consolation.

The Howling and *An American Werewolf in London* came out a few months apart in 1981. The werewolf transformations in both films were, and still are, as jaw-dropping as promised, and the films themselves are now considered classics. Although I find both of them deeply flawed, I prefer *American Werewolf* for the simple reason that it's scarier. The most frightening part of *The Howling* is how casually Christopher Stone slaps wife Dee Wallace when she confronts him about his infidelity. In fact, at least for me, it's much more fun to try to spot Dante's numerous inside jokes* than it is to focus on the film. *American Werewolf* star David Naughton should also get a special prize for agreeing to go full-frontal in the cold London winter.

There's an unintentionally dark moment in the special features on *American Werewolf*'s DVD release. Landis is being interviewed about the climactic scene in Piccadilly Circus when he says, "No stunt is worth hurting someone for." One can't help but flash back to the tragic accident on the set of Landis's *Twilight Zone: The Movie* in which a stunt gone awry claimed

---

* Dante names many of the characters after famous horror film directors. There are also cameos by the likes of Roger Corman and Forrest Ackerman. Various references to other wolf-related ephemera are sprinkled throughout, like a copy of Ginsberg's *Howl* and a cartoon of the Three Little Pigs.

the life of star Vic Morrow as well as two illegally hired child actors.*

Between these two titans of werewolf cinema slipped in another entry, no less unconventional. Michael Wadleigh's *Wolfen* took a completely different approach to lycanthropic lore. In it, transformation is a conscious choice on the part of Native American shape-shifters, as opposed to an unwanted condition inflicted upon them by some unfortunate accident. In a *Fangoria* interview, Wadleigh, a documentarian who won the Oscar for his epic *Woodstock*, calls *Wolfen* a "political thriller" and comes across as kind of an asshole. Despite the director's obvious disdain for the genre, *Wolfen* is actually the scariest of the werewolf film troika. That the killers are actual wolves—albeit imbued with some Indian spirit—as opposed to a human/wolf amalgam, adds a layer of realism absent from similar films.

This is not to say that *Wolfen* is a perfect film. Far from it. The ubiquitous thermal-imaging effect, designed to represent the wolves' point of view and considered cutting-edge at the time, grows old fairly quickly. Half a dozen times I thought it was artifacting on the DVD. There's also a rather extraneous subplot about an antiterrorism organization, which, Wadleigh explains, was watered down by producers and the studio brass at Orion Pictures. Wadleigh also blames Orion for what he perceives as their mishandling of the film's marketing campaign, insinuating the studio's dire financial straits clouded their thinking. No doubt *Wolfen* was a challenging film to sell. But

* Morrow was decapitated by the blade of a helicopter when it crashed on him and the two children. After a nine-month trial, Landis was eventually found innocent of involuntary manslaughter.

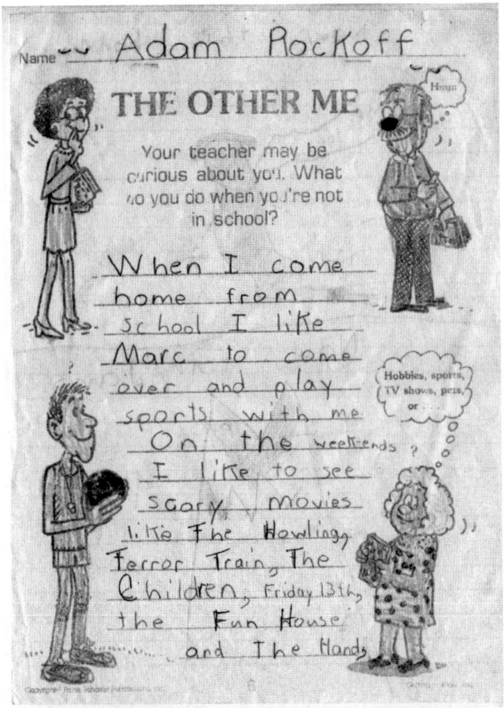

Name Adam Rockoff

THE OTHER ME

Your teacher may be curious about you. What do you do when you're not in school?

When I come home from school I like Marc to come over and play sports with me On the week-ends I like to see scary movies like The Howling, Terror Train, The Children, Friday 13th, the Fun House and The Hands

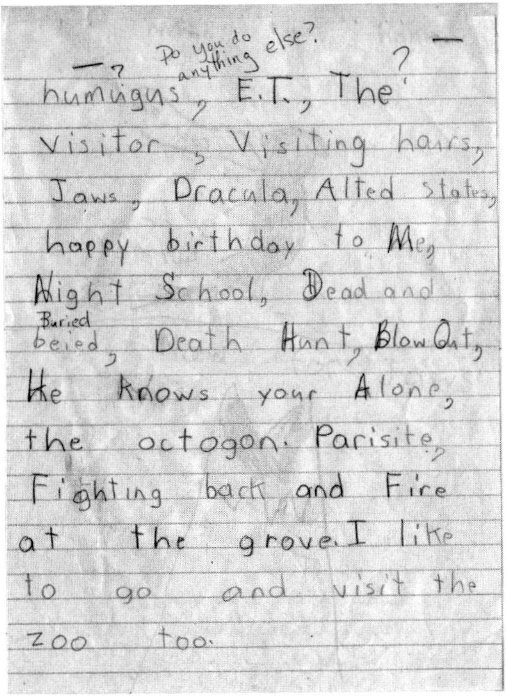

Do you do anything else?

humungus, E.T., The visitor, Visiting hours, Jaws, Dracula, Alted states, happy birthday to Me, Night School, Dead and Buried beied, Death Hunt, Blow Out, He knows your Alone, the octogon. Parisite, Fighting back and Fire at the grove. I like to go and visit the zoo too.

My offending second-grade essay. Far more disturbing than the content is the teacher's haphazard editorial work.

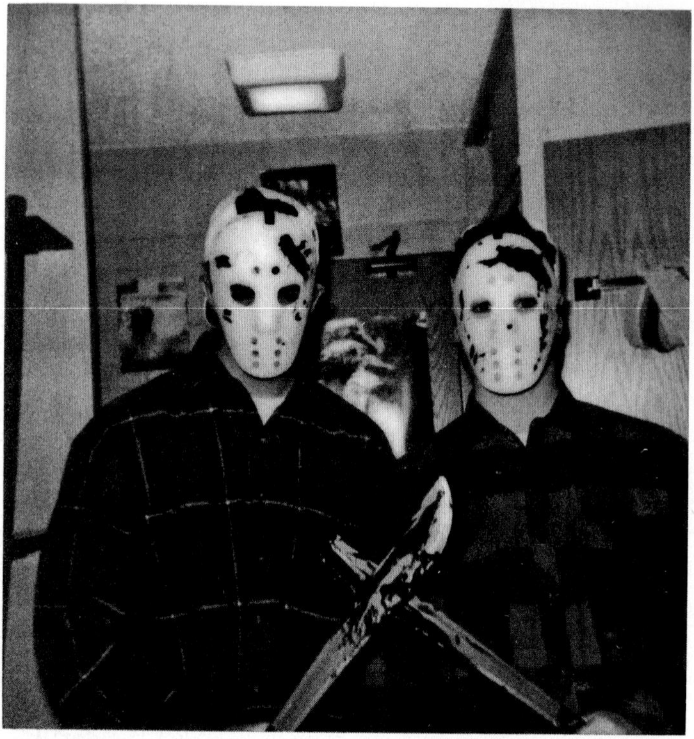

My college buddy Mike Scheer and me, dressed as Jason Voorhees for Halloween. Senior year, the two of us had a *Friday the 13th* marathon where we watched the first eight installments of the series. That same year, Scheer's German girlfriend, whom he had met while traveling abroad, came to stay with us. When I asked if she spoke English, he replied, "She speaks English better than you, Rockoff." Upon arriving, she could barely say "hello" and almost immediately got bitten by a spider, causing a pus-filled, golf-ball-size lump to form on her forehead. They broke up soon after.

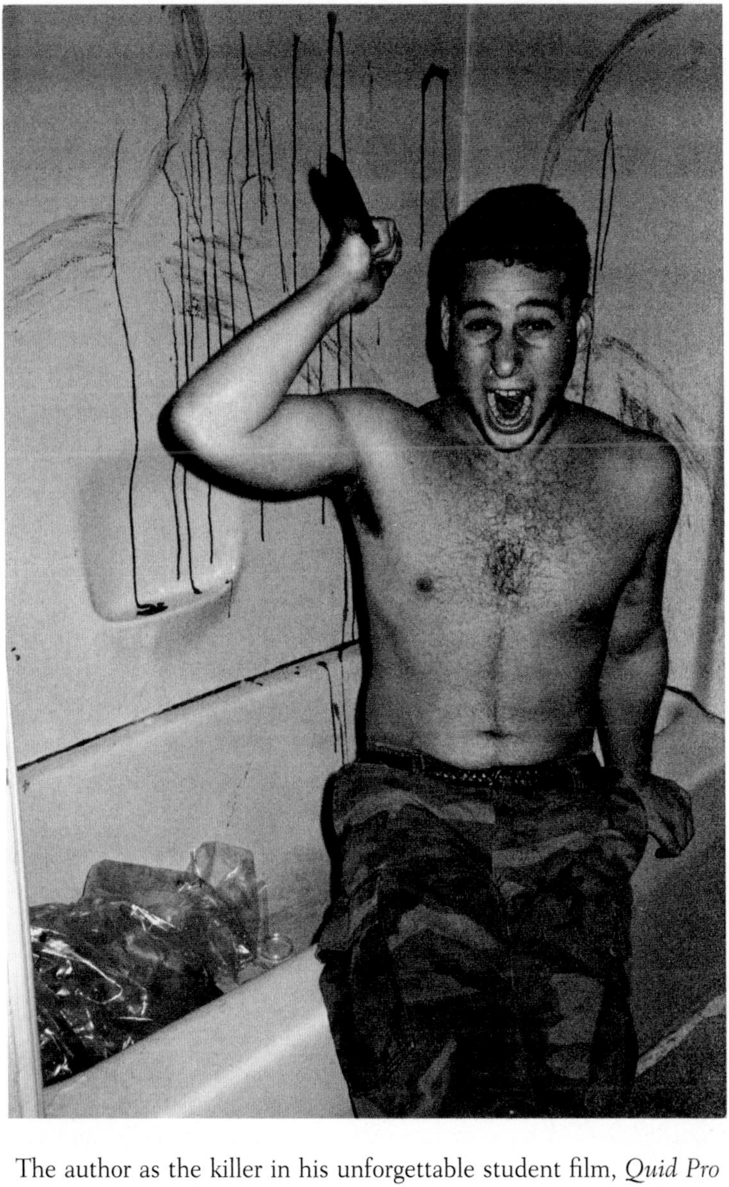

The author as the killer in his unforgettable student film, *Quid Pro Quo*.

Me and my business partner in FlashRock Films, Alex Flaster, at one of the haunted houses we visit during Halloween.

I'm still amazed *Wicked Lake* received this kind of promotion.

Interviewing George Mihalka, director of the original *My Bloody Valentine*.

Aaron Christensen, editor of *Hidden Horror*; me; Rusty Nails; and Joe Zito, director of *Friday the 13th: The Final Chapter* and the slasher favorite *The Prowler* (*left to right*).

Michael Ruggiero and me at the Los Angeles premiere of *I Spit on Your Grave* (2010). A longtime producer and television executive, Ruggiero produced the documentary adaptation of *Going to Pieces: The Rise and Fall of the Slasher Film*.

Me; Rudy Scalese, the producer most responsible for turning *Going to Pieces* into a documentary; actress Lynn Lowry of *The Crazies* and *Shivers*; and Ruggiero (*left to right*).

The lovely Sarah Butler, star of *I Spit on Your Grave* (2010); the less lovely but equally delightful Meir Zarchi, writer/director of the original *I Spit*; and me, sporting a gigantic sweat stain on my T-shirt (*left to right*).

Brian Kirst, founder of Big Gay Horror Fan; some dude I don't know; the legendary Herschell Gordon Lewis; and me, literally five minutes before Herschell yelled at the kid at the adjacent table (*left to right*).

Me and Jon Kitley of Kitley's Krypt, webmaster, author, columnist, collector, and the most knowledgeable horror fan I know.

Feasting on the intestines of Rusty Nails, who, for some inexplicable reason, is dressed as a disemboweled Santa Claus.

since Orion didn't declare bankruptcy until 1991, and didn't close its doors for good until 1998 (picking up a handful of Best Picture winners on the way), Wadleigh's complaints feel more like sour grapes.

Those looking for something a little different from the tongue-in-cheek humor of *The Howling* and *American Werewolf* should really give *Wolfen* a shot. In addition to the surprisingly graphic murders—a severed hand here, a severed head there—and the distinctive urban setting, Albert Finney gives a wonderful performance as a veteran cop slowly coming to terms with the truth behind the carnage. Because *Annie* was one of the only VHS tapes my family had—I know, beyond bizarre for a family who owned a video store—when *Wolfen* finally hit cable it took me a while to get past the fact that Daddy Warbucks was a cigar-smoking, lovemaking, gun-wielding werewolf hunter. That said, if you can buy Gregory Hines as a karate-kicking coroner who moonlights as a sniper, this probably won't be a problem for you.

CHAPTER SEVEN

Reality Bites

Call me a killjoy, but I don't find anything particularly funny about Charlie Sheen.

I realize that most people think of him as a harmless buffoon. He pals around with a harem of porn stars, lays waste to hotel rooms, and babbles on about "Adonis DNA" and "tiger blood." Unfortunately, the public at large—partly responsible for at one time making him the highest-paid actor on TV—and talk show hosts who continue to enable him (particularly nauseating is watching Jay Leno slobber over him, especially since Leno's wife, Mavis, has done such wonderful work on behalf of disenfranchised women) have either forgotten or chosen to ignore his very recent psychopathic behavior. And I'm not even talking about the bizarre 1990 incident in which his then-fiancée Kelly Preston was accidentally shot, leaving her so rattled she was forced to marry John Travolta and become a Scientologist.*

* For years, the story was that Sheen accidentally shot Preston. This version was reported in hundreds of media outlets and neither party did anything to claim otherwise. However, in 2011, Sheen admitted that Preston was injured when a

Sheen is a bigot and a serial abuser of women. In 1996, he was accused of beating girlfriend Brittany Ashland so badly that she needed stitches to close the wound, after which he threatened to kill her if she reported the assault. Years later, he called his ex-wife and the mother of his two daughters, actress Denise Richards, a nigger, wished cancer upon her, and threatened to kill her too. Only his most rabid defenders would have been surprised when two years later, according to a court filing, he told his estranged wife, Brooke Mueller, "I will cut your head off, put it in a box and send it to your mom!" During a well-publicized 2009 feud with producer Chuck Lorre, Sheen continued to refer to him as "Chaim Levine" (Lorre's given name is Charles Levine). To some, it reeked of anti-Semitism. More disturbing to me was the complete lack of self-awareness by one Carlos Irwin Estévez.

Bottom line: Sheen is just a pussy, much like other celebrity abusers (or any abuser for that matter), from Mel Gibson and Axl Rose* to that rapper who showed how tough he was by biting his girlfriend.

But Sheen is also a fucking moron, which is how he plays into this chapter.

As the story goes, in 1991 Sheen was at a party when he was given a so-called snuff film by *Film Threat* magazine founder

---

revolver, left in Sheen's pants, accidentally discharged, shattering the toilet bowl and injuring Preston with the debris.

* Despite all evidence to the contrary—most of all his waiflike body—Axl Rose fashions himself as something of a tough guy. In the GNR song "Get in the Ring," Rose dares a handful of writers who he feels have wronged him to "get in the ring" so he can kick their "bitchy little ass." Even as a kid, I found the prospect of Axl Rose kicking anybody's ass to be laugh-out-loud funny.

Chris Gore. Somehow convinced the murder on the VHS tape was real, a rattled Sheen contacted the FBI, who informed him they were already on the case. According to numerous sources, the tape was then traced to an "early distributor" of the film, journalist Chas Balun, often referred to fondly as the Lester Bangs of the horror set.

In Shade Rupe's marvelous collection of interviews, *Dark Stars Rising: Conversations from the Outer Realms*, Balun gives the definitive account of this monumental misunderstanding. According to Balun, he was approached by an acquaintance who asked for a favor: for his birthday, would Balun send him the most outrageous tape from his extensive collection? Balun went a step further. He filled an entire two-hour cassette with cinematic atrocities, beginning with *Flower of Flesh and Blood*, the second film in the notorious Japanese *Guinea Pig* series. At the beginning of the compilation, Balun also included his name and the quote "Anything worth doing is worth OVER-doing," attributed to himself. A couple of months later, Balun received a call from the acquaintance, warning him that the FBI would probably be contacting him (they never did, despite numerous stories to the contrary). You see, the acquaintance had passed the compilation on to Chris Gore, setting the events in motion.

It didn't take long for *Guinea Pig*'s veracity to be called into question, not least of all because of the accompanying documentary entitled *Making of Guinea Pig*. In fact, were it not for Sheen tripping over the role of good Samaritan, it's doubtful very many people in America would have heard of the *Guinea Pig* films at all. Although a few of the films have what I guess could be called a plot, the majority of it is just ultra-graphic scenes of torture and mutilation. They were made in the 1980s by producer Satoru Ogura and adapted in part from the horror manga of Hideshi Hino, who also directed two of the films.

As competent as most of the effects are, only someone without the most elementary sense of how filmmaking works could possibly think these films are real. And despite what one might think of Sheen as a person, or even as a thespian, he's been around enough sets (and presumably he's been sober on *some* of them) to know what's what. Did it never cross his mind to wonder why a down-and-dirty snuff film would be shot from multiple angles? Or be edited at all, much less competently with establishing shots and close-ups? And why would somebody with no compunction about showing the graphic dismemberment and disemboweling of a woman still adhere to the arcane Japanese practice of avoiding showing genitalia?

Of course, although Sheen might have been the most high-profile dupe, he was hardly the first to be fooled by cinematic slaughter marketed as the real thing. In 1976, a film was released whose very title was predicated on this constructed reality.

It's quite fitting that this sleazy tale begins five years earlier with the husband-and-wife team of Michael and Roberta Findlay, among the most famous—and certainly most unique—exploitation duos. Although their bread and butter was sexploitation films like *The Touch of Her Flesh*, they also dabbled in the occasional horror item; their best known is probably the mad-Yeti favorite *Shriek of the Mutilated*. Roberta was also something of a maverick, graduating to hard-core pornography in the mid-seventies when a female director in the business was a rarity.

In 1971, hoping to capitalize on the Tate-LaBianca murders, which were still fresh in the public's mind, the Findlays hightailed it to Argentina, where they could exploit the cheap local labor and quickly film a story about a Manson-esque cult.

Within a month, they had a film called *Slaughter* in the can. It was amateurish and practically incoherent, and would have undoubtedly died a quick death were it not for Allan Shackleton, a notorious exploitation distributor and lothario. Shackleton owned a small company, Monarch Releasing Corporation, and bought the rights to *Slaughter* in 1972. For three years, the film sat on a shelf collecting dust. Then Shackleton had a flash of pure huckster genius, inspired by current stories about snuff films from the Far East in which prostitutes were killed on camera.

Shackleton's idea was one of those for which the cliché "so crazy it just might work" was created. He grabbed Simon Nuchtern, a local New York filmmaker who had been reediting Monarch's foreign acquisitions, and sent him off to shoot a three-minute coda to *Slaughter* in order to pass it off as a genuine snuff film.

This new scene was shot in a bedroom set rented from porn star and director Carter Stevens—whom Nuchtern calls an "unattractive round man with a cockeyed eye" (insert your own porn joke)—who at the time was trying to go legit. Early accounts of the filming erroneously cite Stevens himself as the director. The new footage begins with a long shot of the production crew. The fictional director is speaking to one of the actresses, who we are supposed to believe is the actress from the previous scene (meaning the previous scene from *Slaugh-*

ter). The two banter about how they were both incredibly turned on while filming a murder; exhibiting the self-control of teenagers on ecstasy, they begin making out on the bed right in front of the entire crew. For some reason, the woman becomes extremely upset once she realizes they're being filmed. So the director does what any reasonable person would do to placate her—he snips off her fingers with a pair of pliers and then saws off her entire hand, before finally stabbing and disemboweling her. He then holds up her intestines—which look like a twisted bedsheet smeared with Vaseline and food coloring—and shrieks as the camera runs out of film. The last thing we hear over black is the crew whispering to each other, wondering if they managed to capture it all.

When the scene was completed, it was tacked on to the finished *Slaughter* and the entire enchilada was retitled *Snuff*. And this is when all the fun began.

In an excellent 1999 article in *Skeptical Inquirer*, "The Snuff Film: The Making of an Urban Legend," Scott Aaron Stine gives the most comprehensive account of the brouhaha over the film. He details how Shackleton paid off Findlay, who had eventually become aware of *Slaughter 2.0*, and then created a phony organization called Citizens for Decency to drum up faux outrage. But in one of those surreal intersections of life and art, a real group also called Citizens for Decency got wind of the controversy and latched on to it. Shackleton himself stoked the flames by telling *Variety*, "If it was real, I'd be a fool to admit it. If it isn't real, I'd be a fool to admit it."

Finally, *Snuff* opened in January 1976, accompanied by the now-classic tagline *Made in South America . . . where LIFE is cheap!* Supposedly, it grossed more than *One Flew over the*

Cuckoo's Nest for three weeks during its New York run. One would think that once the film was out in the open, and its ineptitude apparent for all to see, continuing the hoax would be nearly impossible. But this didn't dissuade those who were as disturbed by the *idea* of a snuff film as they were about the real McCoy. On February 15, 1976, about fifty protesters* picketed the National Theater in Times Square, among them feminist author and activist Susan Brownmiller and US representative Elizabeth Holtzman.

On March 10, 1976, the *New York Times* ran a brief piece reassuring the public that Manhattan district attorney Robert M. Morgenthau had determined that *Snuff* was indeed fake. For some reason, I always find it funny imagining well-heeled Upper East Siders reading this story and freaking out at the possibility of a snuff film—an idea that never would have previously entered their minds. However, around this time, Shackleton also sent the actress who was supposedly killed on an all-expenses-paid Caribbean vacation to prolong the mystery of her identity. When the actress's neighbors noticed her mail was piling up, they contacted the police, who then paid Nuchtern a visit. Nuchtern not only reassured the cops that the actress was alive and well, but he furnished them with on-set photos of her eating lunch on the bed—her guts strewn all around her—smiling and blowing kisses at the photographer. Shackleton's generosity didn't last forever. When the actress eventually returned—unharmed other than a probable

* There's good reason to believe that a majority of the protesters were plants hired by Shackleton, who would then tip off his friends at the local news affiliates to ensure the maximum amount of coverage.

sunburn—Morgenthau announced that there was no cause for prosecution (it's not exactly clear *who* was prosecutable and for *what*). So as not to embarrass those who had made such a stink, he felt compelled to add that he was concerned the "film might incite or encourage people to commit violence against women."

The FBI came to the same conclusion as Morgenthau. In David Kerekes and David Slater's *Killing for Culture: An Illustrated History of Death Film from Mondo to Snuff*, the authors unearthed a fantastic gem in the form of a bureau report that proves, although it didn't have the notoriety of the New York premiere, *Snuff* actually first opened on January 16, 1976, in Indianapolis of all places. According to the report, a source at Monarch Releasing claimed Indianapolis was the perfect American city to test the "playability" of the film. The source also admits to knowing whether or not the on-screen murder was real but is unable to say due to "legal reasons." Although the source's name is redacted, it's clearly Shackleton. Accompanying FBI agents to the Indianapolis screening was a pathologist hired by the bureau to weigh in on the issue. The report concludes with the pathologist "doubting that an actual murder was committed." Now, we don't have the entirety of his remark, and certainly can't hear the inflection of his voice, but how any trained medical professional could, after watching *Snuff*, be anything other than 100 percent convinced that it's phony is mindboggling. If he really only "doubted" it, as in there was still some lingering suspicion or possible chance that it might in fact be real, Indiana's entire medical licensing board should be called into question.

What is so interesting about *l'affaire Snuff* is that all the players had an even greater interest than the filmmakers in maintaining the authenticity of the film. For the feminist critics and outraged citizens, an actual snuff film would validate their increasingly shrill warnings of artistic misogyny taken to its inevitable extreme. Law enforcement, from the DA down to the boots on the street, definitely wanted the film to be real. Which would you prefer? Smashing a nefarious criminal enterprise that preys on vulnerable young women, or chasing rumors to the satisfaction of a bunch of society busybodies? But Shackleton, he didn't really give a shit one way or another. Audiences could come expecting a real death, or they could come already in on the joke. All that mattered was that they came at all.

For being an absolutely delightful man, Simon Nuchtern might actually be the Grim Reaper. In fact, if he were more well-known, the following events might be as famous as other horror movie urban legends, from the *Poltergeist* curse to the death of Brandon Lee. In May 1977, Michael Findlay had just left a brief meeting with Nuchtern, whom he knew casually, and was heading to Manhattan's Pan Am Building, where a helicopter was waiting for him on the rooftop. As the craft was idling, its landing gear collapsed. This caused the copter's blade to snap off, slicing five people to death (including Findlay, who was allegedly decapitated), before it plunged nearly sixty stories to the street, where it killed a pedestrian. A few years later, Nuchtern was scheduled to go jogging with Shackleton, who had since moved to Los Angeles but was back in New York for business. At the last minute, Nuchtern had to cancel. Shackleton went ahead with his run and dropped dead of a heart attack in the middle of Central Park.

So *Guinea Pig* and *Snuff* were fakes. Impressive fakes, at least to some. To others (meaning people not currently in a coma), ridiculous frauds. But both were created in the spirit of preserving the illusion of reality.

But what about those films for which reality is no illusion? I'm not talking about films like *The Entity*, whose main selling point was that it was "based on a true story," which were the most terrifying words ever spoken—that is, until I got my first real girlfriend and they became, "I'm late."

No, I'm talking about films—as well as specific scenes within films—for which the magic of moviemaking does not apply. Because there is no magic. There is only truth. And because this is a memoir about horror, there is death. Death in all its faces.

I've already detailed the relative permissiveness of my mother, at least in regards to my horror-viewing habits. There was one movie, however, that was absolutely verboten—the infamous *Faces of Death*. In one of the few instances where I thought the woman might be off her rocker, I distinctly remember her taking the cassette from me and placing it on the top shelf of our living room bookcase. Why in the world she didn't think that her twelve-year-old son, a fairly accomplished athlete, could procure a stepstool and retrieve the offending video at a later date is completely beyond me. She was probably betting that my guilt at disobeying her would be stronger than my desire to see the film. Lousy bet.

Less perplexing was *why* she didn't want me to watch it. *Faces of Death* is a compilation of alleged real-life "faces of death," from authentic autopsy and slaughterhouse footage to impressively re-created executions, animal attacks, and cult rituals. Although it was readily available in most of the local video stores, in a rather nondescript box warning that it was banned in forty-six countries,* I seem to remember that my friends and I obtained our copy as a grainy bootlegged VHS—exactly the way it was meant to be seen. It was probably passed down to one of us by someone's older brother, an urban legend come to life.

We so badly wanted *Faces of Death* to be real. But even at that impressionable age, we had a sneaking suspicion that most of the carnage was about as real as professional wrestling, another one of our passions. The illusion was permanently shattered when, in college, I met a kid who claimed his father worked on numerous installments of the series (yes, there were sequels galore). Naturally, I branded him a bald-faced liar until we popped in the tape and there he was, instantly recognizable, standing in the background of one of the scenes.

The general consensus is that audiences enjoy horror films because they allow us to confront our fears in a safe and controlled environment. The producers of *Faces of Death* understood that there is also a market for the real thing.

In his commentary on MPI's special edition DVD of *Faces of Death*, director Conan Le Cilaire explains that the film's financiers were encouraged by how well an Italian film called *The Great Hunt*,† replete with graphic scenes of animal slaughter, had done in Japan. For anybody who knows anything about the seedy underbelly of Japanese culture, this shouldn't be the least

---

* Although this number was undoubtedly made up as a marketing ploy, it's certainly not inconceivable. After all, any country that *did* ban movies would have certainly banned *Faces of Death*.

† Le Cilaire is probably referring to the 1975 film *Savage Man Savage Beast*, as it was made only a few years prior and was also known as *The Great Hunting*.

bit surprising. This is a society that fetishizes schoolgirls, elevated tentacle porn to high art, and produces some of the most depraved torture films in existence. They're even perverted in their prudishness; because it's illegal to show unblurred genitals in Japanese films, other forms of less crotch-centric pornography have sprung up, including bukkake, in which a group of men all ejaculate on a woman. Nor is it just their art that is lascivious. As a gift, I once received a coffee table book about the Japanese sex industry (don't ask). Inside, there is a photograph of a menu from a Japanese whorehouse listing as many variations of rim jobs as there are types of sushi.

Anyway, because Le Cilaire was a veteran producer of nature films, the investors hoped he might have footage similar to that found in *The Great Hunt*. But Le Cilaire had a better idea: instead of animals being killed, what about people? Thus was born *Faces of Death*.

In its intended Japanese market, where it was released as *Junk*, *Faces of Death* did gangbusters. According to Le Cilaire, the film hit theaters the same year as *Star Wars* and even outgrossed (no pun intended) Lucas's film in some locations.* In the States, *Faces of Death* played the famous Forty-Second Street grindhouses before starting its run as a midnight movie around the country. But it was on home video, not in theaters, where the film would secure its legacy as one of the most taboo and highly sought-after titles. There's no reliable way to determine how much *Faces of Death* has made over the years. Some esti-

---

* On the DVD commentary, Le Cilaire specifically says "*Star Wars*." However, he probably means *The Empire Strikes Back*, as this was released in Japan around the same time as *Faces of Death*.

mates put the take close to $60 million. Whatever the real number, its $450,000 budget was money well spent. Three official sequels, incorporating much of the "talent" from the original, and the documentary *Faces of Death: Fact or Fiction?* followed. *Faces of Death* also inspired a host of similar films, with almost identical titles, that upped the ante in terms of explicit gore.

As audiences became more savvy about special effects and filmmaking techniques in general, the focus on *Faces of Death* shifted from which scenes were staged to who was actually responsible for the film. Clearly, Conan Le Cilaire was a pseudonym, as were most of the names in the credits. But *somebody* had directed it. Then an interview with one John Alan Schwartz in a 2004 issue of *The Dark Side* magazine shed some light on the matter. Schwartz claimed that he was the codirector, coproducer, and sole writer of the film. His pseudonym, "Alan Black," made perfect sense; "Schwartz" is German for "black" and "Alan" is his middle name. But that still didn't explain the identity of Schwartz's mysterious codirector.

Plus, on the DVD commentary, Le Cilaire takes care to make the distinction between himself and Schwartz, foiling those who claim the two men are one and the same. He even points out both of them at various points in the film; Schwartz plays the cult leader, Le Cilaire plays an assassin. Although Le Cilaire calls Schwartz "a very big part of the film" who "helped direct and helped produce a lot of scenes," he's crystal clear that he alone was the driving creative force.

In 2014, at a time when you can see practically any star's pubes on the Internet, I found it astonishing that the real director had *still* not been named. I'm not saying it's a secret on par with which A-list actresses were once call girls (trust me, *way* more than you think), but I couldn't believe that *any* secret could be kept in Hollywood, even one as minor as this. So I channeled my inner Kolchak and set out to unmask Monsieur Le Cilaire.

First, I reached out to a friend of mine who works for MPI Media, the company that released *Faces of Death* on DVD. Although he knew the actual identity of Le Cilaire, he was like a goddamn safe. The only thing he would confirm is that Le Cilaire and Black/Schwartz were two different people, which was already obvious. I then called in a favor to an old acquaintance who knew someone that worked on the film. Without much prodding, he gave me the answer I was looking for. By cross-referencing various sources and cryptic postings on Internet message boards, I was able, with some certainty, to confirm what I was told. Just to be sure, I downloaded a YouTube clip of this gentleman speaking at an industry conference. I then compared his voice to Le Cilaire's voice on the DVD commentary. It was a match.

But I'm not going to reveal his name.

What I will say is that unless you've worked directly for this man, you've probably never heard of him. So it's not as if I'm holding back a revelation like Conan Le Cilaire is, drumroll please . . . Francis Ford Coppola!

From what I've learned, the real Le Cilaire is an accomplished reality television producer. Apparently, he either feels embarrassed by his association with *Faces of Death* or fears it could negatively impact future business. As ludicrous as I find this—his colleagues would probably be impressed or, more likely, have no idea what the hell *Faces of Death* even is—I'm going to respect his privacy. If he doesn't want the world to know him as Conan Le Cilaire, who am I to out him?

Some may feel this decision destroys my credibility as a journalist. Possibly, but I assure you, when warranted there's nothing I enjoy more than exposing truths others would prefer kept quiet. I recently directed a feature documentary called *The Blue Room*. The film is about Hephzibah House, a boarding school for troubled girls in rural Indiana, founded in 1971 by a fundamentalist Baptist pastor named Ron Williams. Its stated mandate is to help young women find spiritual peace. In fact, dozens of girls have come forward to claim that Williams; his wife, Patti; and their staff ladies have variously beaten, starved, humiliated, and tortured them (both physically and mentally). In 2011, Patti Williams died from what I can only assume was some sort of stomach cancer. I was told in the last months of her life she walked around the house toting a huge colostomy bag filled with shit. There are many, myself included, who saw this as an appropriate metaphor for her life. So maybe God really does have a sense of humor.

Since I'm already off on a tangent, I have one more story that will bring us back full circle to *Faces of Death*.

One of my closest college friends was an American Indian named John Orie. Since I was one of the first Jews he ever met, and he was the only American Indian I knew, we spent a lot of time discussing the particulars of our specific cultures. Understandably, John was very proud of his Oneida heritage. Although this pride was genuine, the reality was that he was a suburban kid from Green Bay, Wisconsin, meaning that his upbringing wasn't worlds away from my own. He was as far removed from battling English colonists as I was from evading Cossacks in Eastern Europe. This is why I found it so preposterous when he claimed that, were he in the right state of mind and given the right mind-altering substances, he would voluntarily undergo the Sun Vow from *A Man Called Horse*.

For those not familiar with the movie, Richard Harris plays the titular character, a white man who is initially kidnapped by and then tries to win the acceptance of the Sioux. To do so, he undertakes the Sun Vow, a ritual in which sharp knives are inserted under his pectoral muscle. He's then hoisted high in the air by the skin of his chest.

John became annoyed when I questioned his ability to endure the ritual. Never mind that the worst he'd had to endure thus far in life was two-a-day football practices during the heat of a Wisconsin August. Still, I figured I might as well drop it as he clearly didn't appreciate my teasing. I was, however, vindicated a few months later when we watched the *Faces of Death* knockoff *Traces of Death*, which, like *Faces*, purports to show real scenes of death and violence. *Traces* is probably best known for its inclusion of the suicide of R. Budd Dwyer, the Pennsylvania state treasurer who blew his brains out during a live news conference.

It was the genuine autopsy footage that really got to John. Some poor sap on the slab was having his face peeled off, starting from his forehead and down past his chin. You could literally see the sinew pulling away from the bone. "I'll be right back," John said as he walked out of the room. I figured he was either going to take a leak or, since it was an unusually warm autumn day, maybe smoke a bowl on our third-floor balcony. Instead, when I went to check on him a few minutes later, I found him in the bathroom hunched over the toilet. I left him to finish vomiting in peace and never mentioned it again. But the implication was clear: if he couldn't make it through *Traces*, he sure as hell wasn't going to survive the Sun Vow.

Years later, I was developing a documentary series about an extreme tattoo artist in Michigan who also specialized in body modification. One of the services he offered was "suspension," in which his victims (uh, customers) were lifted off the ground by large metal fishhooks inserted through their skin. Apparently, the practice is quite common in this subculture. Common, but evidently off-putting, as I couldn't find a single network remotely interested in a show about human bait.

The precursors to *Faces of Death* were the mondo films of the 1960s and early '70s. The best definition for "mondo" (Italian for "world") that I've ever found comes, unsurprisingly, from *Killing for Culture: An Illustrated History of Death Film from Mondo to Snuff*, the most comprehensive study of the subgenre:

> A feature-length mélange of exotic sights and startling incidents, the mondo film professed to show the viewer genuine and spontaneously filmed events from around the globe. These often unrelated episodes would find a continuity in the condescending, haughty, repulsed, or excited commentaries of a narrator. Quite literally a sensationalist travelogue, the raison d'être of the mondo film was to shock the audience with its exposé of bizarre cultural behaviour, fluctuating from the exotic to the erotic to the undeniably repellent.

Mondo has its roots, of course, in documentary filmmaking, which was then the province of cinema clubs, universities, and the mental hygiene films distributed in schools and churches. The first true mondo film was 1962's *Mondo Cane*, pronounced "cah-nay" and loosely translated as "A Dog's World." In it, we're treated to such sights and sounds as the force-feeding of geese to make foie gras; an upscale New York restaurant that serves fried ants, stuffed beetles, butterfly eggs, and other insect dishes; flagellants in the Italian city of Calabria who slice their legs to ribbons in a show of piety; and a Tokyo spa stocked with cutting-edge exercise devices that would seem at home in a medieval dungeon. What's odd is that the strangest and most disconcerting footage comes from then-contemporary America, such as the lunatics at the Pasadena Dog Cemetery who have gathered to pay their final respects to Rover.

Mondo Cane was the brainchild of Gualtiero Jacopetti and Franco Prosperi. Jacopetti was an extroverted and dashing journalist who viewed mondo as a natural extension of his trade. He was bothered by the Italian neorealist films of his youth, which he felt created an artificial realism. With *Mondo Cane*, he wanted to throw back the curtain and expose the darker side of life. His partner in crime, Prosperi, loved the idea. A trained naturalist, Prosperi was Jacopetti's mirror opposite in terms of temperament; the two made for an imposing team. Although they only made a handful of films together, each of these was a pillar of mondo cinema.

Internationally, *Mondo Cane* was a huge hit. Apparently, cultures all across the world have an innate desire to experience those even stranger or more barbaric than their own.

Although he had no desire to retread the same material, Jacopetti felt an obligation to his producers and began work immediately on *Mondo Cane 2*. Even this early in the subgenre's evolution, it faced the same issue of faux reality that would later plague *Faces of Death*. In one of the film's most disturbing scenes, a Buddhist monk is doused with gasoline and set aflame. Not only does it look real (although the color of his robe changes at the last second), but since this exact same scenario was captured a year before in Malcolm Browne's famous photo, there's no real reason to doubt it. After all, isn't this just what Buddhist monks did in protest? Turn themselves into human candles? But according to *Mondo Cane 2* cinematographer Benito Frattari, the monk was actually a mannequin made by renowned special effects designer and Oscar winner Carlo Rambaldi.

Years later, Rambaldi, who's probably best known for designing the iconic creature in *E.T.*, would find himself embroiled in a situation that would illustrate the unequalled realism of his creations. In 1971, Lucio Fulci hired Rambaldi to work on his early giallo *A Lizard in a Woman's Skin*. In the film, Florinda Bolkan plays Carol, a woman plagued by disturbing dreams. Accused of murder and placed in a sanatorium, Carol wanders into a room containing a grisly medical experiment. Four dogs are lashed upright to a metal stand. They've been vivisected, their innards on display and their still-beating hearts fed with blood flowing through elaborate tubing. As the blood pumps and the dogs' organs pulse, their jaws twitching in silent agony, it's easy to understand how almost everybody thought the notoriously unpredictable Fulci had finally gone too far. After all, this was a good decade before films like *An American Werewolf in London* and *The Thing* started doing mind-blowing effects with inflatable bladders. Fulci was indicted for cruelty to animals and faced a two-year prison sentence. Until, in a scene reminiscent of a Hollywood courtroom thriller, Rambaldi showed up at the eleventh hour with one of the prop canines.

Jacopetti and Prosperi watched with disdain as a host of mondo imitators flooded the marketplace. While plotting their next move, they became interested in the geopolitical changes occurring in Africa. The resultant film, *Africa Addio* (*Good-bye, Africa*), sought to document the continent's upheaval as it threw off the yoke of colonialism. As Jacopetti explains in David Gregory's illuminating documentary about the pair, *The Godfathers of Mondo*, "It was not a justification for colonialism, but it was a condemnation for leaving a continent in miserable condition." During the film, in which actual atrocities are filmed, word spread that Congolese were killed by mercenaries either at the behest of Jacopetti or as the result of his camera crew's presence. Although both filmmakers vehemently denied the claim—falling back on the convenient, but probably true, war correspondent defense—the progressive Italian press had a field day.

Eventually, Jacopetti was acquitted of murder, but the entire experience left a sour taste. After being accused of racism, and worse, the pair decided to make a scathing critique of bigotry. If the road to hell is paved with good intentions, then *Addio Zio Tom* (*Good-bye, Uncle Tom*) must have secured the exclusive contract for the whole damn thing. The idea itself had merit: a faux documentary set in the antebellum South that unflinchingly records the horrors of slavery. But somewhere between the conception and execution, things took a hard turn for the worse.

The scenes are legitimately excruciating to sit through. A slave who refuses to eat has his teeth bashed in with a hammer before a steel funnel is shoved into his bloody maw. Epileptic slaves are strung up naked by their feet to "cure" them of their affliction. And, of course, slaves are humiliated, beaten, raped, and murdered en masse. Even if these scenes are staged, the terror in the eyes of the babies and child "actors" is all too real, as is a pathetic scene in which multiple amputees are forced to grovel for food. American distributors forced Jacopetti and Prosperi to cut a particularly surreal fifteen-minute chunk at the end of the film. A militant black man reads *The Confessions of Nat Turner* and imagines the book being played out in the present day; an elderly white couple is axed in their bed, followed by an infant being smashed against the wall, before an all-American family is butchered in cold blood.

The entire film is condescending, exploitative, and in the worst possible taste. The fact that much of it was shot in Haiti, where Papa Doc Duvalier welcomed the crew with open arms, makes me wonder just how voluntary the participation of the locals was at all.

Benito Frattari says, "It was a beautiful film in its intention . . . but it came out *wrong*." Truer words have rarely been spoken.

Jacopetti and Prosperi's ultimate legacy is not only all the subsequent mondo films that flourished in the wake of *Mondo Cane*—*Mondo Bizarro*, *Mondo Freudo*, *Mondo Sex*, *Mondo Magic*, *Mondo Erotico*, *Mondo Candido*, *Mondo Infame*, *Mondo Balordo*—but the *idea* of reality as a genre unto itself. In today's world of *Fear Factor*, that freakin' duck family, thousands of reality shows on hundreds of channels, and millions of user-generated YouTube curiosities, it's nearly impossible to understand just how revolutionary the concept of "reality" once was. Films like *Mondo Cane* held up a mirror to the dark side of the human condition, and although the reflection was usually messy and sometimes constructed, it was never anything less than compelling.

Inspired by the mondo films of his homeland, Ruggero Deodato dropped the neutron bomb on unsuspecting audiences with *Cannibal Holocaust*, generally considered the apex (or nadir, depending on your point of view) of the Italian cannibal subgenre. Using a then-unique narrative device, the film follows the exploits of a New York anthropologist who travels to the depths of the Amazon in order to locate a documentary crew that has gone missing. Half the film is made up of the crew's "found footage," which contains some of the most disturbing images ever captured on celluloid. A native adulteress is raped with a stone dildo and then bludgeoned to death. A pregnant woman's baby is yanked out prematurely and then buried in the mud. The film's most iconic image—which today adorns T-shirts, books, and the DVD I have in my hand—is of a young woman suspended on a stake that has been forced through her vagina and out her mouth.

Right after the Italian premiere of *Cannibal Holocaust* in early February 1980, the film was pulled from theaters by the authorities. Deodato was initially charged with murder. The killing of the documentary film crew as well as the shish kebobbed native looked too real. Allegedly, Deodato compounded the problem by requiring the actors to lie low for a year, allowing him to exploit their "real" disappearance, much like Allan Shackleton had done with his *Snuff* actress. However, in recent interviews, two of the principals deny they ever signed such an agreement, much less vanished from public view. Deodato also had to prove that the impalement was just a special—albeit gruesome—effect. Like Rambaldi in the courtroom less than a decade before, he demonstrated how the nude actress sat upon a bicycle seat mounted on the end of a metal pole secured in the ground. She then tilted her head backward and held a light piece of balsa wood between her teeth, giving the impression that the stake tore through her lengthwise. For such a simple effect, the result is extraordinarily realistic. Just in case there was any further doubt, Deodato also furnished the court with photos of the actress interacting with the crew—after the scene had been filmed.

But *Cannibal Holocaust* was originally banned not because of fake murder but because of actual animal slaughter. The Italian cannibal film has a long history of on-screen critter carnage, initiated by Umberto Lenzi with 1972's *The Man from Deep River*, which includes scenes of cockfighting, a mongoose battling with a cobra, and an alligator being sliced open. Lenzi would recycle the exact same footage eight years later in *Eaten Alive!* His most famous film, the gutmuncher *Cannibal Ferox*, is best known for the scene in which Zora Kerova is strung up by her breasts with metal hooks, but it also features plenty of animal abuse: some type of constrictor smothers a small mammal, a turtle is decapitated and then dismembered, and in a reprise of his other films, another gator is disemboweled.

For some incongruous reason, horror fans tend to be animal lovers. Many who watched *Cannibal Holocaust* really *did* care about a very graphic turtle beheading, as well as a monkey scalping and the shooting of a small pig tied to a pole. Using an old law against animal cruelty originally created to combat bullfighting, authorities charged Deodato with obscenity and he received a four-month suspended sentence.

Deodato claims *Cannibal Holocaust* has made more than $200 million since its original release, even accounting for its prematurely ended Italian run. Although I think this is a wildly inflated estimate, there are no reliable figures for thirty-five-year-old exploitation films, so you can decide if you want to take him at his word. According to an article in *Empire* magazine, while shooting his upcoming cannibal film, *The Green Inferno*—greatly inspired by the Italian cannibal genre—director Eli Roth screened *Cannibal Holocaust* for a group of native Amazonians who had never before seen a movie (not *the* movie, but *any* movie). Apparently, they thought it was the funniest thing they had ever seen, proving that gore, not love, is the real universal language.

The ultimate irony is that sometimes realism is achieved solely by accident, in spite of the filmmaker's best intentions, not because of them.

In late November 2010, firefighters were called to the George Washington Hotel in the small Western Pennsylvania city of Washington. While checking the building, they came across a surprise in room 405. Pittsburgh police chief J. R. Blyth described it as "the most grisly murder scene in [my] thirty-five years in law enforcement."

Empty liquor bottles were strewn across the floor. Vulgar words were scrawled on the wall in blood. There was even a piece of scalp with hair still sticking out of it. "I had no idea what was going on," said Chief Blyth. "There was blood on the floor, the mattress, the walls, the pillow." The room was declared a crime scene and detectives were dispatched to investigate the matter. Eight hours later (clearly this wasn't the crack CSI team of Petersen, Caruso, or Sinise) it was determined that the crime scene was nothing more than the abandoned set from the forgettable horror movie *New Terminal Hotel*, starring the late Corey Haim and scream queen Tiffany Shepis. The hotel owner had left the set intact in case the crew wanted to return for reshoots.

Either he was the most accommodating owner in history, or the George Washington Hotel had more than its share of vacancies. And if it was the latter, he could always have rigged the rooms with hidden cameras, murdered his guests, and sold the ensuing snuff films to make a little extra cash—just like in the movie *Vacancy*.

Because as the makers of *Snuff*, *Guinea Pig*, and *Faces of Death* learned long ago, the specter of real death—no matter how poorly executed—always pays the bills.

CHAPTER EIGHT

Friends in Low Places

Jon Kitley knows more about horror films than anyone I know.

He lives in Aurora, Illinois (made famous by *Wayne's World*), with his lovely wife, Dawn, who designs and bakes the most amazing horror-themed cakes you'll ever see, and twenty-one-year-old son, Nick, who can complete a Rubik's Cube in less than three minutes. As somebody who was obsessed with this puzzle back in the day—but who could never complete more than a single side of the cube—this feat is right up there with splitting the atom. Jon possesses one of the most enviable collections of horror memorabilia I've seen. Some of my favorite items of his include a promotional box cutter from *Blood Cult* (often described, incorrectly, as the first made-for-home-video release), a scale model of the Tingler (I'm trying to convince him to also install Percepto! in his screening room seats), and a gorgeous German poster for *I, Madman*, the first film I name whenever somebody asks me for a little-seen horror recommendation. Although Jon maintains his own fantastic website, Kitley's Krypt, and writes a regular column for *HorrorHound* magazine, it's an absolute crime he's not teaching at a university. Not only is his breadth of knowledge unrivaled, but his enthusiasm for the genre is infectious. His website's tagline is *Discover the Horror*, and there's nothing he enjoys more than suggesting obscure gems to those in need of something a little different. At the University of Wisconsin–Madison, I once took a class on Hollywood genres (with an emphasis on horror) taught by an esteemed professor with a long list of letters after his name and an even longer list of publications to his credit. Madison has an excellent film program, especially for a Midwestern university. This guy was the resident "horror expert." And he couldn't carry Kitley's jock.

Matt Carr is a ridiculously talented local Chicago artist who goes by the name of Putrid. In the days of hand-painted exploitation one-sheets he would have been a legend. Putrid shaves his head, is covered in tattoos (mainly from horror movies), wears his ever-present black leather jacket no matter the weather, and drinks like a fish. He collects vintage horror VHS tapes and his favorite band is NunSlaughter. NunSlaughter! And yet he is one of the absolute nicest guys you will ever meet. By contrast, I know plenty of diehard Deadheads, always babbling on about boxes of rain and how love will see you through, who are some of the biggest jerks in the world.

To horror fans, Aaron Christensen is better known as Dr. AC, the editor of two indispensable critical guides, *Horror 101: The A-List of Horror Films and Monster Movies* and *Hidden Horror: A Celebration of 101 Underrated and Overlooked Fright Flicks*. But aside from his encyclopedic knowledge of the genre, Aaron is a Shakespearian actor who, along with his beautiful and talented actress wife, Michelle Courvais, also performs in independent films. As a rule, I hate the theater. And it's not for a lack of exposure. I've already detailed my family's annual Christmas pilgrimage into New York City. So by the time I moved to Chicago at age twenty-three, I had seen pretty much every major Broadway musical. As much as I looked forward to the preshow meal with my grandparents, aunts, uncles, and cousins, I equally dreaded the show itself. Once in college I got so fucked up the night before we saw *Carousel* that I practically slept through the whole thing, aside from intermission, when I went to the bathroom to vomit. All this is relevant because aside from *Les Misérables* (the one musical I adore) and, strangely enough, an amateur production of Allan Sherman's *Hello Muddah, Hello Fadduh*, the only other play I've enjoyed was *The Quiet Man Tales*, an adaptation of Irish novelist Maurice Walsh's short stories, in which Aaron starred. So this should tell you something about his talent.

What do these folks have in common and why am I mentioning them at all? They're all part of Chicago's robust and vibrant horror community.

It's always risky to analyze a specific subculture, whether it's a fringe political group, motorcycle enthusiasts, swingers, triathletes, bookworms, or lactation fetishists. This is especially true if you're part of said group. You run the risk of making sweeping generalizations and inevitably manage to alienate the very people with whom you want to ingratiate yourself. Writing about an unrelated topic in the September 2013 issue, *Rue Morgue* editor-in-chief Dave Alexander admits, "just the term 'genre community' is problematic due to the vastly different interests and opinions within it." He's exactly right.

That said, I've toiled in the genre long enough that I think

I can speak, with at least some authority, about the soul of the horror community.

In some ways, I'm an outsider in a community of outsiders. I have zero tattoos. I let my three ear piercings* close up over twenty years ago. Although I proudly wear my *New York Ripper* T-shirt to horror conventions, in civilian life I own a television production company and attend meetings in a suit. I'm married, have two young children, and am a pretty conservative parent. I love horror films, but they're not my *entire* life. On the other hand, I wrote a book about slasher films at a time when most horror writers considered this endeavor beneath them. Furthermore, *Wicked Lake* won a Mr. Skin Award for Best Lesbian Orgy and the remake of *I Spit on Your Grave* not only performed well enough to warrant a sequel but earned inclusion in Roger Ebert's *A Horrible Experience of Unbearable Length*, alongside his other least-favorite movies.

I like to think my horror cred is unimpeachable, but all subcultures are exclusionary to some degree, and although my horror brethren might be welcoming to the dude with a nail driven through his nasal bridge, I've also caught them looking my way with thinly veiled distrust.

It's tough to describe a horror convention—at least the major ones—to someone who's never attended. The best analogy I can think of is trying to explain what a small-town carnival is like to someone who's only been to Disneyland. Oh, I can paint a picture for you. The rusty amusements set up in a sin-

* At my most stylish, I wore a *Playboy* bunny, a lightning bolt, and my football number, all at once in one ear.

gle night by freelance meth heads. Malnourished farm animals pumped full of enough downers to prevent them from biting off the fingers of little children yanking on their tails. Concession stands selling combinations of foodstuff that nature never intended. But unless you're there, walking through the hay and shit, breathing in that sublime mixture of fried fat, cigarette smoke, and teenage lust, you can never really appreciate the essence of the place.

But since these conventions are ground zero for the horror faithful, I have to give it a go.

Gone are the days when the cons were held in church basements and rec centers. The last *Fangoria*'s Weekend of Horrors I attended was in the Los Angeles Convention Center. Usually, there's a "guest of honor." The biggest of the big. The kind of personalities who can, and do, command forty bones for an autographed photo. People like John Carpenter, Wes Craven, Dario Argento, and Clive Barker. At one time you could have thrown George Romero or Bruce Campbell into the mix, but they attend conventions so regularly now that the thrill is, if not gone, at least muted. Sometimes there's a "reunion" of the cast from a beloved film. You might find *Re-Animator* alumni Stuart Gordon, Barbara Crampton, Jeffrey Combs, and maybe even writer Dennis Paoli making a group appearance. Then you have about a dozen or so minor celebrities. People like *Hellraiser*'s Ashley Laurence; the Avellan twins from *Planet Terror*; Lance Henriksen; Danny Trejo; Reggie Bannister; Lloyd Kaufman and whichever Tromettes he can round up; one of the *Evil Dead* ladies; P. J. Soles; Kane Hodder, or at least someone who played Jason Voorhees; either Michael Berryman or Robert Z'Dar (of *The Hills Have Eyes* and *Maniac Cop* fame, respectively); and definitely Danielle Harris. If the crowd is strong there will be a line for all these folks. And you hope so. Because there's nothing more depressing than watching Z-list horror actors sitting by themselves, looking down at their iPhones and pretending to be busy, while all their signed headshots and lobby cards lie untouched in front of them.

Every piece of memorabilia seems to beckon as you stroll down the rows and rows of booths. There's a ton of vendors selling posters, press kits, movie stills, and rare DVDs. The crazy thing is, you'll gladly pay thirty bucks for the two-disc set of *Street Trash* when it can be gotten on Amazon for $17.99, simply because *it's there*. The instant gratification is well worth the premium, as is the knowledge that the profit is going to a fellow fan, not an online retail behemoth. Horror collectors meet at the intersection of commerce and nostalgia; in some strange way, the cachet of owning Goblin's *Suspiria* soundtrack on vinyl is just as important as the prog-rock melodies pressed into the spiral grooves. There are the whack-job artists selling replicas of classic monsters built from matchsticks. The rare-book peddlers with first editions of Lovecraft, King, Barker, and Straub. I don't care how many times you've read *The Shining*, it's just scarier housed in the original dust jacket. The vendor with silk-screened T-shirts of *Cannibal Holocaust*, *Nekromantik*, *A Cat in the Brain*, and *Shock Waves*, taking the calculated risk that nobody knows who the hell owns the licensing rights to these images. There are the independent filmmakers hawking their low-budget bloodbaths for ten bucks, telling everyone within earshot that they do it for the art while secretly praying that some low-level distribution executive will give their passion project a quick glance. Jewelry makers and mask designers.

Comic book collectors and black-metal aficionados. A Zuni fetish doll and a scale model of the Lament Configuration.

As Obi-Wan once warned Luke, "You will never find a more wretched hive of scum and villainy." He wasn't talking about the horror convention floor, but he might as well have been.

Of course, I mean this not only affectionately but ironically. After all, and this will be evident to anyone who regularly attends cons (but counterintuitive to everyone else), horror fans are some of the nicest and most peaceful people around.

A couple of years ago I was at a film festival. A movie whose title I don't recall was playing and there was a scene in which the male lead (and not an unlikeable one, I might add) slaps a woman across her face. Hard. In context, it may have been to calm her down from a bout of hysterics (and just so everybody is clear, only in the movies does this *ever* work), but nonetheless, all of us men who were not raised by sociopaths and have even a modicum of decency know that there's *never* an acceptable time to hit a woman.

The audience reaction to the slap heard round the theater was not gasps of self-righteous disbelief; it was near-universal laughter. I was sitting next to a female friend, a strong independent woman. I'd call her a modern feminist if I didn't think that was in some way condescending. Upon hearing the laughter, she muttered under her breath, "Nice, really nice," calling out the misogynists who seemed to find domestic abuse funny. What she failed to understand was the reason for this reaction. It was precisely because the audience recognized just how blatantly inappropriate this behavior was. Most—and I like to think, *all*—of the men watching the film would have rather chewed off their own arm than strike a woman. Play this exact same scene in Saudi Arabia (that is, if they had movie theaters), or some other country where spousal abuse is tolerated and tacitly encouraged, and I guarantee you'd get a very different reaction.

I never thought this needed to be said, but this seems as good a place as any to reiterate that just because a person loves fictitious violence, that person does not necessarily enjoy—or even have the capacity to tolerate—the real thing. I realize this is only anecdotal, but I've experienced literally every type of on-screen cruelty, yet seeing someone in actual pain, however minor, still has a profound effect on me. When our son was born, we opted to have him circumcised in the hospital by an actual doctor, rather than at home in the traditional Jewish ritual of a bris. Because my wife was still recovering from her C-section and had no desire to watch anyway, I held my infant son's tiny hand during the procedure. Or at least I tried to. After the doctor secured him and sterilized the area, the next thing I remember is being wheeled back into my wife's recovery room to shouts of, "Get him on the couch." I had passed out cold. Now, maybe this episode proves nothing except that I'm an extraordinary softy when it comes to my own kids. But I like to think that it's indicative of the horror community at large—all the bloodshed we've seen has not desensitized us, as the popular theory goes, but instead has made us more attuned to the suffering of others.

Horror fans are generally such pacifists that at times it's actually made me uncomfortable. For example, at some revival screening in the dark days right after 9/11, when even most conscientious objectors recognized the need to uproot the Taliban, the event's hosts passed out buttons that read: "Bombs are NOT the Answer" and "An Eye for an Eye Leaves Everyone Blind." As neither a Democrat nor a Republican—but certainly not a part of any of those lunatic-fringe parties either—nor a liberal or a conservative, most people assume I hold staunchly middle-of-the-road views. On the contrary, at the risk of sounding like a fanatic, most of my beliefs are either far left or far right. For example, I'm staunchly pro-choice. Well, more than staunchly. I'd estimate that if 75–80 percent of the people I come into contact with on a daily basis had been aborted we'd all be a lot better off. Plus, I can't think of anything more ghoulish—literally, *anything*—than making a woman who was sexually assaulted carry her rapist's baby to term. On the other end of the spectrum, I'm vehemently pro–death penalty. Right now, even in the most execution-friendly states, capital punishment is only reserved for the most heinous of murderers. I'd expand the list to include child molesters, serial domestic abusers, rapists, and people who pay with a check at the grocery store. This never occurred to me before, but I guess what it comes down to is that I'm really just pro-death. Especially because I'm also a firm believer in euthanasia. If someone, for whatever reason, wants to take that leap into the great beyond, I say good riddance.

Pacifism, however, doesn't preclude righteous indignation. And this is something the horror community has in spades.

In the July 2011 issue of *Rue Morgue*, John W. Bowen, my favorite of all the magazine's excellent writers, penned a piece that created quite a stir, at least in our little universe.

In his monthly "It Came from Bowen's Basement" column, he calls out some horror luminaries—Richard Matheson, William Friedkin, Brian De Palma, Karen Black—for their dismissal of the very genre that made them famous. I could spend this entire chapter deconstructing their reasoning and proving just how ill informed they are. Suffice it to say the quotes from each of them that Bowen supplies make them sound like absolute idiots. (Okay, I can't resist Friedkin's. Regarding *The Exorcist*: "It won ten Academy Award nominations. How can that be horror?") But as Bowen in his own inimitable way writes, "This actually bothers me less, as Friedkin is infamous for being a tactless, abusive, egomaniacal douche, and this is far from the most offensive thing he's ever said."*

Feeling their beloved genre was being disrespected, horror fans circled the wagons. They flooded message boards and wrote letters to the editor (of many different horror periodicals) in support of Bowen's gripe. They heralded the few noble A-listers who embrace their horror past and chastised others who prefer to keep it in the closet. Fans also took issue with the mainstream's ignorance of anything but the most high-profile horror films. For example, when Conan O'Brien once had Jennifer Connelly on as a guest, he showed a clip of *Phenomena* as a gag, to illustrate an early career misstep. Now, in all fairness, out of context—sometimes even in context—I can understand the unintentional humor of *Phenomena*. But for those who would carve Argento's dour countenance into the stone of horror's Mount Rushmore, it felt like a slap in the face. A cheap shot from someone who didn't have the foggiest idea that *Phenomena*, while flawed, was also touched by genius.

---

* Most offensive to me is Friedkin's explanation for the rise of Nazism, which he attributes to demonic possession—and he means this literally, not metaphorically—as it absolves the Nazis and the willing German populace of any responsibility for the Holocaust.

Logically, this anger seems misplaced. I mean, why should we—and by "we," I mean the proverbial horror fans—give a shit what these people think? Matheson and Black are both dead, and Friedkin and De Palma are shells of their former selves (despite their comments about the genre, I'm still holding out hope that either one might have a little magic left). But we *did* care, at least as evidenced by the response to Bowen's column. He unknowingly revealed an insecurity that I fear is all too prevalent in our community, and at the same time exposed a curious irony: we have an almost insatiable need for acceptance and yet profess not to care a lick about the very acceptance we seek.

As a general rule, horror fans embrace their status as cultural outsiders. In fact, many define their identity solely by opposition to the mainstream. We tell ourselves we don't need, or even want, casual endorsements—not from the public or the critics, and especially not from Hollywood suits. The contradiction though is that horror fans seem to be one of the most defensive and thin-skinned groups around. We're so accustomed to being told that horror as a genre is terrible, infantile, less than serious, puerile, a waste of time, and an affront to culture and society that our knee-jerk reaction is to defend it at all costs.

Sometimes this urge is appropriate.

Just recently, in a *Wall Street Journal* review of *Chain Saw Confidential*, Gunnar Hansen's *Texas Chain Saw Massacre* memoir, Christopher Bray writes about the film itself, "Whatever this movie is about, the fact remains that it is a shoddy and shamingly bad piece of work." Say what you want about *Chain Saw*. Call it raw, visceral, disgusting, upsetting, disturbing, hallucinatory. But "shoddy" and "shamingly bad"? Fuck you. *Chain Saw* is in the Museum of Modern Art's permanent collection, not exactly a repository for incompetence.

This is the same reviewer who attempts to compare hard-core horror and hard-core porn: "One seeks to titillate the adolescent mind, the other to terrify and torment it, but the two genres are premised on young people's fascinated shame about their own bodies." As someone who knows *a lot* more about both horror movies and pornography than Mr. Bray, I can safely say that this is nothing more than academic gobbledygook. Besides some of Cronenberg's work, I can't think of more than a handful of horror films that come close to fitting this criterion. And as for pornography, a good deal of my adolescence was spent trying to procure adult material, whether in the form of magazines, videos, or even dirty talk on 1-900 lines. I promise you, I was the furthest thing from ashamed about either my own body or my interest in other people's. Curious, you bet your ass, but certainly not ashamed. Critics like Bray make these sweeping generalizations because it allows them to intellectualize something that can't be intellectualized: the fact that people like to watch other people fuck.

Far more insidious than fools like Bray are those who try to legitimize horror by pretending it's something else. As if it's not good enough to stand on its own, warts and all. A pet peeve of mine (and I have many) is the recent trend of referring to horror films as "genre films." Part of it is the redundancy—*all* films are genre films, from *The Godfather* to *Invasion of the Blood Farmers*. Practically, this is about as helpful as calling a type of cuisine "ethnic," as if there is no difference between a veal scallopini and a porridge made by some tribe in sub-Saharan

Africa, which I bet you anything will soon become the hottest new item at Whole Foods.

It's the connotation that I find so galling, the fact that "genre" is substituted because the user assumes that the term it's replacing—in this case, "horror"—is in itself inherently pejorative. It's the same reason I detest the adjective "urban" used as an alternative for "black." And quite frankly, I don't see how more African-Americans aren't outraged, since in an effort to be PC people are making a gross (and totally false) generalization that all blacks live in cities. The NBC sitcom *The Office* skewers this brilliantly. In the season 4 episode "Local Ad," clueless boss Michael Scott refers to Stanley, the lone African-American in the office, as "the key to our urban vibe." Stanley looks up and replies, "I grew up in a small town. What about me seems urban to you?"

Although I can't pinpoint the first use of "genre" as a straightforward synonym for "horror," I'm guessing it was probably by some distribution executive looking to gussy up his latest direct-to-video release. The sad thing is that by now, it's practically become part of the vernacular, used even by devoted horror fans either oblivious to or unconcerned with the ramifications.

And, sadly, I've found myself succumbing to this inferiority complex far too often. In *Blood Money*, Richard Nowell refers to *Going to Pieces* as a "fan-oriented publication." Naturally, I took offense to his characterization of my book. After all, his insinuation was that by definition *Going to Pieces* was for the slasher fan, certainly not a work worthy of scholarly consideration. Again, it's the old canard that for horror to be taken seriously we must pretend it's something other than what it is.

And by extension, for *writings* on the subject to be taken seriously, they must be geared to an audience far different from the rabble that actually *likes* the subject itself.

But the more I thought about it, regardless of Nowell's intent with his statement, he was absolutely correct. Of course *Going to Pieces* was written for the fans. For the kind of person who would never have been stumped by Ghostface. Who would brave a torrential downpour and a swarm of bloodthirsty mosquitoes to attend a two a.m. screening of *Sleepaway Camp* at one of Chicago's last remaining drive-ins. By contrast, *Blood Money* was written for the scholars and academics. I know I'll never be close to the writer that Nowell is. In a lot of ways, that bothers me. In others, I actually think it's a good thing. After all, I can barely get through a single page of his book without zoning out—and it's a topic about which I'm passionate above all else. On a handful of other occasions, Nowell references *Going to Pieces* to illustrate a point. And even though it's my own book, I have no idea what the fuck the guy is talking about. I'm reminded of a 1994 *Playboy* interview with Howard Stern. The interviewer asked him about a series of *Doonesbury* comics in which he'd recently appeared as a character, to which Stern replied, "I have never understood the comic pages of the newspaper . . . I don't think any of them are funny, *Doonesbury* in particular. I don't even know what the fuck Garry Trudeau is talking about. The guy writes a series of comics on me, and I don't know what the fuck the joke is. I don't get it."*

* Stern goes on to speculate that the smell of Trudeau's wife Jane Pauley's vagina could be the cause of the cartoonist's problems. Although he does so in far cruder terms.

What is most ironic, and I would argue unfortunate, is that oftentimes the most fervent attacks on the genre come from within. Horror fans can be as demanding and tough to please—and I would even add nitpicky—as the worst Philadelphia Eagles supporters (for the non–sports folks, Philly fans are so awful that they famously booed Santa Claus). It's axiomatic that the only thing America loves more than building up its heroes is tearing them down once they become too big. And the horror community, to be sure, is certainly not immune to this phenomenon.

Nowhere is this more apparent than in the career of Eli Roth, who first came to the attention of horror fans thanks to his entertaining commentary on the late-nineties Troma release of Joel Reed's *Bloodsucking Freaks*. Roth had been toiling in the entertainment industry for years, but once he exploded onto the scene it made for better copy to pretend he came out of nowhere. His 2003 film, *Cabin Fever*, about a group of campers ravaged by a flesh-eating virus, was made for less than $2 million and grossed just north of $21 million domestically. But it was his 2006 film, *Hostel*, which opened at number one at the box office and went on to earn more than $47 million, that really thrust him into the public consciousness. The story of a group of friends backpacking through Slovakia who stumble upon a criminal enterprise in which wealthy patrons can indulge their most sadistic fantasies, *Hostel* (along with *Saw*, released a year before) was deemed responsible for ushering in the subgenre colloquially known as "torture porn." Film critic David Edelstein is usually credited with coining the phrase in a February 2006 article in *New York* magazine. However, I've found it used in an October 2005 article from the *Guard-*

ian and then a few months later in the *Commercial Appeal*, a Memphis newspaper, in reference to the Aussie slasher *Wolf Creek*.

Naturally, critics loved this term, as it combined the two things guaranteed to engage viewers: sex and violence. They could also spit it out derisively, reaping the benefits of discussing it while allowing them to feel morally superior to those who enjoyed it. I, on the other hand, hated the term the first time I heard it. Some of it was jealousy. Previously, I had tried to coin a similarly descriptive one: "ArtGore." It was both a play on the word "hard-core" and an attempt to indicate that gore can in fact be artistic. "ArtGore" never caught on as anything, much less a universal expression, partly because, having no platform to promote it, I told all of two people, but more importantly because it just wasn't that clever.

But mainly, "torture porn" (the term, not the subgenre) is reductive and negates Roth's immense talent as a filmmaker.

Now, admittedly, there's more than a few reasons for the average horror fan to dislike Roth, none of which have anything to do with his films. He's extremely good-looking and charismatic, he's a shameless name-dropper (especially about his friendship with Tarantino), and he's slept with more than his fair share of young ingénues.

Even before *Hostel: Part II*, Roth's equally well-made and even more beautiful-looking sequel that pretty much just substituted the male backpackers of the original for a trio of girls, the backlash began. Once horror's enfant terrible, Roth delighted in a balls-to-the-wall violence that was seen as no longer an asset but a detriment. The *Saw* series experienced a similar phenomenon. The difference was that there was no single person set up as the fall guy, mainly because there was no single person identified with the series: James Wan only directed the first installment; Darren Lynn Bousman was too nondescript and Leigh Whannell too likeable.

This made Roth a convenient target. And this would have been fine if the criticism had come from the usual suspects who took every opportunity to disparage the genre. Romero had endured it. Carpenter, Craven, and Hooper had endured it. Roth could endure it too. But, instead, the barbs came from the people who should have known better. In half the interviews I read with filmmakers who have made a movie filled with graphic uncomfortable violence, the director will inevitably state his desire to create something more than "just a *Hostel* clone." The irony is that *Hostel* is still a smarter and much better film than 99.9 percent of those made by people who shudder at the comparison.

It's not just Roth, or even torture porn in general, that is attacked as soon as it becomes too successful. Every subgenre is fair game. Pick up any horror magazine and read the interviews. Watch how the directors try to differentiate their films from the competition. "It's smarter than the typical slasher." "Our film doesn't rely on jump scares." "Blood and graphic gore grow old quickly." And the worst of all, "It's really more of a psychological thriller." Director Jason Eisener came onto the scene with his 2011 exploitationer, the Rutger Hauer starrer *Hobo with a Shotgun*. It's vintage Carpenter by way of Troma. *Hobo* garnered tons of positive press and a *Rue Morgue* cover story. Based at least in part on this success, Eisener became involved with the *V/H/S* films, lo-fi anthologies that jettisoned the yucks of *Creepshow* and *Tales from the Crypt* for piss-your-pants frights. In an article about *V/H/S/2* in the August 2013 issue of *Fangoria*, Eisener says, "There's so much shit in the *Paranormal Activity* movies where they're just filming random stuff. It doesn't do anything for the characters; they bore you, bore you, bore you until something flutters in the curtain and you're like, 'Ohh!' because something is finally happening." Is Eisener entitled to his opinion? Of course. But he didn't need to disparage what I consider the most frightening modern-day horror franchise in order to prove the worth of his film. Maybe it's just human nature to be dismissive of others' success. And horror filmmakers, like horror fans, instinctively push back whenever a film becomes too big. As Tony Timpone notes, "Horror fans want horror films to be just theirs. So when these films have mainstream appeal . . . and when Joe Schmo and middle America and the rest of the world embraces these films, horror fans get jealous."

Sometimes, however, the attacks on our own are justified. For years, I had heard rumbles that the well-known writer and horror personality Lianne Spiderbaby had been passing off other writers' work as her own. I knew nothing of Spiderbaby (obviously not her real name, but an homage to Jack Hill's cult classic), other than that she absolutely detested my *I Spit on Your Grave* remake, but I figured most of these ad hominem attacks had more to do with the fact she was not only gorgeous but currently dating Quentin Tarantino. After all, most horror geeks never got to fuck the head cheerleader (or any cheerleader, or any girl for that matter) and relished the opportunity to take a beautiful colleague down a peg. This woman was a contributor to *Fangoria*, *FEARnet,* and *Video Watchdog*, in addition to other well-respected publications, so obviously, I thought, she knew how to write. Plus, if these allegations were really true, they would be fairly easy to prove.

Turns out, they were. In July 2013, the blogosphere erupted with hard evidence that Spiderbaby was a serial plagiarist. The examples cited were so egregious they were almost comical; entire paragraphs were lifted verbatim. The reaction was swift and predictable. She was crucified by fans and fellow writers alike.

Generally, I take no pleasure in the misfortune of others, unless those others are people I actively dislike—then I revel in it. But I didn't have much sympathy for Spiderbaby either. After all, she was irrefutably guilty. She broke the cardinal rule—or at least one of the cardinal rules—of journalism. That said, I wasn't nearly as enraged as most people were. Call me a cynic, but once her crimes were pointed out, all it did was bring more attention to the original writer. If somebody ripped me off, as long as everyone knew it, I'd come out smelling like a rose. If imitation is the sincerest form of flattery, then outright plagiarism is the sincerest form of sycophancy.

I wasn't particularly surprised that Spiderbaby (the more I write it, the more ridiculous her name seems) had no ethical barrier to taking a shortcut. Sad to say, but I've long stopped being shocked by the moral failings of others. What was far more stupefying was that Spiderbaby thought she could get away with it. That she weighed the cost-to-benefit ratio and decided it was worth the risk. As writers, the one thing we can control is our integrity. You might think I'm an untalented hack and an irredeemable asshole, but at least I've led you to that conclusion honestly. Oftentimes, to the detriment of a sentence's construction, I'll ineloquently make reference to other works from which I've drawn, even if I've done so obliquely. Other times, I actually refuse to use a certain phrase because, although I can't place it, I'm certain I've heard it somewhere before. I'm completely terrified someone will call me a fraud. It's similar to the reason I could never wear a toupee, even though I'm under no illusion about the fact that I would look far better with the thick curly hair I once had rather than the thinning remnants I now sport. However, were I to opt for a piece, I would feel compelled to tell every single person I met that I was in no way trying to be coy about the pelt sitting atop my head. Or else I'd go fucking crazy, like the dude from "The Tell-Tale Heart," obsessed with continuing the charade.

In the long run, the only person this whole episode really affects is Lianne (I can't bear to write "Spiderbaby" anymore) herself. She made her bed and now she has to lie in it. That she's sharing it with Tarantino might mitigate the sting of her banishment to some degree. But one thing is certain: it's going to take a long time—and a few genuine mea culpas (which admittedly she's already given)—before any periodical will even think of hiring her again.

While we're on the subject of magazines, it seems that there's nothing horror fans enjoy more than griping about those that cover the genre. And when I say "those" I'm really talking about the big two—*Fangoria* and *Rue Morgue*—because honestly, none of the other ones matter. I'm not saying that none of the others are *good*; some of them are quality publications. But even the ones that are uniformly excellent, like Tim Lucas's *Video Watchdog*, lack either the distribution or influence to be representative of the genre the way that *Fango* and *Rue Morgue* are.

The most frequent complaint about *Fangoria* is that it covers bloated, big-budget studio horror at the expense of smaller indie films or forgotten classics from the past. For *Rue Morgue*, it's an almost too-cool-for-school attitude exhibited by a stable of writers who would rather call attention to their own snark than offer an honest critique.

Both criticisms are equally invalid.

Even before Chris Alexander took over in 2010 as editor-in-chief of *Fango*—and, truthfully, *did* put more of an emphasis on retro shit—the magazine always made sure to balance its contemporary coverage with retrospectives. I remember *Fango*'s longtime, even-keeled managing editor Michael Gingold becoming apoplectic because of a reader's letter making this charge. I'm too tired to go back through a decade's worth of "Postal Zones" to find the exact exchange, but basically Gingold's rebuttal was that *The Beyond* had been featured on the cover of the magazine two times in the past year—not bad for a fairly obscure European film over twenty years old. And he was absolutely right. As for *Rue Morgue*, their writers *are* opinionated. Sometimes obnoxiously so. They're also incredibly well versed, they're passionate, and they don't suffer fools (or shitty films, books, or albums) gladly. You want pabulum? Read the film reviews in *Us Weekly*.

Like every other ill of the twenty-first century, we can blame the horror community's penchant for self-flagellation on the Internet. Specifically, on the Internet's ability to give every asshole with an opinion an anonymous forum in which to air it. Read a review, any review, from one of your favorite websites. Then scroll down to the comments. I guarantee you, it will seem like someone's offering a prize to whoever can be the most offensive. As Rodrigo Gudiño told me, "Social networks are vehicles for people to express their dislike or negative ideas about anything. They're used as a tool to bitch."

The Internet has also democratized the medium so the fans, and not just the critics, can separate the wheat from the chaff. Many would say this is a good thing, a true meritocracy where the great unwashed alone can decide the fate of a movie. Maybe.

On the other hand, what is being lost is the kind of Us vs. Them mentality that used to pit the horror faithful against the mainstream press. Did anybody give a shit what reviewers from the *New York Times* and the *Washington Post* had to say about *Friday the 13th Part V*, if they said anything at all? Of course not. It was taken as a matter of faith that they would hate it. In fact, that's what added to the appeal. When *Interview with the Vampire* started receiving rave reviews and Oscar buzz began building for the stars, I knew it was the kiss of death. And sure enough, that movie sucked.

One might argue this criticism is healthy. That it proves a genre is strong enough to withstand the brickbats of even its most ardent supporters. Possibly. There's no question that the Internet, as a technology, has been infinitely more boom than bust for horror films, especially in terms of disseminating information. Back in the day, breaking horror news came via monthly updates in *Fangoria* and, if it was big enough (meaning it involved a star or a juicy scandal), possibly through general-interest entertainment periodicals and industry trades. But if the issue was published three weeks after the news was out, it was hardly "breaking." Today, websites like Bloody Disgusting, Dread Central, Shock Till You Drop, and thousands of others of varying quality churn out updates by the minute. As far as reliable sources go, *Fango* and *Rue Morgue* can't compete. The reason, I pray, that neither will go the way of *Variety* and the *Hollywood Reporter*—venerable trade magazines decimated by Deadline Hollywood—is because both offer the kind of analysis and access that no website can currently provide.

Nor is there any question that the Internet has made everything having to do with horror much *easier*. For the content creators, the financing, producing, distributing, and marketing of horror movies has been irrevocably changed—unless of course we're talking about huge studio films, but even these are starting to take cues from their low-budget brethren, especially on the promotional front. For the consumers, you can meet like-minded fans, purchase rare imports, and buy, sell, or trade any type of memorabilia online. The only thing that's missing is the human element. In the good old days, third-generation SLP VHS tapes used to be traded in person—from the trunks of cars and in the backs of old bookstores—not shipped through the US Postal Service from some gigantic central warehouse. I'm convinced that this is one of the main reasons the convention scene has thrived in recent years. Despite the notion of horror fans being something of vampiric loners, only crawling out of our basement lairs after sundown, we're really a pretty social subculture. We crave the human connection that can't be duplicated by purchasing something on eBay.

Let's assume I owned zero VHS cassettes, DVDs, Blu-ray discs, or any other piece of physical media. With an Internet connection, I could still watch more than 75 percent of the films I've mentioned in this book without ever leaving my couch. How fucking crazy is that? Whether it's Netflix, Amazon Prime, YouTube, Crackle, Hulu, or some other obscure streaming service, a few clicks of the mouse can bring me any number of illicit thrills. Eat your heart out, *Videodrome*.

It's a far cry from when I was writing *Going to Pieces*, way back in the late nineties, and needed immediate access to a number of obscure titles that I didn't own. This was a sad time for the home video industry. The majority of the mom-and-pop video stores were being shuttered, and although the large national chains were still plugging along, everyone saw the writing on the wall. A few indie stalwarts like Big Brother, Blast Off Video, and Darkstar Video held out for as long as they could before they were forced out of business by market conditions beyond their control. I don't expect these names to mean anything to anybody outside of Chicago—and really, few people in it—but if only for posterity I want to give them the tiny bit of recognition they deserve.

The best of the bunch was an independent video store located in the Hyde Park neighborhood. For the life of me, I can't remember the name. And now, it's long gone. Hyde Park is a beautiful oasis of brick and greenery surrounded by strife, not unlike Columbia University before Harlem became chic and relatively safe. It is home to Barack Obama and the University of Chicago, which means it's usually teeming with police officers and college students in porkpie hats.

Late at night, once rush hour was long over, I would drive from my home on the north side of the city down Lake Shore Drive into Hyde Park, singing the Aliotta Haynes Jeremiah song "Lake Shore Drive" at the top of my lungs. I've been told that hard-core Chicagoans hate this song and find it ridiculously cheesy. I think it's beautiful. *And the blue lights shining with a heavenly grace, help you ride on by . . .*

The store was poorly organized and understaffed. To make matters worse, because it was in a bad area—it was the only video store I've ever been to in which it was not uncommon for a fight to break out—only the empty boxes were displayed. So even if a case was on the shelf, that was certainly no guarantee that the clerk could locate the corresponding cassette. The entire experience was inconvenient, annoying, and somewhat dangerous. To add insult to injury, I don't think anybody in the store had any idea how to properly price a rental, resulting in my having to pay exorbitant fees to keep *Headless Eyes* for the weekend. But looking back, the oddball moments in the store are what I remember. Not lying on the couch in my warm apartment with a glass of wine while *Final Exam* played on the flat-screen but sitting on the cold linoleum floor of that video store, my eyes wide with glee like a kid's on Christmas morning as I stumbled across the working box* for *Microwave Massacre*.

For a fleeting moment, I was transported back to the Book Swap. Mark Cichowski was telling me to hurry up so we could go watch *Mausoleum* for the umpteenth time.

I felt someone tap me on the shoulder. But it wasn't Mark. It was one of the store employees, telling me to get my ass off their floor.

* This was the ne plus ultra of big box marketing from the VHS era. From what I can recall, the cover actually had working lights and sounds.

CHAPTER NINE

Postmodern Blues

In 1997, Miramax was the epicenter of the independent film world. Just a few years earlier, it had upended the economics of the business with its $60 million sale to the Walt Disney Company. A year after that, it upended the very definition of indie film itself with the release of *Pulp Fiction*. This was no minor hit along the lines of *Sex, Lies, and Videotape*; it was a blockbuster by even the strictest definition of the word.

The Weinstein brothers stood at the intersection of art and commerce, like two fat ill-mannered colossuses. Their mother ship churned out art house classics like *The Crying Game*, *The Piano*, and *The English Patient*, while their horror label, Dimension Films, printed money with hits such as *The Crow* and *From Dusk Till Dawn*, as well as forgettable sequels to the *Halloween*, *Hellraiser*, and *Children of the Corn* franchises.

To any kid worth his salt who wanted to make it in the New York City film industry, there was no better place to start. Thanks to a summer internship I'd had at a rival company, I was able to finagle an interview with Bobby Cohen, then Miramax's senior vice president of production. Cohen seemed like a nice enough guy (an impression confirmed years later when he agreed to read one of my scripts) and I came in brimming with confidence. And why not? After all, the company was still riding high following the success of *Scream*, a sleeper horror hit from Wes Craven that came out of nowhere to become Dimension's top-grossing film. And I was the ultimate horror fan. Clearly, this was a match made in heaven. I had absolutely no doubt that the two of us, me and Dimension Films, were going to reinvent the genre. Greatness was within my grasp.

The interview started off fine. Cohen laid out some of the position's responsibilities and I rattled off the appropriate responses about how I was willing to do anything to learn and how if I had a fault, it was that I worked too hard, was too much of a perfectionist, and would probably be too dedicated to my job. Later in the interview, after I casually mentioned that I was a rabid horror fan, Cohen asked me what I thought of *Scream*. Assuming most of the other candidates would have answered the same question with, "I loved it!" or "It was great," I opted to go the other way. I took a deep breath and explained how *Scream* was a fraud. How it pretended to operate at some higher level while exploiting the same conventions that made its less ironic predecessors so successful.

Soon after, the interview concluded. The crazy thing is that while walking to my car I was completely convinced that I had the job (the crazier thing is that I actually passed by *Scream* creator Kevin Williamson, who was standing in the parking lot smoking a cigarette, although I didn't recognize him at the time). If anything, my critical analysis of *Scream*, compounded with my unfiltered honesty, sealed the deal.

After all, there was a reason I had been the film critic for my college newspaper, the *Daily Cardinal*.* Who in their right mind *wouldn't* be desperate for my opinion? It never occurred to me that a high-powered film executive in the real world wouldn't just love a precocious postgraduate trying to discredit his cash cow.

Not surprisingly (to anybody except for me), I didn't get the job. At least I learned from my mistakes. From then on, I told every prospective employer that whatever they had done was nothing short of the greatest movie since *Citizen Kane*. And since the film industry as a whole is so self-deluded, some of them actually believed me.

The thing is, I wasn't wrong about *Scream*. I might have been an insufferable little prick, but I wasn't wrong.

To understand the *Scream* phenomenon, and to appreciate its importance to the horror genre as a whole, you really have to go back a good ten years or so before the film came out. By the mid-eighties, the horror film as a whole was in trouble. The slasher franchises that had so dominated the horror landscape for the first half of the decade were former shells of themselves. Financially, they were still earning a pretty penny, which is why they continued to be made. But soon they started deviating from the formula that had made them so successful. Conventional wisdom holds that slasher films eventually petered out

* My career at the *Cardinal* came to an ignominious end. I was assigned to cover the making of the Keanu Reeves starrer *Chain Reaction*, which was shooting at the Wisconsin State Capital on campus. However, it was an early-morning shoot and by the time I woke up the production had long since wrapped for the day. My editor was not amused and I was never asked to write another review for the paper.

because audiences tired of the same old story lines. In reality, hard-core fans only lost interest when their beloved films were bowdlerized beyond recognition. It was bad enough that in *Friday the 13th Part V: A New Beginning* the killer wasn't even Jason Voorhees. But in *Part VIII*, he actually traveled to Manhattan. It would only be a few more years before he went to hell and then reappeared in outer space!

To make matters worse, no new franchises were stepping up to replace the old guard. Sure, films like *Witchboard*, *Pumpkinhead*, and *Maniac Cop* spawned sequels, but not only were these far from the windfalls that the *Friday*s and *Nightmare*s were, but they never crossed over into popular culture. My grandmother knew who Freddy Krueger was; Malfeitor (the evil spirit in *Witchboard*) was about as well-known as Cal Ripken Jr.'s backup.

During this time, there was also a dearth of "adult" or "serious" horror films. No *Exorcist* or *Rosemary's Baby* that captured the zeitgeist and made the cover of *Time*. In fact, the most successful movies were kid-friendly offerings like *The Goonies*, *Ghostbusters*, *The Monster Squad*, and *The Lost Boys*. The rise of horror lite dovetailed with the inception of the PG-13 rating. Implemented after *Indiana Jones and the Temple of Doom* and first used on *Red Dawn*, the rating sought to pacify parents who wanted some designation to bridge the gap between family-friendly scares like *Star Wars* and *E.T.* and a film like, say, *Straw Dogs*. Studios loved the new rating. They could still make horror films, but by excising only a few seconds of sex and blood, and maybe a "fuck" here and there, an enormous new demographic was now accessible. Horror fans, on the other hand, viewed the PG-13 rating as a warning of their own—a warning to stay clear of the watered-down frights ahead.

Nor did it help that horror's reigning grand masters failed to produce anything close to the quality of the films that made them famous. Wes Craven whiffed with *Deadly Friend* and a few episodes of the revamped *Twilight Zone*. John Carpenter had *Prince of Darkness* and *They Live*, which were both considered huge disappointments at the time. I don't even know what the fuck George Romero was doing after *Day of the Dead* other than the tepid *Monkey Shines*. There were, however, a few stellar remakes. David Cronenberg's *The Fly* and Chuck Russell's *The Blob* were big improvements over their B-movie progenitors. But these were single movies, nothing that spoke to the long-term viability of the genre.

Another devastating blow to the horror genre was the rise of the psychological thriller. Using 1987's *Fatal Attraction* as the blueprint, these films appropriated horror tropes but scaled back the blood and supernatural undertones, allowing them to target a much larger audience. For the next five years, it felt like these were the *only* types of films in theaters. I saw *Pacific Heights*, *Unlawful Entry*, *The Hand That Rocks the Cradle*, and *Single White Female* in packed houses. By contrast, I endured *Popcorn* alone and *The Lawnmower Man* with a homeless person who I assume snuck in before the theater opened and proceeded to fall asleep in the back row.

None of this is to say that there were *no* good horror films made between the years 1986 and 1996. *Near Dark*, *Dead Ringers*, and *In the Mouth of Madness* would have been solid in any year. But the truth is, I had to struggle to come up with just these three names. And really, none of them have the gravitas of a *Halloween* or a *Texas Chain Saw Massacre*, or even an *Evil Dead* or a *Re-Animator*.

For me, the one good thing about this "lost decade" was that it coincided with my college years and allowed me to become a pretentious asshole. A lack of new horror films meant that I was forced to dabble in other genres. So on one hand, I was exposed to some wonderful films that previously I would have ignored. On the other, I said things like "All *real* films have subtitles," and claimed my favorite movie of all time was *Battleship Potemkin*.

Still, I was never able to fully escape my horror roots. My junior year in college, I took a class in advanced film production. For the final project, we had to make our own five-to-ten-minute student film. Inspired by whatever historical film movement we were studying that week, most of the kids chose to channel their inner Truffaut and make some unintelligible piece of shit. Besides myself, the only two exceptions were Lance Hori, my future haunted house buddy, who made an excellent film, and one strange girl who used this assignment as an opportunity to explore her own sexuality. For the majority of her moody black-and-white film, she crawled around a forest half-naked with the handle of a whip shoved up her ass. Of course, I giggled uncontrollably the entire time. When the lights came up, most of us were speechless. Our professor said it was one of the bravest examples of filmmaking she had ever seen. Then she glared at me and added it was unfortunate that some members of the class were not mature enough to handle it.

Naturally, I chose to make a horror film. It was called *Quid Pro Quo*. The flimsy, unoriginal plot followed three roommates who accidentally kill their fourth. As they're arguing about what to do with the body, it disappears, only to reappear later, very much alive, and take its revenge. Writing this, it actually sounds far more interesting than it was. I borrowed music cues from *Psycho*, *The Shining*, and *Children of the Corn*, and re-created some of my favorite shots from famous horror movies. As one of the actors walks down a darkened hallway in a long shot, I zoom in as fast as possible at the exact moment the killer jumps out of the shadows; it's an homage to one of the all-time best "jump scares," from *The Exorcist III*. From *Black Christmas*, I cribbed the slow zoom into the killer's eyeball as he's hiding behind a door. And of course, I had to re-create *Psycho*'s shower scene, which in my film was about six times as long and charitably 0.00001 percent as effective.

When the film was over, after a few seconds of uncomfortable silence, it was time for my fellow auteurs to weigh in. Finally, one dude spoke up. "Well, I guess we know who's going to Hollywood," he said. The entire class erupted in laughter and for a few seconds I beamed—until I realized they were all making fun of me. In Advanced Video Production, "going Hollywood" meant that I had sold out. I was a fraud, a hack, because I dared make a film that was commercial and fun (albeit terrible) rather than suffering for my art by inserting objects into my rectum. It's too absurd to even be pathetic, but most of the students in my class really did believe that they would go on to change the face of cinema like their uncompromising heroes. Only the cloistered world of academia could foster, and encourage, such delusions.

I'm not going to pretend this episode didn't bother me. My feelings were hurt. But I decided then and there that never again would I be ashamed of my love of horror. As David

Crosby would say, I was going to let my freak flag fly. After all, my sloppy, ridiculous, inept, and sad little slasher film was infinitely better than any of the sloppy, ridiculous, inept, and sad little wannabe art films my classmates made.

I like to think that I got the last laugh. After graduation, most of these kids went home to their farms in Oshkosh, Sheboygan, or Appleton. If they were lucky, maybe they got an unpaid internship at the local PBS affiliate. Or a firsthand look at the exciting world of public access. I went to New York City. And eventually sat down with Bobby Cohen to plot the future trajectory of the horror genre.

The genesis of *Scream* is one of those stories that has been told so many times it has become apocryphal. Struggling screenwriter Kevin Williamson was house-sitting for a friend when he saw a Barbara Walters special about the Gainesville Ripper, a serial killer who murdered and mutilated five Florida coeds in the summer of 1990. Alone and terrified, Williamson called his pal David Blanchard for some moral support. Blanchard told him that there was a very real chance that Freddy, or Michael, or Jason, could be waiting right outside the window because, well, that's what friends do. The good-natured ribbing turned into a trivia contest, with Williamson and Blanchard quizzing each other about horror films.

Williamson survived the night. Now inspired, and with the kernel of an idea, he took off for Palm Springs and sequestered himself in his hotel room for the weekend. By the time he resurfaced, he had written a script titled *Scary Movie*, as well as a five-page treatment for the second and third installments of what was always planned as a trilogy. A bidding war ensued for the script—which would eventually be rechristened

Scream near the end of production—with the Weinsteins besting Universal, Paramount, Morgan Creek, and a not-yet-clinically-insane Oliver Stone. Wes Craven signed on to direct after initially passing. In one of their characteristically ballsy moves, Miramax (technically Dimension) released the film over Christmas, and Old St. Nick rewarded their gamble with a $100 million payout. A new horror franchise was born, the first legitimate one since *Child's Play* nearly a decade before.

Scream was a bona fide blockbuster, which meant that despite being a horror film, it couldn't be dismissed so easily. It was also the right *kind* of horror film, tailor-made for critics who practically trampled each other in an effort to overuse the term "postmodern." What they meant, of course, was that *Scream* was self-conscious. It was aware of itself, playfully acknowledging that it was not only a horror film, but a horror film that belonged to a specific lineage of similar films.

This self-reflexivity is on display from the get-go. In the opening scene, slightly reminiscent of *When a Stranger Calls*, Drew Barrymore is terrorized by a prank caller. Along with the requisite threats of disembowelment, the caller challenges her to a horror trivia quiz to save the life of her boyfriend. She gets the first question right (the name of *Halloween*'s villain) but boots the second by incorrectly naming Jason as the killer in *Friday the 13th*, as opposed to Jason's mother, Mrs. Voorhees.

Craven was praised for having the cojones to cast a recognizable star in Barrymore for the scene, only to knock her off in explicit fashion. The comparison was made to *Psycho*, although in Hitchcock's film Janet Leigh is not murdered until more than forty-five minutes in, while Barrymore is dispatched in just over ten.

Then there's Jamie Kennedy, the resident film geek whose main purpose is to lay out "the rules" of slasherdom to his fellow characters: 1) you can never have sex, 2) you can never drink or do drugs, and 3) never ever ever under any circumstances say, "I'll be right back." Again, critics found this meta shit unspeakably clever. I found it much more entertaining to try to spot all the other in-jokes peppered throughout the film, such as VHS tapes from other Miramax releases strewn all over the set.

What nobody seemed to remember was that *Scream* was hardly the first horror film to actively reference the films that preceded it. Abbott and Costello were meeting all sorts of famous monsters in the forties and fifties, while *Young Frankenstein* proved that a comic genius could understand the genre as well as anyone. Much more recently, the early eighties were rife with slasher parodies. What was unique about this batch was that they spoofed *contemporary* films, which, looking back, is probably the reason none of them were too successful. After all, the slasher film was at its peak, still years away from the point where saturation gives rise to satire.

It is a shame, however, that most of these parodies have long been forgotten. As individual films, their importance is debatable; as a group, they're invaluable for understanding just how pervasive the slasher had become.

The first out of the gate, in 1981, was *Student Bodies*, written and directed by (at least according to the opening credits) Mickey Rose, a close friend and early collaborator of Woody Allen. Rose actually met his wife on a blind date facilitated by Allen, as she was close friends with Allen's wife at the time (not

Mia Farrow, or the daughter he's currently fucking*). However, *Student Bodies* was probably codirected and produced by Michael Ritchie (taking the pseudonym Allen Smithee), who found far more success with a bigger spoof a few years later in *Fletch*.

Student Bodies takes place at Lamab High, where a killer dubbed "the Breather" has been knocking off promiscuous students in a number of unusually creative ways, using items such as paper clips and an eggplant. There's no shortage of suspects. Could it be the shop teacher who's obsessed with horsehead bookends? The school psychologist, played by actor Carl Jacobs, who has exactly zero other film credits to his name and is as good a straight man as Leslie Nielsen? Or most memorable of all, Malvert the janitor, who has the "IQ of a handball"? Malvert is played by an actor known only as "the Stick." He reprised the same type of imbecilic role on Nickelodeon's early Dave Coulier–hosted sketch comedy show, *Out of Control*, giving credence to the idea that he was actually a moron. I had never heard of *Out of Control*, even though it was targeted to my exact demographic, but after watching an old episode on YouTube it seems to have been made for the type of people who think *Full House* is the height of comedy.

The jokes in *Student Bodies* are more perceptive than outright funny. For example, the movie is set on a number of im-

---

* Before all the Allen apologists—a pathetic group that includes many of Hollywood's most famous faces—completely freak out, I concede that Allen isn't technically fucking his daughter (although if you believe the recent allegations of his adopted daughter, Dylan, he may very well have molested her). Instead, he slept with, and then married, the multiple-decades-younger adopted daughter of his longtime girlfriend. Nothing untoward about that.

portant dates: Halloween, Friday the thirteenth, and, wait for it . . . Jamie Lee Curtis's birthday. Looking back, it's remarkable that by 1981 Curtis's reputation as a scream queen was already solidified; *Halloween*, *Prom Night*, and *Terror Train* had been released, with *Halloween II* hitting theaters a few months later. Another running gag is that after each murder, the number of the victim is flashed over the scene, a commentary on the high body count of the slasher. If this kind of stuff gets your goat, you might find *Student Bodies* hysterical. Personally, I never even found *Young Frankenstein* that clever, so I might not be the best judge of comedy.

In fact, I was much more amused by a scene in which a horny couple can't go all the way because the girl's mother found her diaphragm. I'm not trying to be funny, this is a serious question: has anybody actually ever used a diaphragm? Does anyone even *know* anybody who's used one? In health class, we learned that as a mode of contraception the diaphragm was revolutionary, since it allows the woman to take a more proactive role in her sexual health, but the entire idea of such a device seems more suited to the realm of late-night talk shows and edgy sitcoms. The crazy thing is that because my parents were very open-minded about sex and furnished me with a seemingly unlimited supply of "what's happening to my body" books, I actually knew a lot about this Byzantine device. What I can't imagine is how anyone ever thought it was a good idea. A condom is annoying enough but, as we all know, a necessary evil and not too difficult to slip on. But is there anything more potentially mood-killing than a rubber ring that you have to fill with some sort of spermicide and then shove all the way up against the cervix? The only device I find more unwieldy is the dental dam, which, in layman's terms, is basically a sheet of cellophane that is placed over the vagina in order to prevent the transmission of pathogens during oral sex. Unless your fantasy is to pretend your partner's genitals are Thanksgiving leftovers, this seems like a lot more trouble than it's worth.

The next of these early slasher spoofs, *Pandemonium*, was created ostensibly as a vehicle for Tom Smothers, which is curious since he's hardly in it. I didn't know much about Smothers, other than he was one of the Smothers Brothers, a comedy team whose *Smothers Brothers Comedy Hour* aired on CBS in the late sixties. Apparently the show was quite controversial at the time for its antiestablishment bent. Unfortunately, there's nothing nearly as interesting about his role as a Mountie investigating a series of murders at an Indiana cheerleading camp. In fact, the only thing even remotely noteworthy is that his sidekick is played by future public masturbator Paul "Pee-wee Herman" Reubens. Still, in addition to the requisite sight gags, puns, and complete inanity, there really are some fairly clever inside jokes. For example, Carol Kane plays a Carrie White–like student whose mother references her "dirty pillows." But here, they're actually filthy pillows, not breasts. And bringing the joke full circle, they belong to a bum played by Sydney Lassick, who was Sissy Spacek's high school teacher in *Carrie*. There's also a nice homage to Kevin Bacon's death in *Friday the 13th*, only it's pom-poms, not an arrow, that make the fateful deathblow. The best part of the film, however, is its refreshingly politically incorrect humor that would never fly in today's climate of nervous production executives and diversity czars. Case in point: when Judge Reinhold is shot into the stratosphere by an exploding trampoline, he comes across a plane full of Japanese tourists who, upon seeing a human projectile, naturally giggle excitedly and start snapping photographs with their ever-present Nikons.

The slasher parody with arguably the most star power is, ironically, one of the least known. *Wacko* features Joe Don Baker as an obsessed and unhinged detective tracking down the pumpkin-headed Lawnmower Killer (years before both *Pumpkinhead* and *The Lawnmower Man*, neither of which have anything to do with this). George Kennedy plays an incestuous doctor (it's as weird as it sounds, and hardly funny) and in the best surprise, Andrew Dice Clay—credited here just as Andrew Clay—is greaser Tony Schlongini. It's a role no different from the persona that would one day make him famous as the Dice Man. In fact, he's nearly impossible to watch without anticipating his trademark "Oh!" after every one of his lines.

Alex once pointed out to me that Dice's enduring legacy is to have ruined—or improved—Mother Goose for an entire generation of parents. No one I know can ever read these bedtime tales to their kids without thinking about Old Mother Hubbard bent over, Mary's hairy snatch, or Little Boy Blue sucking cock. There was also that bizarre incident when Dice broke down and cried on *The Arsenio Hall Show* and the equally strange 2003 CNNfn interview where he became irate with an interviewer for asking him about managing a gym. Still, I prefer to remember him as the filthy, leather-clad, chain-smoking troubadour of old. A couple of years ago, Dice went on a rant about Charlie Sheen, so I have even more respect for him today.

Besides being a bit wackier (pun intended), *Wacko* is no better or worse than its fellow slasher parodies—although having the Birds of Alfred Hitchcock High School suiting up for rival De Palma's Knives is a nice touch.

National Lampoon's Class Reunion was made at a time when National Lampoon films were still funny. But sandwiched between *National Lampoon's Animal House* and *National Lampoon's Vacation*, *Class Reunion* suffered by comparison. Hated by critics and virtually ignored by moviegoers, the film hastened writer John Hughes's metamorphosis from parody scribe to chronicler of teen angst. It takes place at the ten-year reunion of Lizzie Borden High School's class of 1972 and uses virtually the same plot as 1978's similarly named but off-the-wall *Class Reunion Massacre*. Despite everything said about it (or not said about it), *Class Reunion* is nowhere near as bad as advertised. If anything, its fatal flaw is that it can't out-*Airplane! Airplane!* That and the fact that it's afflicted with a severe case of "*Grease* syndrome." According to the Centers for Disease Control, this condition is characterized by the casting of actors no less than a generation older than their on-screen personas. Have you seen *Grease* recently? Olivia Newton-John was pushing it as a high school senior and John Travolta was patently absurd. But the most ridiculous had to be Stockard Channing, who, at the time, might have even been older than her costars Eve Arden and Sid Caesar.

Speaking of getting old, I can't believe we're approaching *Scream*'s twentieth anniversary. I recently watched it again and it was all the more apparent why I disliked it so much. There's something so off-putting about it. A smarminess that, as I would later tell Bobby Cohen, looked like a slasher film, quacked like a slasher film, but had art house pretensions.

Less apparent is why I was so charitable in *Going to Pieces*. I wrote, "[*Scream*] walks a fine line between poking fun at the classic slasher films and paying homage to them." Okay,

I guess you could make that argument. "The dialogue was witty, self-referential, and seemed to capture the authenticity of modern teenage jargon." Hardly. It was more mean-spirited than anything. The characters all joke about the deaths of their friends who were brutally murdered over the weekend. Even the biggest assholes I know wouldn't be this tone-deaf. "The characters were well-drawn and three-dimensional, hip enough to understand the conventions of the slasher film and still young and naïve enough to ignore them." Nope. In fact, *Scream* has some of the most unlikeable characters in any teen-laden film. In the lineage of distinguished douche bags that stretches from Damone in *Fast Times at Ridgemont High* to Stifler in *American Pie*, Matthew Lillard's Stu might be the douchiest of all. His weird twitchiness is more performance art than acting and I honestly have no idea how he managed to get through the shoot without any of his costars physically attacking him. Skeet Ulrich's character isn't much better. On the anniversary of the murder of his virgin girlfriend's mother, he basically tells her it's time to get over the loss and just fuck him. Then after he finally convinces her to give it up, he reveals he's actually her mother's killer! For crissakes, Wes, even *Last House on the Left* had a more uplifting ending.

Sometimes I think I just don't understand irony. For example, I'm pretty sure the Janis Joplin ditty "Mercedes Benz" is meant to be ironic, right? I mean, why would the quintessential hippy chick be pining for a Benz? But I've heard the song literally hundreds of times and listened closely to the lyrics. And to me, it sounds like nothing more than a girl who wants a luxury automobile.

This must be the reason I prefer all the irony-free slasher

films that followed *Scream*. For one thing, critics hated them just as much as they loved *Scream*, which in turn made me appreciate them even more. With *Scream*, they could at least pretend it was something more intelligent than a typical slasher (just as they did with *Halloween* nearly twenty years before), while completely dismissing the new crop as derivative crap (as they did with *Friday the 13th* and its clones). Although the laziest of the tastemakers grouped all these films together under the umbrella of "postmodern slashers," it was clear to even the most casual observer that *I Know What You Did Last Summer*, *Urban Legend*, and *Valentine* were much different. They didn't wink at the audience or go for knowing laughs. Although they didn't perform as well as *Scream* at the box office, they still brought in an impressive take, giving credence to the idea that it was the Weinsteins' marketing muscle more than anything that was responsible for *Scream*'s success.

One unfortunate result of the critics' renewed hatred of slasher films was that the directors who made them got a raw deal. And none more so than Jamie Blanks. The Australian wunderkind actually received some nice notices for his Hollywood debut, *Urban Legend*, mainly because of its clever premise: a killer murders his victims based on well-known urban legends. When Blanks chose the more traditional *Valentine* as his follow-up, the critics pounced. There's nothing particularly groundbreaking about *Valentine*, but it certainly didn't deserve anywhere near the vitriol it received. To use an analogy from the golden age of slashers, it was a *Terror Train*, a *Night School*, or a *Graduation Day*—fine films that defined but didn't transcend the genre like a *Halloween* or *Friday the 13th*. To those who were watching—and cared—it was obvious that Blanks's real sin was not following up *Urban Legend* with a project the critics deemed worthy. For his trouble, Blanks was sentenced to purgatory until 2007, six years later, when he directed the underrated *Storm Warning*, which played various festivals before receiving a release from Dimension Extreme. The very next year, Blanks took a thankless job—the remake of *Long Weekend*. Admittedly, few films warranted a remake less, as the original is a brilliant Australian gem that nearly thirty years later still doesn't feel the least bit dated. It's as unsettling a film as you'll find, mainly because nothing really happens and yet up until the very last frame it's impossible to shake the feeling of impending doom. With the remake, Blanks was shrewd enough to leave well enough alone. He understood implicitly which scenes not to touch and which would benefit from a small tweak. I'm not going to go as far as to say that Blanks's version is superior, or even concede that a remake was in any way necessary, but I can't imagine anyone tasked with the assignment doing a better job. In recent years, Blanks has worked on two of the very best documentaries ever made about exploitation films, Mark Hartley's *Not Quite Hollywood: The Wild, Untold Story of Ozploitation!* and *Machete Maidens Unleashed!*, about the Filipino film industry.

I'm fairly certain that Santayana could not have foreseen the rise of the slasher film when he wrote, "Those who cannot remember the past are condemned to repeat it." But if he did, he probably would have included an addendum that said, "And those who do remember it can profit handsomely."

Just as the early-eighties slashers spawned the first wave of spoofs, so did their late-nineties progeny. The big difference was that thirty years ago, the spoofs were a fraction as successful as their targets; combine the lifetime grosses of *Student Bodies*, *Pandemonium*, *Wacko*, and *National Lampoon's Class Reunion*, and you'd have the domestic take of a mediocre slasher of the time. But when 2000's *Scary Movie* took in more than $150 million—50 percent more than *Scream*—Dimension knew it had a new golden goose.

Created by the Wayans brothers—Keenen Ivory, Shawn, and Marlon—the *Scary Movie* series spoofs whatever the most popular horror films are at the time; the original focused on *Scream* and *I Know What You Did Last Summer*, while the most recent entry, *Scary Movie* 5, targeted *Mama* and *Paranormal Activity*.

Objectively, the *Scary Movie* films aren't as terrible as you would expect something featuring multiple Wayans to be. Like any spoof, each has its moments. In *Scary Movie* 2, James Woods plays a Father Merrin–like priest who takes Regan's exhortations of "Fuck me" literally and, well, fucks her. It's a little uncomfortable in light of Woods's fondness for much younger (but legal) girls but, if you're not easily offended, kind of funny. *Scary Movie* 3 opens with a scene in which Pamela Anderson and Jenny McCarthy are dressed as Catholic school girls. And because Pamela Anderson and Jenny McCarthy are dressed as Catholic schoolgirls, I completely forgot what it's a parody of. Also for *Part* 3, David Zucker replaces Keenen Ivory Wayans, who directed the first two installments. Not only does he bring in Leslie Nielsen, who does what Leslie Nielsen does best, but he's not even above throwing in a sly *Airplane!* reference or two. In 2013, Marlon Wayans produced and starred in *A Haunted House*, a new horror spoof that mainly targets the *Paranormal Activity* films. Although Wayans won't call the film a parody, it's virtually indistinguishable from the *Scary Movie* franchise in which he made his name (and fortune).

If *Scream* can lay claim to one thing, it's igniting the current horror Renaissance, which, nearly two decades later, shows no signs of abating. Young horror fans have absolutely no recollection of a time when the fields of horror were anything but bountiful. Rod Gudiño is often asked how he keeps *Rue Morgue* relevant in times of famine. His response: "There are no times of famine." And for a magazine that premiered less than a year after *Scream*'s release, there really haven't been.

But the geezers among us remember all too well. We would wait months and months for a new theatrical release—only to be given *Dr. Giggles*. "In the late eighties, early nineties before *Scream*, we'd be pulling our hair out trying to find a movie to put on the cover of *Fangoria*. It was really slim pickings a lot of months," recalls Tony Timpone. "If it wasn't for *Scream*, we wouldn't have had this flood of product."

This is why all of us who hold this genre dear owe *Scream* a debt of gratitude. And if I could go back in time, I'd have a completely different answer ready for Bobby Cohen. Asked what I thought about his company's new movie that was taking the country by storm, I'd look him in the eye, smile, and say, "It sure beats a sequel to *Dr. Giggles*."

CHAPTER TEN

A Decade That Dripped Blood

Bob Adelman loves horror movies.

He sees more of them than anyone I know who isn't professionally involved in the industry. As a successful lawyer with a family, he obviously doesn't have that much free time. So a few times a month, once the wives and kids are asleep, we head out to our local theater to catch the last show of the night. We've been doing this for over a decade now and have seen plenty of modern classics (*Paranormal Activity*, *The Last Exorcism*), just as many stinkers (*Primeval, Dead Silence*), and everything in between.

Usually, we're the only two jokers in the theater. After all, how many people are going to go see *Saw VI* at a suburban multiplex at 10:20 on a Tuesday night? We have dissimilar tastes; as a rule, I'm creeped out by movies about ghosts or the occult, while Bob is terrified of flesh-and-blood murderers and home invasion films. Still, we've had a lot of fun together. And there's no one else I would rather have had as a wingman for the last ten or so years to witness the genre's evolution.

What's unique about horror in the first decade and a half

of the millennium is its variety. We all know that genres are cyclical. But in the past, every decade seemed to be defined by a single *type* of horror film. There were the Universal classics of the thirties and forties. In the 1950s, horror melded with sci-fi for a slew of alien-invasion and atomic monster movies that everyone agrees were fairly blatant allegories for Cold War paranoia. The sixties were a mishmash—it seemed like the decade's cultural upheaval was reflected in its idiosyncratic horror output—while the seventies conjured up Satan in various forms and Mother Earth sought revenge with nature-run-amok warnings. Slasher films dominated the eighties before horror, as we saw in the preceding chapter, went into hibernation.

But following *Scream*, the genre rose from the ashes like a phoenix—or more appropriately, a hydra, where from every stump there sprouted multiple new heads of cinematic terror. And the amazing thing was that none of them overshadowed the others. Instead, it was as if the various subgenres fed off of one another, creating something far greater than the sum of its parts. Think of it as a giant storm front, comprised not of a single cell but dozens of separate squalls spinning at their own speed but still contained within a larger weather system.

That said, a few of these trends have had a much more profound cultural impact than others, and none more so than the humble zombie. Vampires have placed a close second. However, I've never seen a *Twilight* film or a single episode of *True Blood* or *The Vampire Diaries*, and have never read so much as a paragraph of any pop-lit teen vampire novel. As much as I loved *30 Days of Night* and *Daybreakers*, I know very little about bloodsuckers, pubescent or otherwise. If this pisses you off, go out and pick up Liisa Ladouceur's *How to Kill a Vampire: Fangs in Folklore, Film and Fiction*. I assure you, you'll learn more about the undead than I could ever offer.

On the surface, zombies seem like a strange choice for the monster du jour. They don't have the literary pedigree of Dracula and Frankenstein's monster. Nor are they rooted in history or myth like the Mummy and the Wolf Man. Instead, their emergence can be traced back to the slave trade, when West Africans were rounded up in their homeland and shipped across the ocean to work the Caribbean plantations. The island colony of Haiti (then Saint-Domingue) was especially fertile ground for this particular fiend and its accompanying magic, known colloquially as voodoo, thanks in large part to French king Louis XIV's decree that upon arrival all slaves abandon their African religions and convert to Roman Catholicism. As a result, a wonderfully colorful potpourri of African mysticism and Christianity was born.

I always assumed that pre-1968 the entire zombie subgenre was comprised almost solely of the Bela Lugosi starrer *White Zombie* and the Jacques Tourneur/Val Lewton collaboration *I Walked with a Zombie*, which is far classier and less exploitative than its title would lead one to believe. However, Jamie Russell's *Book of the Dead: The Complete History of Zombie Cinema* (as accurate a subtitle as you'll ever find) disabused me of that notion. Turns out, Hollywood's Poverty Row studios were actually churning out zombie films throughout the 1940s with titles such as *The Ghost Breakers*, *King of the Zombies*, *Revenge of the Zombies*, and *Voodoo Man*.

Even more interesting (at least to me), it seems that *White Zombie*'s most important contribution to pop culture wasn't the eponymous band it inspired but one of the first instances of experiential marketing. When *White Zombie* opened at New York's famous Rivoli theater, actors dressed as zombies walked along a platform above the theater's marquee performing a "series of thrilling dramatic sequences." Apparently, thousands of onlookers packed the sidewalks to gawk at the spectacle, which also included sound effects of "the screeching of vultures, the grinding of the sugar mill and the beating of the tom toms and other nerve wracking sounds." It's not too hard to draw a line from this early PR stunt to the ubiquitous zombie events of today.

Then, in 1968, *Night of the Living Dead* happened. If you need me to explain what this means, why the hell are you even reading this book? (My apologies to friends and family who are doing so out of interest or obligation.) Even after *Night*'s phenomenal success—not to mention that of its sequels *Dawn of the Dead* and *Day of the Dead*—zombies remained something of a blue-collar fiend, appearing mainly in ridiculous Italian gut-munchers. There were exceptions along the way. Spanish expat Jorge Grau's *The Living Dead at Manchester Morgue* is always a favorite among zombie buffs, though I find it overrated. The *Blind Dead* films of Amando de Ossorio—*Tombs of the Blind Dead*, *Return of the Blind Dead*, *Horror of the Zombies*, *Night of the Seagulls*—are also beloved, but to me they're tedious and dull. Two of Bob Clark's early films, *Children Shouldn't Play with Dead Things* and *Deathdream*, are both zombie films, the former explicitly while the latter much more subtly, although the main character does die and then returns as something much different from what he was before.

But now, zombies are everywhere. Like, well, a plague of zombies, munching their way through pop culture and carving out their place as the first great monster of the millennium.

The modern zombie Renaissance can be traced back to two films, *Resident Evil* and *28 Days Later*. Based on the blockbuster video game franchise of the same name, *Resident Evil* initially started out as a vehicle for George Romero. After nearly a twenty-year hiatus, the king was returning home, back to the ghouls whose fortunes were inextricably linked to his own. The homecoming lasted all of one draft of the screenplay. Eventually, Paul W. S. Anderson took over the project. Anderson was an avid gamer who had cut his teeth on *Mortal Kombat*, another film adapted from a wildly popular video game. Unsurprisingly, *Resident Evil*'s flaws were a result of its source medium. It was sprawling and sterile. And although it eventually spawned four sequels to date (with a fifth currently in development), it was considered something of a joke among horror fans and was not nearly as successful as generally assumed (domestically, it barely made back its budget). On the other side of the coin (and the pond) was Danny Boyle's *28 Days Later*, a British zombie film about the outbreak of a man-made virus. *28 Days Later* was down and dirty, like a modern-day Dickens novel, albeit one with zombies who moved *fast*. This analogy sounds a lot less ludicrous after recent mashup novels such as *Pride and Prejudice and Zombies* and *Sense and Sensibility and Sea Monsters* found an audience by grafting horror elements into public-domain works of classic literature.

If *Resident Evil* and *28 Days Later* were the sparks that ignited the zombie apocalypse, then Romero himself was the gasoline. At first, it was indirectly. Zack Snyder's 2004 *Dawn of the Dead* was a remake in name only. A big, glossy Hollywood popcorn flick with plenty of style, it divided the horror community down the middle; some embraced it as a brilliant reimagining, while others remained loyal to Romero's plodding proletariat. The traditionalists didn't have to wait long. Later that year, Romero's long-rumored *Twilight of the Dead*—eventually retitled *Land of the Dead*—was finally released. Where *Night* had touched on race relations, *Dawn* on consumerism, and *Day* on the military industrial complex (to *really* simplify the underlying themes), *Land* was a commentary on social class.

Whereas Romero needed three decades to make his first three *Living Dead* films, he only needed the better part of one to make his final three. After *Land*, *Diary of the Dead* (2008) and *Survival of the Dead* (2010) were released in (relatively) short order. *Diary of the Dead* is shot in the first-person documentary style that was the flavor of the day. Romero has never exactly been subtle about his politics, but *Diary* feels almost like a polemic, a blatant critique of America's media-saturated culture. This heavy-handedness does not serve the story, as the characters act more disturbed by the *filming* of the zombie atrocities than by the atrocities themselves—as if only by capturing them on video do they become real and, by extension, exploitative. In stark contrast to *Diary*, possibly Romero's most nihilistic film since *The Crazies*, *Survival of the Dead* is a zombie retelling of the Hatfields and the McCoys, for some reason set on an island off the coast of Delaware. Romero wanted *Survival* to be the wackiest of his zombie films. Mission accomplished, George. It's also his worst, by far.

The zombies continued to multiply, invading every nook and cranny of contemporary life. Living-dead video games were everywhere, from old-school nineties franchises that kept churning out new versions (*House of the Dead*, *Doom*, *Resident Evil*) to completely new apocalypses like *Dead Rising*, *Dead*

Island, *Left 4 Dead*, and *Splatterhouse* (although an early iteration of that one hit arcades in 1988). And this is to say nothing of the hundreds of social media zombie games designed for the iPad and smartphone platforms. Under the eye of Frank Darabont (at least initially), Robert Kirkman's comic *The Walking Dead* was adapted into the highest-rated basic cable drama of all time. Funnyman Mel Brooks's son Max Brooks published *The Zombie Survival Guide*. After this became a bestseller, he followed up with *World War Z: An Oral History of the Zombie War*. In 2013, the filmed adaptation, the most expensive zombie movie ever made, was finally released after well-publicized production problems. Those who hated the fast-moving zombies of *28 Days Later* and the *Dawn of the Dead* remake absolutely despised those in *World War Z*, which attacked less like reanimated humans than swarms of pestilence. Most surreal of all—and the bar is set pretty high in a world of zombie lollipops and toilet seat covers—in 2011, the Centers for Disease Control released a graphic novel to instruct the populace about how to deal with a zombie plague. According to US assistant surgeon general Dr. Ali Khan, "if you are generally well equipped to deal with a zombie apocalypse you will be prepared for a hurricane, pandemic, earthquake, or terrorist attack." I don't know what's most disturbing, the thought of an actual zombie invasion or the fact that people need disaster preparation fed to them under the guise of entertainment.

I know this is going to sound like one of those made-up anecdotes, or at least tweaked to make it chronologically convenient, but I swear to god it's completely true. I just took a break from writing to tuck my daughter into bed. She was reading a book and before she inserted the bookmark to save her spot, I caught a glimpse of it. It was an age-appropriate cartoon of a grinning, rotting corpse, accompanied by the text "READ TO A ZOMBIE . . . IF YOU DARE."

When my eight-year-old daughter who's far more interested in American Girl dolls than anything horror related can casually incorporate a living-dead tchotchke into her bedtime ritual, clearly something is in the air. But what is it?

An essay in the April 6–7, 2013, weekend edition of the *Wall Street Journal* attempted to answer this very question. It was titled "The Lessons of Zombie-Mania" and was written by Daniel W. Drezner, a professor of international politics at Tufts University. At first, it kind of pissed me off, which is usually how I feel whenever horror issues seep into the mainstream and somebody with no apparent expertise in the genre attempts to contextualize these trends. If anybody was going to write about the current zombie craze, it sure as hell shouldn't have been some stuffy academic. After I put aside my self-righteous indignation and read the article, I had to admit, the guy actually knew what he was talking about.

While I might call bullshit on Drezner's theory that "zombies thrive in popular culture during times of recession, epidemic and general unhappiness," you'd have to be a fool not to acknowledge that at the very least, they're a metaphor for *something*. But what is this something? Is it the ever-present threat of terrorism in post-9/11 America? Global pandemics? Climate change, whose resulting Frankenstorms are as unpredictable and relentless as zombie hordes?

If you think about it, zombies are the *most* political monsters because they're actually the *least* political. They're a blank slate onto which anybody can project their pet anxieties. To those on the right of the political spectrum, zombies are terrorists, monstrous creatures devoid of human emotion that must be immediately destroyed. To the left, they represent the great unwashed masses, shuffling along mindlessly as their civil liberties—and individuality—are stripped away. The first act of 2004's *Shaun of the Dead* plays upon this conceit quite cleverly; the characters remain oblivious to the zombie menace around them because, at least on the surface, those infected don't act particularly different.

Which is the correct interpretation? Like all art, that depends on both the intent of the creator and the way in which audiences choose to process the information.

But one thing is certain: there are far less interesting ways to look at popular culture than through the prism of flesh-eating ghouls with no conscience and a taste for brains.

This answer—or more accurately, this nonanswer—might be a bit nebulous for some. For pundits like Drezner, it's taken as gospel that violent entertainment—specifically horror films—really does thrive in times of societal strife.

As any first-year science student will tell you, correlation does not imply causation. However, I think we can all agree on two things: 1) in the past ten years or so, we've seen a resurgence of uncompromising horror films, ones that are less a harmless roller-coaster ride than a vessel to explore the darkest recesses of the human condition, and 2) the last decade has been especially stressful: The war in Iraq. A floundering economy. A nation divided fairly evenly between red and blue values—sometimes it seems like the very fabric of America is coming apart.

I've already detailed the reason I dislike the term "torture porn" being used to identify a specific subgenre of horror films, but, I'll admit, the term still gives us a pretty accurate idea of the types of films we're talking about. Although blame for this movement is usually laid right at the feet of Roth and *Hostel*, *Saw* was actually released a year before in 2004. And a year before that, both Rob Zombie's *House of 1,000 Corpses* and *Wrong Turn* began the inexorable march toward a harder, more in-your-face brand of horror film. Seventies über-nasty exploitationer *I Spit on Your Grave* was remade (with a brilliant script reminiscent of *Citizen Kane*!). Although it lacked the shocking realism of its predecessor, the revenge murders were far more graphic. Its unfairly dismissed 2013 sequel upped the rape and torture even further. *The Human Centipede*, its sequel, and its upcoming third "sequence" explore the nauseating possibilities of the titular creature, created by surgically connecting a train of human beings ass-to-mouth. Even if this sounds like your thing, trust me, there's nothing even remotely sexual about the scenario. For sheer nihilism, however, nothing can touch *A Serbian Film*. It's the story of an aging male porn star who's blackmailed into one last performance. And, um, things don't go well, which led to bans of the film in a handful of countries. *Philosophy of a Knife* would come close if the torture wasn't so over-the-top that it actually diminishes the impact. Shot documentary-style, the film re-creates the human experiments of imperial Japan's notorious Unit 731. Teeth are extracted, flesh is burned, and an enormous live insect is inserted into a victim's vagina. One of them—either the animal or the vagina—has to be fake (I guess/hope), although I'll be damned if I can tell which it is. Then there is the seemingly never-ending supply of direct-to-video offerings whose one-word titles should tell you everything you need to know about the film: *Broken*, *Scar*, *Vile*, *Chop*, *Hunger*.

These films offered an even bleaker vision than their seventies counterparts. In the original *I Spit on Your Grave*, Jennifer is brutalized beyond comprehension, and ostensibly changed forever. But by the end of the film, her four attackers are taking dirt naps while she's cruising the lake in a motorboat—deranged but alive. Even Wes Craven's two early revenge flicks end on somewhat of an upbeat note. In *Last House on the Left*, Mari's parents off Krug and co., while in *The Hills Have Eyes* the civilized city folks make the rural mutants pay.

But today, it's all so fucking grim. Most of the victims in *Saw* die horribly, while Jigsaw returns to kill again (and again, and again, and again . . .). Although the main character in *Hostel* survives, he's knocked off in the first scene of the sequel. The ending of *A Serbian Film* is so soul crushing I can't even bring myself to write about it.

So the question isn't *if* the horror film has become more downbeat, but *why*. Is it simply a logical progression, a way to up the ante for a generation becoming rapidly desensitized to traditional violence? Or is it a reaction to the zeitgeist, a safe way to process the new realities of terrorism, disease, and natural disasters?

One answer came from an unlikely place: television. Since 2002, Mick Garris had been organizing a series of informal dinners where his friends and fellow horror filmmakers would meet to catch up and swap war stories. This led to a partnership with Showtime for *Masters of Horror*, a series that ran for two seasons between 2005 and 2007. Thirteen "masters" were each given $1–2 million and carte blanche to do what they wanted.

No studio interference, no meddling producers, no rules. In return, Showtime got more than it bargained for.

Joe Dante's episode "Homecoming" was a scathing attack on the war in Iraq and the Bush administration, at the time one of the few mainstream films to take such an unapologetic point of view. Less graphic than ideologically combustible, "Homecoming" aired intact. But other episodes weren't so lucky. Dario Argento's "Jenifer" was trimmed of a "penis chewing" scene. Takashi Miike's contribution was shelved altogether.* His graphic scenes of torture—including cringe-inducing shots of needles being inserted under fingernails and into the gum line—were deemed far too offensive even for a series designed to shock and disgust. Dante may have said it best, not just about *Masters of Horror* but about the past ten years in general: "In the world we live in, we like to push the envelope, so today's gory horror movies are gorier than the last generation's horror movies. There is a limit to what you can do to horror, and frankly I thought we had reached it in the mid-'80s. But apparently not."

I've been talking about the changes taking place within the horror film as if they were exclusively an American phenomenon, hardly surprising since I'm an American author writing in America. However, concurrent to the boom in the States, horror was exploding in all corners of the globe.

The most obvious place was Japan, which had a long history of supernatural films. The modern crop inspired the moniker

* The episode was eventually released on DVD with the rest of the series and currently airs uncut on numerous streaming services.

"J-horror," as unimaginative a descriptor as there ever was. We coined "Spaghetti Horror" for Italy and "Kiwi Horror" for down under, and "J-horror" is the best we can come up with for Japan?

For whatever reason, we seem to view foreign horror as single homogenized entities specific to each country. An illustrative analogy would be our conception of aliens. Regardless of the medium (film, literature, video games), and their home planet, the alien visitors all look exactly the same. Of course, their appearance differs from work to work—the creatures in *Alien* are worlds away from those in *Close Encounters of the Third Kind*—but rarely, if ever, within the works themselves. It's as if a race of beings who have mastered the technology to travel light-years to visit us has already ferreted out all the artificial constructs that keep us apart—gender, ethnicity, religion, class, creed. By contrast, what would an alien find if he landed on Earth? It depends, of course, on *where* he landed. How could he reconcile a bunch of Orthodox Jews in Brooklyn with the indigenous tribes of the Amazon? What does a Bedouin of the Sahara have in common with a Hong Kong businessman?

How is any of this relevant? Well, if we apply this concept to J-horror, the face of the genre was unquestionably a pale-as-death ghost girl with long black hair, especially after the release of 1998's *Ringu* and its American remake, *The Ring*. To be sure, this specter, which has deep roots in Japanese culture, was pervasive, but it certainly wasn't representative of *all* J-horror. Professional provocateur Takashi Miike was well on his way to sucker punching unsuspecting audiences long before Sadako climbed out of her watery grave. In fact, in a way, Japan mirrored the American horror scene in that the only thing consistent was its inconsistency. On one end of the spectrum, you had the brethren of *Ringu*, subtle yet terrifying ghost stories such as *Ju-on* and *Kairo*. On the other were some of the wildest and most ridiculously over-the-top movies ever made; films such as *Tokyo Gore Police* and *The Machine Girl* make Peter Jackson's *Bad Taste* feel like a Robert Bresson film. At the dawn of the new millennium, Japan was plagued by a precipitous spike in youth crime. You had kids killing each other, their respected elders, and even themselves in a spasm of violence that until now was thought to be an exclusively Western problem. As the island nation struggled to make sense of these crimes, films such as *Battle Royale* and *Suicide Club* reflected the hopelessness of the times.

If Japan had a challenger for most notable horror resurgence it would have to be France. Let me tell you something right off the bat—I can't stand the French. There's no point in going through all the reasons; they're the same reasons other fair-minded people have for hating them. I've only visited the country once. It was for business in Cannes. I pictured the French Riviera as a ribbon of white-sand beaches where Bardot clones sunbathed topless while washing their hair with Perrier. When I got there, it stunk of fish and looked like Massachusetts.

Not a single Frenchman I met in Cannes managed to change the opinion I already had of them. When I was in tenth grade, we had two foreign exchange students stay with us. I thought it was a terrible idea from the beginning, but since it was through my sister's private school and my parents were fully supportive, there wasn't much I could do. Everyone knows that the French don't wear deodorant, so naturally I warned my family that the boy, named Jean Michel, was going to smell like shit. My parents dismissed my concerns and called me narrow-minded. "These are Parisians from the city," my mother said, admonishing me. "They're sophisticated people. They're going to smell better than you." Flash-forward to the first, and I mean the *very first*, day. By nighttime, my mother had to open all the windows in our house in the dead of winter to air out the stench. Better than me indeed. To make matters worse, the kid ended up falling in love with our neighbor's au pair. We spent one frantic night scouring the neighborhood, wondering where a lovesick Frenchman would be most inclined to hide out. Luckily, the girl exchange student proved less unpredictable. Instead, she spent the majority of her stay alternating between bouts of crying and vomiting. So don't tell me I have no firsthand experience with the French.

That said, I can put aside my animus toward those snail-eating bastards and appreciate their first real attempt at horror since the films of Jean Rollin and their most important cinematic movement since the French New Wave. Historically, horror was never much of a Gallic mainstay, although Clouzot's *Les Diaboliques* and Georges Franju's *Eyes Without a Face* are certainly among the best the genre has to offer. This all changed in 2002 with Gaspar Noé's *Irréversible*, which has the dubious distinction of containing the longest, and most disturbing, rape scene in mainstream cinema. Things kicked off in earnest a year later with Alexandre Aja's *Haute Tension*, a gialloesque mind-fuck with a final twist that divided both viewers and critics alike. *Ils* (*Them*) is an overrated home invasion film that is actually inferior to its American clone, *The Strangers*. *Frontière(s)* was the country's attempt at backwoods horror. Many called it a sly political allegory; I found it silly. *Martyrs* received the most press for its relentless misanthropy and final scene in which a character is skinned alive (as unsettling as it is, it's not much more graphic than similar scenes in the *X-Files* episode "Hellbound" or the *Buffy the Vampire Slayer* episode "Villains"). The best of this entire bunch, and, in my opinion, one of the twenty greatest horror films ever made,* was *À l'Intérieur* (*Inside*), a relatively straightforward story about a pregnant woman, alone in her house at night, who will do anything to protect her unborn child. The first time I saw it, I was completely blown away. Written and directed by Alexandre Bustillo and Julien Maury, it's absolutely criminal that the film was released straight to DVD on the Dimension Extreme label. At least it's better than not being released at all, I guess.

From Argentina to Australia, Spain to Serbia, Ireland to Israel, homegrown horror industries were percolating everywhere. The Internet offered an unparalleled opportunity for audiences to sample the local cuisine in far-flung places. Horror had truly become a global phenomenon. And conveniently, it had never been more accessible.

Arguably, the most important development of the past decade (actually, the past fifteen years) was not even a thematic or contextual trend but a stylistic one. It was initiated at the 1999 Sundance Film Festival when a little movie from Eduardo Sánchez and Daniel Myrick, two friends who had met at the University of Central Florida School of Film, became

---

* Whenever I say this to other horror fans, they immediately grow indignant, even if they too love the film. They'll laugh and say, "Oh, so you think it's better than *The Exorcist*? Oh, so you think it's better than *Rosemary's Baby*? Oh, so you think it's better than *Texas Chain Saw*?" Uh, no, no, and no. All I said was it's one of the *twenty* best. Jeez.

the sleeper hit of the festival. Inspired by the 1970s television series *In Search of . . .*, as well as the documentary style of drive-in favorite *The Legend of Boggy Creek*, the conceit of *The Blair Witch Project*, while not completely original, certainly felt fresh. The text on the poster said it all: "In October of 1994, three student filmmakers disappeared in the woods near Burkittsville, Maryland, while shooting a documentary . . . A year later their footage was found." Their entire story is told through the "found footage" discovered by police the following year. To mimic the look of footage shot by a real amateur crew, *The Blair Witch Project* uses a shaky-cam aesthetic. The technique added a layer of gritty realism not seen since the last of the grindhouses closed its doors. There were reports of people vomiting in the theater, unaccustomed to the effect. Stephen King admitted it might have been the only film he has ever been too scared to finish watching.* Lots of people who viewed *Blair Witch* sight unseen, and had not been privy to the marketing blitz, thought it was a genuine documentary.

Although the exact numbers are hard to come by, most accounts peg the film's entire budget at around $35,000. So when Artisan Entertainment acquired *The Blair Witch Project* for $1.1 million and promised to put a substantial marketing push behind it, it was obvious the plan was to treat the film as something more than a typical microbudget festival pickup. With a combination of promotional savvy and dumb luck (far more of the former than the latter), the film exploded. It also

* According to his essay "What's Scary" in *Fangoria* 289, King eventually finished watching *The Blair Witch Project*. After subsequent viewings, he still found it absolutely terrifying.

had the good fortune to be released at a time when the Internet was transitioning from the domain of the technologically savvy to an indispensable communication tool for even the most unconnected Luddite. A woman I worked with at the time was so obsessed with the film and its mythology that she spent hours each day exploring *Blair Witch*'s then-cutting-edge website. A Sci-Fi Channel special, *The Curse of the Blair Witch*, stoked interest in the film before it even opened. It was featured on the cover of *Time*, *Newsweek*, and dozens of entertainment periodicals—solidifying its place as a true old media/new media crossover.

When *The Blair Witch Project* was finally released, it grossed almost $250 million worldwide—the most profitable film in history up to that time.*

Like clockwork, the backlash began almost immediately. Since the film wore its low-budget aesthetic on its sleeve, it was practically immune from attacks on its professionalism. But its originality was fair game. Hard-core fans point to its similarity to *Cannibal Holocaust*, in that both films use faux documentary footage, allegedly discovered by fictional characters in the film. Both Sánchez and Myrick denied having seen the film until *Blair Witch* was finished. There's no reason not to believe them, since *Cannibal Holocaust* is not a film typically found on most bookshelves, even among devotees of the genre. Still, Sánchez admits that had he previously seen Deodato's film, he might not have made *Blair Witch*.

* I'm excluding *Deep Throat* because despite the fact that some crazy numbers are thrown around—the most common being $600 million—there are no reliable figures for its lifetime gross.

More damning were reports that the duo had actually ripped off *The Last Broadcast*, an even lower-budget film that came out less than a year before. Again, Sánchez and Myrick pled ignorance. If you ask me, *Blair Witch* was the best thing to ever happen to *The Last Broadcast*, because as a film, it's barely watchable. Plus, it's not even the same idea. *Blair Witch* is *all* found footage. *The Last Broadcast* is played as a straight documentary about a murder that occurs during a search for the Jersey Devil.

Of course, the general public knew nothing of these mini-scandals. To them, *The Blair Witch Project* was something very, very new, and they embraced it wholeheartedly (although probably not the viewers who vomited in the aisles). The inevitable ancillary gravy train followed: books, comics, Blair Witch action figures (despite the fact that she's never shown in the film), video games, clothing, jewelry in the shape of the ubiquitous stickmen, and even a "soundtrack" purported to be a mix tape found in the car of one of the missing filmmakers.

Then there were the parodies, from the legally-mandated-to-be-unfunny Pauly Shore–hosted *Bogus Witch Project* to the breast-obsessed *Bare Wench Project*. My favorite, however, is the homemade *Blair Warner Project*, about the most fuckable *Facts of Life* character, who in real life became a born-again nut and child abuse advocate (just to be clear, not an advocate *for* abused children, but a proponent of abusing them). Before she completely disappeared from the public eye, she came down with West Nile virus and had a mental breakdown on the reality show *Survivor*.

The Blair Witch Project's most enduring legacy, however, was the impressive number of high-quality films that co-opted its handheld, faux-documentary style, from modestly budgeted domestic terror (*The Last Exorcism*, *The Devil Inside*, *The Chernobyl Diaries*, *Apollo 18*) to foreign films and their inevitable American remakes (the *REC* series and *Quarantine*) and Hollywood blockbusters (*Cloverfield*) to cable television specials (Animal Planet's *Mermaids: The Body Found*). None of these, however, captured the public's imagination like *The Blair Witch Project*—that is, until a film of even humbler means came along.

Displacing its stylistic predecessor as the most profitable film ever made (over $193 million on a budget of $15K), *Paranormal Activity* has an even simpler premise than *Blair Witch*: a young couple use their camcorder to record the ghostly goings-on in their home. Never had a static camera been used to such terrifying effect.

Paranormal Activity didn't just launch the directing career of Oren Peli, then a software developer; it also marked former Miramax executive Jason Blum's first foray into horror. Ever since, no one has been more synonymous with the genre. Through his company Blumhouse Productions he's been the driving force behind many of the most successful films and franchises in recent years.

Unlike nearly every other film series, in which the law of diminishing returns inevitably kicks in, the *Paranormal Activity* films continue to get better. I liked the sequels even more than the original. And I *loved* the original. The third installment is my favorite, followed by *Paranormal Activity 4* and then 2. In January 2014, the spin-off *Paranormal Activity: The Marked Ones* debuted, while another chronological sequel is in the works.

It seems inconceivable, but *Paranormal Activity* almost never saw the light of day, at least in its current incarnation. Initially, DreamWorks acquired the film, always intending to remake it with a far bigger budget. After all, in 2002 they had remade *Ringu* as *The Ring* to the tune of nearly a quarter-billion-dollar gross worldwide. Plus, who ever heard of a studio actually releasing a film that cost less than a typical day of craft services? However, Peli and Blum convinced studio execs—usually not known for their foresight—to first screen the original film with an audience. When the suits saw the reaction, they wisely decided the most prudent course of action would be to simply release it as is.

While we're on the subject, I guess it's as good a time as any to discuss easily the most polarizing post-*Scream* trend. I'm probably in the minority here, but I don't have a visceral hatred of remakes. Of course, they're no longer called remakes but "reimaginings," as producers feared the connotation of the former. I echo the sentiment of Stephen King, who when asked by George Romero what he thought about Hollywood ruining his books replied, "My books have not been ruined. They're on the shelf right behind you. You can read 'em if you want to."* There might not have been a good reason to redo *The Omen*—other than a cash grab—but I can promise you that the next time I watch the film my enjoyment of it will in no way be lessened because of the dreadful Liev Schreiber/Julia Stiles version. Plus, it's easy to forget that some of the genre's most beloved offerings—from Carpenter's *The Thing* to Cronenberg's *The*

* I'm unable to find the original source of this quote. But it's been printed so often I have to believe it's something King has said. And if it's not, I wish it was.

Fly to any number of Hammer's monster movies—are themselves remakes.

Although Joel Silver's Dark Castle Entertainment was founded in 1999 with the mandate—at least at the beginning—of updating William Castle's oeuvre for the twenty-first century, it was Marcus Nispel's 2003 remake of *The Texas Chain Saw Massacre* that opened the floodgates. Instead of embracing the low-budget roots of the original, the new *Chainsaw** looked like the $10 million production it was. Sweaty old Franklin was replaced by the beautiful people, and Tobe Hooper's reliance on insinuation was replaced by exsanguinations. Purists cried foul while a new generation pushed it past the $100 million mark, epitomizing the discrepancy between the *perception* of the film (and remakes in general) and its actual *reception*. Additional sequels followed, but one was a prequel and another was simply a remake in 3-D (I think, but, honestly, I've lost track).

Lest one assume that *Chainsaw* was an anomaly, Zack Snyder's *Dawn of the Dead* remake all but laid that theory to rest. The announcement of *Dawn* was met with an even greater uproar than that of *Chainsaw*, primarily because of *Dawn*'s status within the community. *Chain Saw* is a classic, for sure, but

* I can't believe I actually have to address this issue, but horror fans are beyond obsessive about things like this. Throughout this book, I've used two words, "*Chain Saw*," when writing the title of the original *Texas Chain Saw Massacre*. This is how the film's title appears on-screen and in the copyright. However, on the film's poster, and on some other marketing materials, *Chainsaw* is written as a single world. In *Going to Pieces*, I wrote *Chainsaw* as such, simply because I thought it was more aesthetically pleasing. Some critics freaked out and attacked my horror knowledge. I've rectified the spelling for this work, even though said critics can go fuck themselves. For the 2003 remake, I will write it as *Chainsaw* since this is the proper spelling of the title for this specific film.

Dawn is one of the genre's "message" movies. Although I personally might not subscribe to the theory that every shopping-mall ghoul with a taste for flesh is a wry comment on consumer culture, Romero's legions of fans do. Ironically, once the re-imagined *Dawn* came out, it was received fairly well, possibly because it was so far removed from the look and feel of its predecessor that fans had no reason to feel protective.

Similar to *Chainsaw*, *Dawn* grossed just north of $100 million at the US box office. Whatever uncertainty there may have been about the viability of sequels was now put to rest. They came out of the gate fast and furious. Within the next ten years, we had remakes of *The Toolbox Murders*, *The Amityville Horror*, *The Fog*, *When a Stranger Calls*, *The Hills Have Eyes*, *The Omen*, *The Wicker Man*, *Black Christmas*, *The Hitcher*, *Halloween*, *Sisters*, *April Fool's Day*, *Day of the Dead*, *Prom Night*, *Terror Train*, *My Bloody Valentine*, *Friday the 13th*, *The Last House on the Left*, *The House on Sorority Row*, *The Stepfather*, *The Crazies*, *A Nightmare on Elm Street*, *Piranha*, *I Spit on Your Grave*, *Night of the Demons*, *Mother's Day*, *Fright Night*, *The Thing* (again), *The Evil Dead*, and *Carrie*. And this is to say nothing of all the American remakes of successful foreign films, from *The Grudge* and *Pulse* to *Quarantine* and *Let Me In*.

With so many, the quality ran the gamut. *Prom Night* and *April Fool's Day* were watered-down versions of their predecessors, while ironically, *Train* was much meaner and unrelated to the original *Terror Train*. *Piranha* and *My Bloody Valentine* were fun updates. Some, such as *The Wicker Man*, *Halloween*, *Friday the 13th*, and *A Nightmare on Elm Street*, were completely unwatchable. One or two, such as *The Hills Have Eyes*, even came close to surpassing the original. For whatever reason, I seemed to like the ones that everybody else hated the most; call me crazy, but I really enjoyed *Black Christmas* and *The Amityville Horror*. Read some of the reviews; you'll clearly see I'm in the minority.

There is, of course, a big difference between a straight remake, which updates a film's basic story, themes, and/or characters for a contemporary audience, and trying to recapture the zeitgeist from long ago. It's a lesson Quentin Tarantino and Robert Rodriguez learned the hard way.

It was one of those can't-miss ideas that was so perfect there was no way it could succeed. The two friends and collaborators were screening a double feature in Tarantino's home when they decided to make one themselves. It would be called *Grindhouse*, a love letter to the titular temples of bad taste that inspired so much of their careers. The package would include two feature films—Rodriguez's *Planet Terror* and Tarantino's *Death Proof*—as well as faux trailers directed by their spiritual collaborators Rob Zombie, Eli Roth, and Edgar Wright.

Despite the remake fever in the air and surprisingly positive reviews from critics—who probably didn't much care for the films but wanted to seem hip to their appeal—*Grindhouse* didn't even earn back half its modest budget on its initial release. This was shocking to almost everybody except those who actually understood the appeal of the grindhouse—some people actually *like* their turds unpolished.

It was like Woodstock '94—bigger, louder, and safer than the Summer of Love. But sometimes, you just want to fuck in the mud.

Give the Weinsteins credit (Dimension distributed)—they refused to allow *Grindhouse* to die a slow death. They split up the two films for their foreign theatrical release, tried the same tactic for the domestic home video premiere, and finally slapped them back together as they originally appeared for a bonus-feature-laden special edition Blu-ray. All of this helped recoup some of the losses, but it didn't ease the sting of what was ultimately a very expensive—and foolish—bet on nostalgia.

In the end, isn't this what all these remakes are really selling—nostalgia at the expense of quality?

I don't think anybody believes in the posterity of *any* of these remakes—be they the good, the bad, or the downright ugly. As Tony Timpone wrote in a 2007 *Fango* editorial (as quoted in *Reel Terror*), "Will we really want to watch the *Texas Chain Saw Massacre* remake (the one that started the craze) ten years from now when the original is still far superior?" The answer is self-evident. And in twenty, thirty, and forty years, new generations of horror fans will *still* seek out the original. In many ways, this is good. Not only will it foster an appreciation of horror cinema for successive cinephiles, but objectively, Hooper's film is simply better.

Now, here's where things get tricky. Show of hands: how many of you have seen the film *ATM*? Although I can't see you (unless you're reading this on some sort of E-reader with a front-facing camera and high-speed Internet connection, and we've worked out a really creepy arrangement), I assume not many, since after playing in a couple of theaters the film went straight to home video and then Netflix, which is where I discovered it. Don't ask me what compelled me to watch it one night over the thousands of other low-budget movies I could have chosen to stream. But I'm glad I did. Directed by David Brooks, *ATM* is unquestionably one of the most accomplished debut features I have ever seen, an absolutely terrifying tale about three coworkers trapped by a psychopath inside an ATM vestibule. At the risk of sounding like *ATM*'s press rep, it's a nearly flawless film.

Unfortunately, unless Brooks eventually becomes Wes Craven, once Netflix chooses to bump *ATM* from its lineup, very few people are ever going to see it. To again quote Timpone, "Entertainment and movies have become so disposable. They don't have the staying power they used to have . . . There's not enough time for these gems to shine and build up a fan base. They don't have the staying power of the classics."

Now let's take a film like *Eaten Alive*, Tobe Hooper's follow-up to *The Texas Chain Saw Massacre*. It's a fun film, grimy and sleazy. You can almost feel the bayou heat radiating from the screen. Yet by any conceivable metric, *ATM* is a far superior film. But getting back to our point about longevity, which of these films will be screening at retrospectives when all of us are long gone?

Maybe I'm comparing apples to oranges. Some might even accuse me of having no appreciation for the classics—and I'm including esteemed trash like *Eaten Alive*, which has been elevated to cult status, among the classics. On the contrary, I have tremendous respect (even an unhealthy admiration) for such films. Even for ones that make *Eaten Alive* look like *The Rules of the Game*. I think they *should* be remembered, celebrated, and preserved.

My fear is that in elevating the lesser films of the past, we're liable to overlook the best of the present. The danger in this isn't so much that we're going to miss out on some wonderful films—although this is certainly unfortunate—it's that the already meager funding for horror films is going to dry up. For investors with no particular affinity for the genre, their involvement becomes a value proposition. It used to be that prospective financiers would gravitate to horror because of the historically high returns. Today, this is no longer true; comedy is just as appealing a genre on which to roll the dice.

I've seen this scenario play out firsthand in the career of a director friend of mine, Jeremy Kasten. Since his 2001 debut feature, *The Attic Expeditions*, Jeremy has forged a nice career for himself with the subsequent horror movies *All Souls Day*, *The Thirst*, and the remake of H. G. Lewis's *The Wizard of Gore*. All his films have a kind of European sensibility, at once beautiful and thematically challenging. They might not be everyone's cup of tea, but there's no denying he's an impressive talent. And yet, Jeremy struggles tooth and nail to get his next film off the ground, taking editing gigs and directing episodes of reality television. Now, of course there's nothing wrong with this—in fact, it's how I make my living—but in an earlier time he would have had the career trajectory of a Stuart Gordon or a Richard Stanley, visionaries whose films, good or bad, were always *interesting* and who could afford to ply their trade outside of traditional channels. If Hollywood didn't want to finance their films, then fuck 'em, they would make 'em another way. That's how it felt back in the day, when you never had to wonder if Carpenter or Romero would make their next film. It was expected as a matter of course. But now there are no guarantees, and even the masters struggle to get their films greenlit. More and more, it seems as if there really are only two types of pictures being made today: the $200 million blockbusters that can leverage their marketing and distribution muscle to virtually guarantee a profit, and the microbudget films that can't help but make money. The middle is getting squeezed. Although I can already think of a handful of films that are the exception, I promise you that nobody—and I mean *nobody*—in Hollywood is optimistic about the future of midsize horror productions.

The counterargument is that there's a current crop of filmmakers who are consistently creating important and provocative work, and they seem to have no trouble getting their films made. Eli Roth and Rob Zombie can practically have their pick of projects, while Jason Blum seems incapable of failure. The team behind the *V/H/S* films also appears to be doing fine for themselves. Ti West has carved out a niche as a master of quiet horror (*The House of the Devil*, *The Innkeepers*) after a disastrous turn with the sequel to Roth's *Cabin Fever*. Adam Green's *Hatchet* was a love letter to the horror films of his youth and the first real slasher franchise of the new millennium (although I much prefer his excellent survival film *Frozen*). With *Dog Soldiers*, *The Descent*, *Doomsday*, and *Centurion*, Neil Marshall could become his generation's Jeff Lieberman, a highly respected but idiosyncratic director who expertly skips between genres and whose films are more admired than they are successful. Lucky McKee may never again duplicate the pathos of 2002's *May*, but he seems more than content to continue to adapt the novels of Jack Ketchum to critical acclaim.

In my proposal for this book, which you've just slogged your way through, I originally planned to call this final chapter "Through the Crystal Ball"—a forecast about what the future of horror holds.

It would have been a *very* short chapter.

My final question to everybody I interviewed—from the people who make the movies to the fans who pay their hard-earned money to see them—was, "Where do you see the genre going from here?" I want to yet again invoke William Goldman's enduring maxim "Nobody knows anything." And nobody did. Tony Timpone was the only one who even attempted something specific. He hopes we'll see a quality big-budget horror film that spares no expense in service to the story and manages to transcend the genre itself, like how *The Godfather* is far more than just a mob movie and *The Searchers* hardly just a Western. As an example of a film that could possibly fit the bill, he cites Guillermo del Toro's long-gestating *At the Mountains of Madness*.

The truth is, Tony has no idea. And if he doesn't, then nobody does.

I certainly don't. In fact, I have a legal pad right next to my computer on which I was jotting down ideas. Here are some of the random thoughts and non sequiturs scribbled on the page: *Clowns. Priests. Resurgence of what classic monster? Mummy? Creature from Black Lagoon? Technology—how can it hurt us? Cronenberg—body mod? Cheap movies made on iPhones. Movies by request—one maker, one viewer.* (Author's note: I have no idea what that could possibly mean. I think I wrote it down when I was drunk.) *Sharks? People love sharks but no one can outdo* Jaws. *Will* Green Inferno *bring back cannibal films? No, animal rights groups now too powerful. Remake* The Funhouse *and Aussie* Fortress. *Cool invisibility experiments happening. That news story about kids in London taking experimental drugs—looked like Elephant Man. Gotta be something bad about those e-cigs. Mind control shit? Anthologies? Gotta break out,* V/H/S *great but too small.*

Brilliant prognostication indeed. And this is just a sampling of what I wrote. Most of it was far less intelligible.

One thing I'm fairly certain of, however, is that we're never going to return to the dark days before *Scream*. The wellspring will never again be that dry. The ghetto that horror once was forced into has gentrified. It's not just hip to be square, it's hip to be *scared*. The geeks have inherited the earth.

There are too many movies, too many TV series, too many reality ghost-hunting shows, too many horror conventions, too many film festivals, too many up-and-coming horror novelists, too many comics, too many toys—just too much horror in the ether for the genre to ever disappear.

The trick now becomes how to separate the crap from the quality. And the best part is, like a long road trip, the journey is half the fun.

In the epilogue to the paperback edition of *Fargo Rock City*, Chuck Klosterman explains how his love for Radiohead—despite their genius—could never approach the love he had for Mötley Crüe at fifteen. It's a poignant piece of writing on the powerful yet ephemeral nature of teenage passion.

I know exactly how he feels. As terrifying as I still find *The Watcher in the Woods*, the image of a blindfolded Karen Aylwood will never again give me a sleepless night. I could watch *A Nightmare on Elm Street* sitting on Wes Craven's lap while being fed grapes by Heather Langenkamp and it wouldn't come close to approaching the excitement I felt during that night in seventh grade when I had a girl under each arm. Michael Myers is now old enough to receive his AARP card.

But what's different, and wonderful, about horror is that you never really grow out of the one thing that drew all of us to the genre in the first place: *the love of being scared*. The triggers are different, but the feeling is the same.

Recently, I was trying to find an appropriate horror movie to watch with my sixteen-year-old niece. It had to be scary enough for a teenager but without the profanity or sexual situations that would make the viewing beyond uncomfortable. *Poltergeist* seemed like the perfect choice. Best of all, she had never even *heard* of it. I've seen *Poltergeist* well over fifty times, and I can recite the "You only moved the headstones!" rant verbatim. But since it's been more than a decade since I last watched it, I decided to give it a quick spin.

Obviously, it was as great as I remembered. It's a classic and classics are timeless. But what I was struck by was how differently I identified with the characters. In the past, it was the famous clown scene that made my blood run cold. I could totally see myself as eight-year-old Robbie Freeling, absolutely convinced that the crazy-looking toy sitting on my rocking chair was going to come alive and strangle me—which of course it does.

But this time, it was the scene where Carol Anne first goes missing that was the most traumatic. I could literally feel the panic rise inside me as Steven and Diane search the house in vain for their missing daughter, reaching a crescendo when they assume she's been killed by the freak storm that just ripped through their neighborhood. Until I became a parent, I had absolutely no idea how gut-wrenching the thought of losing a child could be.

When the movie was over, I walked quietly up the stairs and stood outside my daughter's door. Slowly, I opened it and peeked inside. Only her head was visible above the covers. She was snuggling her stuffed piggy—as she always does when she's asleep or tired—drifting peacefully across some distant dreamscape. I closed her door and headed toward my son's room. Boys are different. He too was fast asleep, sprawled out pretzel-like on top of the covers, a twisted bundle of extremities, exhausted from his subconscious battles with Herobrines and Creepers.

I hate pop psychology. So I'm certainly not going to write something as trite as, say, *To appreciate the light, you have to embrace the darkness*. That's such a cliché, and not even true.

But I will say that for those fleeting moments, as I gazed upon my sleeping children, it was a horror movie—one of those wonderful, awful, crazy, wild, brilliant, absurd, and unforgettable movies—that reminded me how much I loved them.

That's not bad for a genre most people view with contempt. That's not bad for any genre.

Acknowledgments

As a rule, nobody gives a shit about acknowledgments except for the people being acknowledged. So instead of offering up thanks, I contemplated calling out those who have in some way wronged me throughout my life. But I reconsidered for two reasons. One, I could already hear my mother accusing me of refusing to let go of a grudge. And two, it would be a disservice to the many people who have been indispensable to me throughout the course of writing this book.

Besides myself, there's no one more responsible for the creation of *The Horror of It All* than Brant Rumble, my editor at Scribner. From the moment I sent him my initial query, I could not have imagined a more enthusiastic, patient, supportive, and savvy partner in crime. In short, he's the editor that every writer dreams of having.

In an analogy keeping with his amateur career as a football star, my agent Jud Laghi took a project in the red zone and powered it across the goal line.

The entire team at Simon & Schuster worked tirelessly on my behalf and I cannot thank them enough for their efforts. John Glynn curbed my more self-indulgent impulses and offered valuable editorial advice. Aja Pollock is not only a brilliant copy editor but saved me countless times from undoubtedly incurring the wrath of horror fans everywhere with careless mistakes (I really do know the difference between Ken Russell and Chuck Russell, I swear). Jason Heuer designed a cover I fell in love with the first time I saw it. Attorney Elisa Rivlin kept me on the straight and narrow and convinced me that a memoir about horror films might not be the best place to take revenge on some awful elementary school teachers.

Photographer extraordinaire Kristin Reyer made me look much better in my jacket photo than I do in real life.

Although I've never met or even corresponded with Chuck Klosterman, *Fargo Rock City* gave me hope that if an ordinary kid from rural North Dakota could write an indisputable classic, then maybe an ordinary kid from suburban New Jersey could write something almost readable.

Tony Timpone, Rodrigo Gudiño, Shade Rupe, Darren Good, and Noah Agay generously gave their time and provided much-needed information.

My business partner Alex Flaster was nothing but supportive about what I'm sure he considered an annoying diversion keeping me from our core business of making television shows. But he never once said a word and even allowed me to screen the Blu-ray release of *Snuff* in his apartment.

And finally, no debt of gratitude would be complete without mentioning the three most important people in my life: my loving wife, Lori, who incredibly requested only a handful of changes to this manuscript, and our two amazing children, Noah and Hailey. All parents think their kids are the best. You're all wrong.